D1742703

# Palm Handhelds!

## *I Didn't Know You Could Do That...*™

### Second Edition

Neil Salkind

SYBEX®

**San Francisco • Paris • Düsseldorf • Soest • London**

Associate Publisher: Richard J. Staron

Contracts and Licensing Manager: Kristine O'Callaghan

Acquisitions and Developmental Editor: Ellen Dendy

Editors: Donna Crossman, Pete Gaughan

Production Editor: Kylie Johnston

Technical Editor: Maryann Brown

Book Designers: Franz Baumhackl, Kate Kaminski

Electronic Publishing Specialist: Maureen Forys, Happenstance Type-O-Rama

Proofreaders: Nanette Duffy, Nelson Kim, Laurie O'Connell, Nancy Riddiough

Indexer: Lynnzee Elze

CD Coordinator: Christine Harris

CD Technician: Kevin Ly

CD Production Tech Assistant: Erica Yee

Cover Designer/Illustrator: Daniel Ziegler

Cover and Chapter Photographs: PhotoDisc

An earlier version of this book was published under the title *PalmPilot and Palm Organizers! I Didn't Know You Could Do That...* © 2000 SYBEX Inc. First edition copyright © 2000 SYBEX Inc.

Library of Congress Card Number: 2001089810
ISBN: 0-7821-2936-6

Manufactured in the United States of America

10 9 8 7 6 5 4 3 2 1

*Dedicated to the cool sharks who swim in lane 5:*
*Brenda, Lori, Maureen, and Dave*

# Acknowledgments

Thanks to Ellen Dendy for giving me the opportunity to complete this project and for her guidance, patience, and good advice throughout its development. Thanks also to the Sybex book team for their contributions, especially Donna Crossman, Kylie Johnston, Pete Gaughan, Maryann Brown, and Maureen Forys. Special thanks to Janet Majure, a friend and fellow writer, and Jennifer Miller for help with the B-I-G table in the appendix. Warm thanks to David and Sherry Rogelberg for all they do for me, and happy everyday to Leni, Sara, Micah, and Pepper. Thanks, thanks, and more thanks for their good nature and unending smiles.

# Contents

# Introduction

**S**o, you think you and your Palm have seen it all? Take a look at some of the new things you can do with your Palm:

- Use Documents To Go to read and edit that letter to the editor you created in Word on your Palm (see the section on tools and utilities)

- Use PopUp Calculator to calculate any values while in any program without leaving the main program (see the section on calculations)

- Stay in touch with your homebase Palm files using MyPalm (see the section on making connections)

- Keep track of Fido, Miss Kitty, and Pumpkin the Bird with Pet Assistant (see the section on fun and unique applications, or apps)

- And my favorite: Use Kodak's PalmPix to take pictures (no kidding!) with your Palm that are as good as those taken with a reasonably priced digital camera (see the Sybex Web site at www.sybex.com for this appendix content)

Your Palm handheld does more than just allow you to read Word (and Excel) documents, calculate values, and keep track of Fido. In fact, your Palm is a business tool, a travel companion, a tutor, a graphics tool, and even a game machine that rivals many of the dedicated ones now available. Your Palm is a personal digital assistant that can do more things than you are aware of, and that's just the reason why we've created this book.

*Palm Handhelds! I Didn't Know You Could Do That...* shows you some of the best, most easily available Palm applications. They can increase your productivity in business, make your traveling more enjoyable, and give you hours of fun playing games. Among these applications, you'll find calculators that compute the correct tip for each person in your dinner party, databases that can help manage your book collection, and masterpieces such as Baum's *The Wizard of Oz*—all on your Palm, regardless of how old or new it is. And, these programs work with any PDA (personal digital assistant) using the Palm operating system (Palm OS). This includes such successful PDAs as the Handspring and Sony Clio line.

# What's in This Book

This book contains an in-depth description of 128 different Palm applications that represent the far-reaching capabilities of the Palm handheld. These applications can be used with any Palm that uses Palm OS 3.5 or later.

The different applications are organized into the following sections:

◆ Getting the Most from Your Palm: Utilities and Tools

◆ A Place for Everything: Information Management

◆ 1,234,567: Calculate Anything and Everything

◆ Does Anyone Really Know What Time It Is?: Clocks and Calendars

◆ Worth a Thousand Words: Writing and Language Utilities

◆ Get Smart: Education and Learning

◆ Health and Fitness

◆ Just Plain Fun: Who Would Have Thought Palm Could Do *This!*

◆ Having Fun: Games and Entertainment

◆ Seeing It All: Graphics Applications

◆ Taking Care of Business: Business' Best

◆ Connectivity Applications

◆ Travel Applications

Each section contains a description of Palm applications that have been through tried-and-true testing methods by a crack team of fun-loving, Palm-loving experts (by me, and my family and friends), who can endorse each one as fully functional and very useful. Once you find an application that you like, just download it to your Palm and it's there for you to use.

The appendices include even more information:

◆ The best Web sites for finding more Palm stuff (see the Sybex Web site at www.sybex.com for this content)

◆ A H-U-G-E table of Palm applications, many of which are included on the CD contained in the back of this book

◆ A brief description of cool add-on tools (see the Sybex Web site at www.sybex.com for this content)

# The Application Descriptions

Each program description in this book and on the CD-ROM contains the following information:

**Name of Program**   The name as it appears on the Internet or as indicated by the developer or manufacturer

**E-Mail Address**   The e-mail address to which you can write for more information about the application should you have any questions or comments (which are, for the most part, always welcome)

**Web Address**   The Web site where you can download the program, find additional information about the application, learn of other applications offered by the same company, retrieve online manuals (if available), and often find tons of other goodies you might want you consider

For those applications covered in the book, you will also find these features:

**Version**   The official version of the software that was available at the time of this book's printing (some programs don't have a version number so that information will not be included for those apps)

**Type of Software**   Such as shareware, commercial, or freeware

**Cost**   The price to register or buy the product, if any, at the time of this printing

**Description**   Details about what the application does and its special features and such

**Getting Started with...**   These are just the basic steps on how to use the application

**Important commands**   These will allow you to see at a glance which commands perform which functions (won't be available for all programs)

## Icons Used in This Book

Within these application descriptions, there are three main icons used that tell you even more. These icons include the following.

This icon indicates that the application is included on the book's accompanying CD-ROM.

This icon indicates that a software application supports color.

This icon represents applications that support mobile functions.

## Try Before You Buy

Each of the software programs that you find on the CD-ROM accompanying this book falls into one of three categories: commercial, shareware, and freeware.

Commercial software is the kind of software that you pay full price for through some kind of distributor, at a local store, from a national chain, or directly on the Internet. As the software becomes more sophisticated, it gets more expensive.

Shareware is software that is widely available and has been developed based on the philosophy that if a good product is introduced to the marketplace at a fair price, then users will be willing to pay a nominal fee for its use. The idea of shareware got started when individuals realized that commercial software was too expensive and the channels through which it was distributed were inefficient. Shareware developers encourage users to share applications with other users so that the potential for more registered users increases.

The majority of the programs in this book and on the CD are shareware. The way it works is as follows:

**1.** You download the program you want to try.

**2.** If you like it, you send the requested fee to the developer.

Why pay? It's simple: If developers continue to be paid (and rewarded) for their efforts, then the result is a better version of the original application. For

$10 (the approximate average shareware price for Palm applications), you get an application that does what you want, the developers benefit from their hard work, and you are informed of future upgrades and improvements. Everybody wins. So, if you download Palm applications, try them and like them, then pay the small fee and keep a nice example of capitalism alive.

Freeware is software that is absolutely free for the asking and taking, and there's a ton of it available on the Internet. The developer expects nothing in return, save for your appreciation for a fun and useful product. Freeware sometimes becomes shareware once it has found its place in the market.

# Getting New Applications

This book brings you the information you'll need to obtain hundreds of different applications for use on your Palm, and there are tens of thousands more available on the Internet. And it's amazingly easy to get and use each and every one. In this section of the introduction, you'll learn how to get an application from your Desktop computer to your Palm. Then you'll learn how to get a program from the Internet to your Desktop.

## From the Disk to Your Palm

To transfer an application to your Palm, you just need to follow these steps. These steps apply no matter where the application files are located, be it on your hard drive, a floppy drive, or the CD-ROM that accompanies this book. Most application files will come to you compressed, or zipped. If this is the case, you must first unzip them using an application such as WinZip, which will be discussed later in this introduction.

**NOTE**  I'm assuming that you have already installed the Palm software, your Palm cradle is attached and working, and that you know how to HotSync or transfer files from your Palm to your Desktop computer.

**1.** Locate the file you want to download. Palm files almost always have the following extensions, or three-letter characters, after the name of the file: PRC or PDB. If you see a file with this extension (such as doodle.prc), you'll know that it is a Palm application.

**2.** Click Start ➤ Programs ➤ Palm Desktop ➤ Install Tool, and you will see the dialog box shown below.

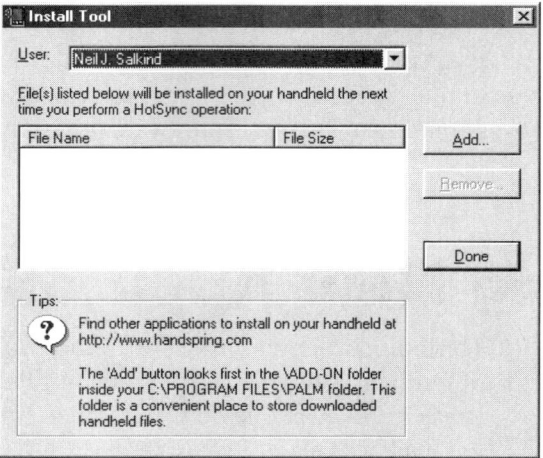

**3.** Click Add, and locate the file you want to install.

**4.** Click Open.

**5.** Click Done.

**6.** Press the HotSync button on your Palm, and the files that you identified will be transferred from the Desktop to your Palm.

The newly installed programs are now ready to use. When you tap on the Applications button on your Palm, they should appear in the screen.

## From the Internet to Your Desktop

To use any of the millions of Palm applications available on Internet sites (see the Sybex Web site at www.sybex.com for this content), you'll first have to download them from the Internet to your Desktop and then transfer them from your Desktop to your Palm (see steps above). Files on the Internet are usually in a compressed form, so the one other step you'll need to take after they are downloaded is to expand the file (see next section).

To download a file from the Internet, follow these steps:

**1.** Locate the file on the Internet.

**2.** Download the file by either clicking the filename or clicking the appropriate on-screen phrase. You will then be asked whether you want to open the file or save it. Click Save.

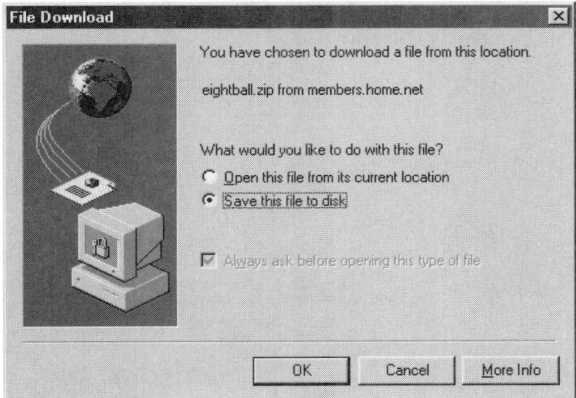

**3.** In the Windows Save dialog box, indicate where you want the saved file to be located. Use the Browse button to find the appropriate folder, or just use the default location.

**4.** Click Open, and the file will be saved to that location. Palm application files are often very small and, depending upon the speed of your Internet connection, can be downloaded very quickly (almost faster than you can see).

**5.** Once the file is downloaded, it is ready to be HotSynched to your Palm, unless it has to be unzipped.

## Using WinZip

WinZip is an ingenious shareware product. It takes a file and compresses it to be a fraction of its size, making the transfer from one computer to another (such as over the Internet) much, much faster. While WinZip (the shareware or evaluation version of which is contained on the CD-ROM) is very powerful and has many different features, uncompressing a file is relatively uncomplicated.

WinZip comes with an easy-to-use wizard that works with files you are downloading from the Internet. The WinZip Wizard automates almost all of the work normally associated with downloading compressed files from the Internet. When you click an archive (which appears as the Zipped File icon you see here) using Netscape Navigator or Microsoft Internet Explorer, WinZip takes over and automatically moves the downloaded file to the download folder (which is initially set to C:\download) and then opens the file.

eightball

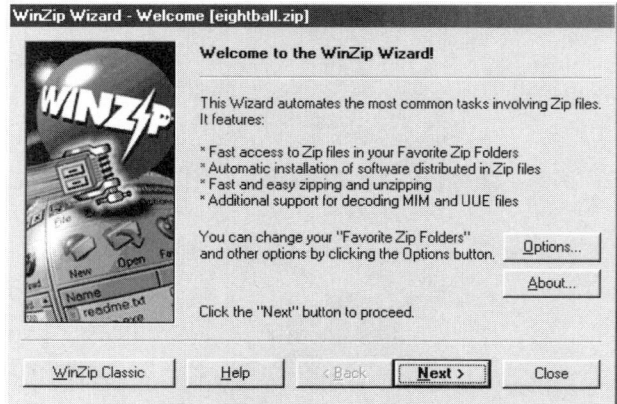

You can also right-click the archive's Zipped File icon, click the Extract To function, and extract it to a new folder or to the one that currently contains the WinZip file.

That's it! That's all you need to know to get started with *Palm Handhelds! I Didn't Know You Could Do That...* So go and have lots of fun—both of the serious and the not-so-serious kind. If you can imagine it, there's a Palm application that can do it.

# Getting the Most from Your Palm: Utilities and Tools

You can do a lot with your Palm and, with the utilities and tools covered in this section, you can learn to do even more. These helpful little programs are sure to increase your productivity and, in the long run, save you precious time.

Two of the utilities covered here, X-Master and DA Launcher, manage system extensions and Desk Accessories. They both allow you to switch from application to application faster and easier. But the really exciting thing about Desktop Accessories and their managers is that you can run them on top of your standard Palm applications, so you don't have to shut one application down in order to run another. If you have these programs, particularly X-Master, you can choose among literally hundreds of little applications that can run while you're running other programs.

Other tools, such as Documents To Go, let you use your Palm device to read regular Desktop documents, such as those produced using your word processor or spreadsheet.

You'll also appreciate the helpfulness of the utilities that can eliminate duplicate entries, beam anything (well, almost), and let you switch back and forth between applications without having to return to the Applications screen.

# 1 Beam Everything Up: BeamWare

Name of Program: BeamWare
E-Mail Address: HiroyukiOkamoto@yahoo.co.jp
Web Address: http://members.tripod.com/~hokamoto/BeamWare.html
Version: 2.03
Type of Software: Shareware
Cost: $5

BeamWare increases your beaming options beyond those that are built in to your Palm. It beams just about anything of the database variety—database applications, files, Desk Accessories, Hacks, and more—to any infrared-equipped Palm device, even if that user doesn't have BeamWare.

Exchanging data doesn't get much easier. Not only does BeamWare let you beam that software, but it also lets you send several files at a time. A special feature is that BeamWare lets you send ROM-based applications, such as your Date Book, which most applications won't allow (although you still can't beam copy-protected software).

BeamWare has some handy functions that make sharing easier. For example, it lets you designate your favorite data to beam, and allows you to send multiple items in a single transmission. It also lets you sort by category and search several ways, but you cannot send an individual record or database entry. Imagine using HanDBase, which is covered in the section of this book titled "A Place for Everything: Information Management," to create an inventory and then using BeamWare to beam it to your new employee!

One curious aspect of BeamWare is that it also lets you delete whole databases. You should, therefore, be sure that you are deleting what you intend to before you select an item and tap the trashcan!

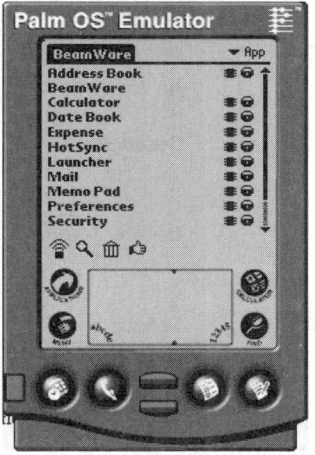

## Getting Started with BeamWare

To beam those database files, follow these steps:

**1.** When you launch BeamWare, BeamWare scans your Palm, selects those applications and database-related files that are eligible to be beamed, and shows you this list. Tap the item you wish to beam.

**2.** Tap the Beam icon (the box with the radiating arcs) and aim your Palm device at the receiver's.

**3.** You're done!

**4.** Additionally, you can tap the Magnifying Glass icon to search for a particular item, or you can tap the triangle in the upper-right corner of the screen to look at different software by type (such as application, Hack, etc.).

**5.** To add an item to your list of beaming favorites, select the software in question and tap the Favorites (thumbs-up) icon.

## BeamWare: The Important Commands

Here's a table of handy shortcuts.

| Menu | Command | Shortcut | What It Does |
|------|---------|----------|--------------|
| DB | Beam Selected | /B | Beams item currently selected |
| DB | Beam All | /A | Beams all items currently on the screen |
| DB | Delete Selected | /D | Deletes selected item from your Palm device |
| DB | Search | /S | Lets you search for a particular item or group of items |
| Favorites | Add/Clear Selected | /F | Adds selected item to or deletes selected item from Favorites |
| Favorites | Add/Clear All Favorites | None | Adds all items on the screen to Favorites, or deletes all Favorites |
| Options | Preferences | /P | Lets you display database size |

# 2 Word and Excel (and Even Mail!) on Your Palm: Documents to Go

Name of Program: Documents To Go
E-Mail Address: info@dataviz.com
Web Address: http://www.dataviz.com
Version: 3.0
Type of Software: Commercial
Cost: $49.95 (Professional Edition); $29.95 (Standard Edition)

This is a truly excellent addition to your Palm arsenal of utilities. Documents To Go allows you to view and edit Word documents and Excel spreadsheets right on your Palm in the original format. No special formatting or translations are needed. Documents To Go automatically converts your Desktop documents so that the next time you Hotsync, the selected files end up on your Palm.

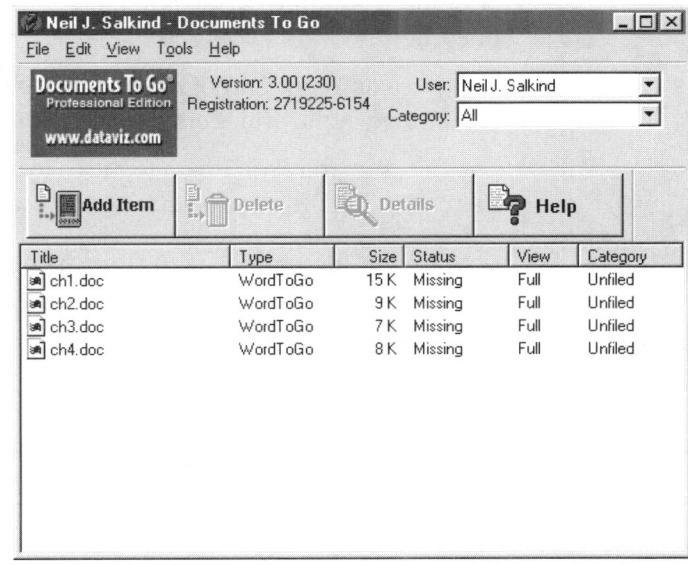

But that's not all. The Professional Edition also lets you edit these documents on your Palm and update the originals when you Hotsync. And this version of Documents To Go contains DataViz Mail, which allows you to Hotsync your mail along with any attachments. The Standard Edition of Documents To Go is available only through the Web site and has no editing capability.

## Getting Started with Documents To Go

To move a document from your Desktop to your Palm, follow these steps:

**1.** Open the Documents To Go program on your Windows Desktop.

**2.** Drag the file representing the document into the Documents To Go window, or click the Add Item button, to select the file.

**3.** HotSync your Palm and PC, and the document you chose in step 2 will be copied to your Palm.

Here are some additional tips for working with word processing documents on your Palm:

◆ Tap on the top half of the document to scroll up and on the bottom half to scroll down.

◆ To scroll continuously, tap and hold in the bottom half of the document.

◆ To go to a different part of the document, tap on the drop-down Percentage menu and identify where you want to go to.

◆ Use the Find and Find Again features by first tapping the menu and then selecting the option you want to use.

And try these tips for working with spreadsheet documents on your Palm:

◆ To move to the next range of cells in a spreadsheet, drag the stylus up, down, left, right, or diagonally.

◆ To get to a particular cell, tap the Go command.

◆ To move between different spreadsheets, tap the drop-down menu on the top-right portion of the screen.

◆ To freeze cells or adjust column width, tap on a column header.

## Documents To Go: The Important Commands

Use these commands to read Word and Excel files on your Palm.

| Menu | Command | Shortcut | What It Does |
|---|---|---|---|
| Record | Add Item | None | Adds an item |
| Record | Delete Item | /D | Deletes an item |
| Record | Beam Document | /B | Beams a document to other Documents To Go users |
| Record | Beam Application and Doc | None | Beams a document to users who do not have Documents To Go |
| Options | Find Application Add-Ons | None | Finds the type of document to be viewed |
| Options | Preferences | /R | Defines the find options |
| Options | About Documents To Go | None | Offers information about Documents To Go |

# 3 The Mother of All Hacks: X-Master

Name of Program: X-Master
E-Mail Address: info@linkesoft.com
Web Address: http://linkesoft.com/
Version: 1.0
Type of Software: Freeware
Cost: Free

If you've read much about Palm software, you've probably heard of
Hacks. Hacks are system extensions, or software programs that add to the

functionality of your Palm. And if you've heard of Hacks (and a few are mentioned in this book), you've most likely heard of HackMaster. The successor to HackMaster is called X-Master and, like its older sibling, X-Master is a system extension manager, which allows you to install Hacks that can, for example, capture screens (ScreenShot), speed up your graffiti writing (TapType), and back up your Palm's contents (Databag).

When you install X-Master, it takes over all existing extensions, so upgrading to X-Master from HackMaster should go smoothly. It's free, so you might as well try it!

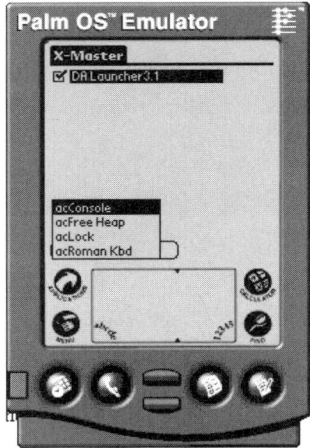

## Getting Started with X-Master

X-Master rules! Give it a whirl by following these steps:

**1.** If you've already downloaded and installed X-Master, but you still have HackMaster on your Palm device, it's not a problem. Go ahead and launch X-Master. It will alert you that you already have HackMaster and ask whether you'd like X-Master to replace it for you. Tap Yes to complete the launch and delete HackMaster from your Palm device.

**NOTE** If you are nervous about deleting HackMaster from your Palm, remember that you can always reinstall HackMaster if you don't like X-Master. But if you tap Cancel, X-Master exits and you can't try it out!

2. X-Master will show you a list of your existing Hacks. Tap the box next to any Hack you want active.

3. Select any Hack on the list by tapping it, and then tap Details to find out more about that particular Hack.

   Tap OK, or tap Configure, to go to that Hack's Configuration screen (which is also accessible from the main X-Master screen).

4. Review and change any preferences, if you wish, in the Configuration screen. Tap OK.

5. Tap Info to see basic information about a Hack that you've selected. This information includes the developer's name, the version number, and contact information. Tap OK.

6. Tap your Palm device's silk-screened Application/Home button. Carry on!

## X-Master: The Important Commands

Here's a table of handy X-Master shortcuts.

| Menu | Command | Shortcut | What It Does |
| --- | --- | --- | --- |
| Extensions | Delete | /D | Deletes extensions |
| Extensions | Beam | /B | Beams extensions |
| Extensions | List All Active | /L | Displays all active Hacks in the X-Master main screen |
| Extensions | Deactivate All | /R | Deactivates all extensions |
| Extensions | Create Set | /S | Creates a Set of Hacks (defined as those that you currently have active so that you can turn extensions on and off as groups) |
| Extensions | Soft Reset | None | Resets your Palm device |
| Options | Preferences | /R | Allows you to set your own preferences |

| Menu | Command | Shortcut | What It Does |
|------|---------|----------|--------------|
| Options | Tips | None | Provides tips on using X-Master |
| Options | Copyright | None | Gives copyright information on X-Master |
| Options | About X-Master | None | Gives information about X-Master |

# 4 Hackety Hack: DA Launcher

Name of Program: DA Launcher
E-Mail Address: piloteer@usa.net
Web Address: http://member.nifty.ne.jp/yamakado/da/
Version: 3.1
Type of Software: Freeware
Cost: Free

No question about it: Palm devices are super-cool. After you've used yours awhile, however, you realize that it would be even cooler if only it could do more.

And it's Desk Accessories, or DAs, that respond to those "if only's." Want to see your handheld's clock while in the middle of a memo? You can with a DA, and that's only the beginning. DAs also make it quicker and easier to switch from one program to another.

**NOTE** DA Launcher's developer notes that DAs do much the same thing as many Hacks do, but they work in such a way as not to interfere with your Palm device's speed and stability, as Hacks often do (even when they aren't running).

To run a DA, you need a DA launcher like the one covered in this section. (The site listed at the beginning of this section also offers alternative DA launchers for downloading.) DA Launcher lets you install those little DA programs that you can quickly pop up on top of a regular Palm application.

DA Launcher comes with these 10 DAs you can try out:

- ◆ acHelloWorld.prc does nothing more than display "Hello World."
- ◆ acDateClock displays date and time.
- ◆ acFreeHeap shows free heap memory.
- ◆ acBaklit turns on or off the backlight, but runs on PalmOS 2.0 only.
- ◆ acConsole allows users to enter into Debugger mode (for developers).
- ◆ acGraffitiRef shows Graffiti Help and runs on PalmOS 2.0 only.
- ◆ acLock locks and turns off the Palm device.
- ◆ acRomanKbd shows a keyboard.
- ◆ acNumKbd shows a numerical keyboard.
- ◆ acWordc shows the number of characters in the field. You should set the cursor before launch.

If you like any of these and want to know how they work, you can go to the Web site above to download these and lots of other DAs.

## Getting Started with DA Launcher

Follow these steps to launch away with DA Launcher:

1. If you don't already have X-Master, install it first.
2. Install DA Launcher and as many of the sample DAs as you'd like.
3. Launch X-Master.
4. In the X-Master Extensions screen, check DA Launcher 3.1 to make it active.
5. Press a hardware button, or return to the Home/Applications screen and launch a program.
6. Tap one of two places on the silk-screened portion of your Palm's face: either in the space to the left of the Applications and Menu buttons or to the right of the Calculator and Find buttons.
7. A pop-up list of Desk Accessories will appear. Select the one you want, and it will appear on top of the screen in which you were working.
8. Tap OK to leave the DA.

# 5 Pulling a Switcheroo: SwitchHack

Name of Program: SwitchHack
E-Mail Address: SwitchHack@deskfree.com
Web Address: http://www.deskfree.com/
Version: 1.62
Type of Software: Shareware
Cost: $5

Here's a slick little Hack extension that will smooth your way from one application to another without having to go back and forth to the Palm device's Applications screen. SwitchHack lets you, with a stroke of your stylus, toggle back and forth between two different applications. Maybe, for instance, you need to keep looking at your calendar while reconstructing your expense account. Maybe you need to look as though you're studying your notes when your boss passes by when you're actually playing a game. SwitchHack will also let you schedule an appointment, for instance, without quitting your memo. Very slick indeed. As with any Hack extension, you need to have HackMaster or any similar program (such as X-Master) installed.

## Getting Started with SwitchHack

Quick switches are easy when you follow these directions:

**1.** Install X-Master if you don't already have it.

**2.** Install SwitchHack.

**3.** Launch X-Master, and tap the box next to SwitchHack to activate it.

**4.** Work on your Palm device and switch from one application to another a few times in order to test out SwitchHack.

**5.** Drag your stylus or your fingertip from the Applications/Home button to the Graffiti area. Poof! The last application you were using appears.

6. Drag from the Applications/Home button to the Graffiti area again. Poof! You're back where you started.

7. Drag your stylus or fingertip from the Menu button toward the Applications/Home button. Up pops a list of the last 10 applications you used, not counting the Launcher.

8. Select the app you need, and you're there.

# 6 Cutting Two (!) Much of a Good Thing: UnDupe

Name of Program: UnDupe
E-Mail Address: support@stevenscreek.com
Web Address: http://www.stevenscreek.com/palm/
Version: 1.6
Type of Software: Commercial
Cost: $7.95

Does it drive you crazy when you look in your Address Book and find the same name entered three times? Maybe you entered it once on your Palm device and twice on your Desktop.

Maybe you don't do that sort of thing, but the rest of us do. And sometimes appointments seem to get duplicated for who-knows-what reason. For this, there's UnDupe, a handy little application that will examine your Date Book, Address Book, Memo Pad, and To Do List. With a couple of taps, UnDupe will search any or all of these applications and eliminate exact duplicates; any variations will be safe.

One shortcoming with UnDupe is that it can't read your mind. For example, if you entered the same name twice in your Address Book, but in one record you showed the phone number as the home number and in the other record you showed the same phone number as the work number, UnDupe will see these as two different records and won't eliminate them. (In your mind they may be the same, but in your database, they are definitely different.)

You might as well know, too, that the unregistered version merely counts your duplicates; it doesn't remove them for you. Still, recognizing a problem is the first step toward a remedy, right?

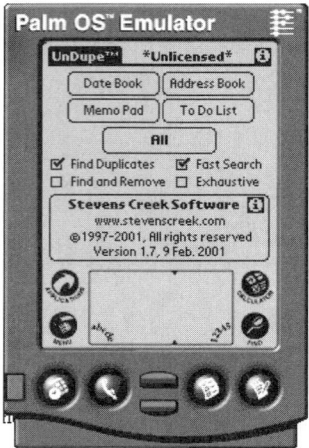

## Getting Started with UnDupe

Follow these steps to eliminate those overlapping files:

1. After launching UnDupe, you will see four check boxes in the middle of the screen. Leave Find Duplicates checked, since Find and Remove isn't available in the unregistered version.

2. Tap the Information button (*i*) in the upper-right corner of the screen for an explanation of the differences between Fast Search and Exhaustive. Tap Done after you've read the explanation.

3. Tap the box next to your choice: use Fast Search to compare each entry with the ones next to it, or use Exhaustive to compare each entry with every other entry.

4. Tap the database that you want searched, or tap All if you want all four basic databases searched for duplicates.

5. Depending on the size of the database(s) searched, UnDupe will take a few or several seconds to do its search.

6. After it gives the results, tap OK.

# 7 Bet You Didn't Think You Could Do This: PalmPrint

Name of Program: PalmPrint
E-Mail Address: pilotsupport@stevenscreek.com
Web Address: http://www.stevenscreek.com/palm/palmprint.shtml
Version: 3.0 (beta version)
Type of Software: Shareware
Cost: $39.95

If you think it would be handy to print your Palm device's contents directly from your device, you're right. You're especially right if you use your Palm device for taking orders, recording expenses, or doing other business that may require you to be away from your Desktop version of Palm software.

PalmPrint makes it easier than you might think. This little program lets your handheld communicate via the infrared port with any infrared-equipped printer, of which there are many. If your printer isn't fitted with infrared capacity, you'll have to use a cable, but printing is still a very nice idea.

The manual that PalmPrint provides thoroughly discusses all possible permutations of printers and Palm devices, and you can try PalmPrint for free. PalmPrint even comes with SnailMail, a related application that lets you print address labels or envelopes from your Address Book.

What is more, lots of other developers have made their applications so that they'll work with PalmPrint. If you have the HanDBase database program, for instance, you can print its contents using PalmPrint. Check PalmPrint's home page (listed above) for a huge listing of applications and corresponding programs for printing.

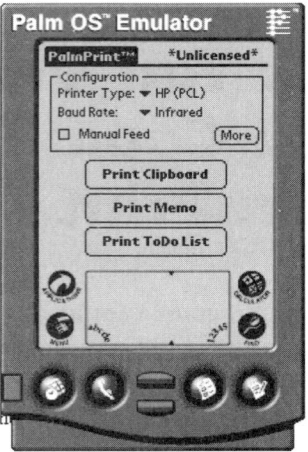

## Getting Started with PalmPrint

To print documents created on your Palm, follow these steps:

**1.** Your first job after launching PalmPrint is to configure it in the screen presented. Tap on the arrow next to Printer Type and select the appropriate printer. If you aren't sure, see the PalmPrint manual for guidance, or check in your printer's manual.

**2.** Now tap on the Baud Rate arrow and select the appropriate baud rate (the rate of transmission from the Palm to the printer). Check the PalmPrint manual or your printer's manual for this information.

**3.** If you want to choose additional configuration settings for the printed page, you can tap the More button. Then Tap OK.

**4.** If you're using the infrared port, you'll now want to test your connection. Set your Palm device about a foot away from your printer's infrared port.

**5.** Tap the silk-screened Menu button and select Test IR Communications. After a few seconds, the PalmPrint Status window will either display some kind of printer identification or tell you that no IR devices were found within range. (If you get the latter message, make sure the printer is turned on and adjust the Palm's distance a little closer to or farther from the printer. Or see the PalmPrint manual.)

**6.** Tap Print Clipboard, Print Memo, or Print To Do List.

**7.** If you choose Print Memo, a dialog box opens and you can select the memo or memos you want to print. If you choose Print To Do List, select the category and specify whether you want to print notes or only completed items. Tap OK.

## PalmPrint: The Important Commands

Here are some PalmPrint shortcuts.

| Menu | Command | Shortcut | What It Does |
|---|---|---|---|
| Options | Test IR Communications | /T | Tells you whether your Palm device is communicating with another infrared device |
| Options | About PalmPrint | None | Tells you all about PalmPrint |

# 8 Top Secret Agent 99: PalmPassword

Name of Program: PalmPassword
E-Mail Address: support@palmpassword.com
Web Address: http://www.palmpassword.com/security.htm
Version: 1.55
Type of Software: Commercial
Cost: $29.95

No one wants to use the same password for a whole bunch of accounts, right? It's too easy for a thief who discovers one to put you out of business altogether. On the other hand, it's pretty tough trying to remember those 30 accounts and their associated passwords.

PalmPassword allows you to set up an account name and password combination just once (what a relief), then link it to the Web page or Authentication window where it is supposed to be used. From then on, whenever you go to that same Web page or Authentication window, PalmPassword will recognize that the account name and password are from your PalmOS-compatible PDA, and you'll be ready to go.

PalmPassword uses a unique password: one that is for every account you have and that is kept in a safe place (the innards of your Palm). In effect, it remembers everything you enter regarding account names and passwords.

PalmPassword offers the following features:

◆ Any and all account information that is stored in PalmPassword is encrypted with special, secure algorithms.

◆ You can use up to 30 characters in a password.

◆ None of your account information is stored on your PC.

◆ PalmPassword enters the information in the username and password fields of the account you are accessing.

PalmPassword is installed on both your Palm and your Desktop computer, and it syncs the passwords that you create on either one. Pretty cool, huh?

## Getting Started with PalmPassword

Follow these basic steps to use PalmPassword:

**1.** Tap PalmPassword.

**2.** Enter a name for the account you want to secure. You can use anything for a name, but be sure that it clearly differentiates this account from others.

**3.** Enter your username. (This has probably been assigned already.)

**4.** Enter your password for this username.

**5.** Enter any specific notes and an expiration date for the account.

**6.** Tap OK.

## PalmPassword: The Important Commands

Here's a table of handy shortcuts.

| Menu | Command | Shortcut | What It Does |
|------|---------|----------|--------------|
| Edit | Undo | /U | Undoes your last action |
| Edit | Cut | /X | Cuts selected text and saves it to the Clipboard |
| Edit | Copy | /C | Copies text and saves it to the Clipboard |
| Edit | Paste | /P | Pastes text from the Clipboard |
| Edit | Select All | None | Selects all entries on the screen |
| Edit | Keyboard | /K | Allows you to use the keyboard to enter information |
| Edit | Graffiti Help | /G | Displays graffiti strokes |
| Help | Help | None | Provides PalmPassword Help |

# 9 Saving Yourself Lots of Strokes: CoLauncher

Name of Program: CoLauncher
E-Mail Address: support@mapletop.com
Web Address: http://www.mapletop.com/#CoLauncher
Version: 1.0
Type of Software: Shareware
Cost: $8 (what a deal!)

The longer you own your Palm, the more you may realize that you need some help with managing all those cool applications you have installed. Instead of going back to the Applications screen every time you want to start a new application, why not try CoLauncher? This neat little program

allows you to use a single graffiti shortcut or any one of the hardware buttons to launch an installed Palm application. CoLauncher does not use any Hacks or system patches, so you can save even more space and more memory.

If it is not enough just to work smoothly, CoLauncher also offers these features:

◆ Instant launching from any application

◆ Up to 62 apps launched via graffiti shortcuts

◆ Up to 39 apps launched via hardware buttons

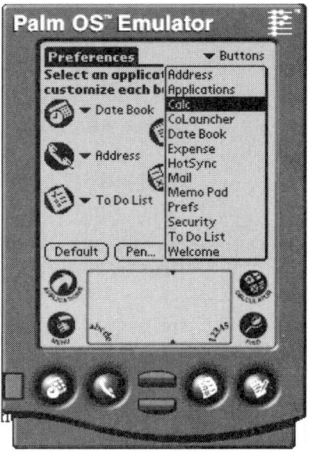

## Getting Started with CoLauncher

You can save lots of time launching what you want when you need it. Just follow these steps:

**1.** Start CoLauncher.

**2.** Assign CoLauncher to one of the four hardware buttons on your Palm. If you want to wait, after two seconds CoLauncher will enter the Setup mode, which is where you can assign CoLauncher and anything else to buttons or strokes.

**3.** Simply select the application that is already installed on your Palm, and select the button or graffiti stroke you want to use to start that application.

## CoLauncher: The Important Commands

Here are some handy shortcuts.

| Menu | Command | Shortcut | What It Does |
| --- | --- | --- | --- |
| Options | Start | /S | Starts CoLauncher |
| Help | Instructions | /I | Explains how to use CoLauncher |
| Help | Tips | /T | Gives tips on using CoLauncher |
| Help | About | /B | Tells all about CoLauncher |

# 10 Palm Icons to Fit Your Mood: IcoEdit

Name of Program: IcoEdit
E-Mail Address: support@mapletop.com
Web Address: http://www.mapletop.com/#IcoEdit
Version: 1.0.1
Type of Software: Shareware
Cost: $10

Don't like that ugly icon for your calculator, calendar, or address book? Change it with this handy utility. You can use a little drawing tool to design or modify existing icons to look exactly as you'd like. It's amazing how much you can accomplish with this tool. Not only does it allow you to change the appearance of icons, but it also does the following:

◆ Works with any app on your Palm

◆ Allows you to move the most often used apps to the top

◆ Allows you to add icons to small applications that don't come with them

◆ Tracks installed apps and notes their size, name, and version on the Memo Pad (very handy)

◆ Backs up selected applications to your Desktop

◆ Works with all application launchers (such as CoLauncher, which is made by the same company)

◆ Allows you to restore the original icon at any time

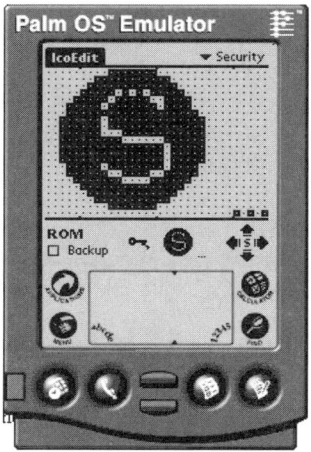

## Getting Started with IcoEdit

Create icons of your own design by following these steps:

**1.** Tap the IcoEdit icon on your Palm.

**2.** From the drop-down menu in the upper-right corner, select the icon representing the application you want to change.

**3.** Use the stylus to change the tiny black squares to white—and the white to black—as you design the image you want. The results are instantly shown on the bottom of the Palm screen.

# IcoEdit: The Important Commands

Here's a table of handy shortcuts.

| Menu | Command | Shortcut | What It Does |
|------|---------|----------|--------------|
| Edit | New | /N | Starts a new design |
| Edit | Undo | /U | Undoes the creation of the new design (reverts to the default) |
| Edit | Copy | /C | Copies text and saves it to the Clipboard |
| Edit | Paste | /P | Pastes text from the Clipboard |
| Edit | Invert | /I | Inverts the colors |
| Edit | Name | /M | Shows name of icon |
| Edit | Version | /V | Tracks version of revision |
| Options | Grid | /G | Toggles grid on and off |
| Options | Sound | /S | Turns sound on for each edit |
| Options | List Sort | /L | Sorts icons |
| Options | Restore | /R | Restores icon to default |
| Options | Restore All | /A | Restores all icons to default |
| Options | Forbid Restore | /F | Forbids a restore |
| Options | Export | /X | Exports the application list to the Memo Pad |
| Options | Datebk3 Icon | /D | Edits the new Date Book icons |
| Help | Note | /W | Attaches a note to the revision |
| Help | Tips | /T | Displays tips |
| Help | About | /B | Gives info about IcoEdit |

# A Place for Everything: Information Management

**Y**our Palm device's Address Book is just the beginning of the information management that's possible on your handheld. Developers have created some remarkable database programs that will handle all your data-managing needs. Some of these managers are elegantly simple. Others are complex, relational, and offer many options.

A handful of the best managers are covered here so you can be sure to find one that fits your needs and your style of working. Or maybe you'll want two: one for reading existing databases created by others and another to create your own personal database application. Either way, you're sure to be impressed by the amount of information you can store, sort, filter, and otherwise manage on your Palm device. You'll have access to a world of information in the palm of your hand.

# 11 Install a Powerful Database on Your Palm: HanDBase

Name of Program: HanDBase
E-Mail Address: support@ddhsoftware.com
Web Address: http://www.ddhsoftware.com/
Version: 2.5
Type of Software: Shareware
Cost: $24.99

This section starts off with what might be the industry standard—and what is now, in its newest version, greatly improved. Besides the usual database features that you will find on almost any Palm database application, this new version of HanDBase is extra special because it offers such useful tools as the following:

◆ It can link two databases together (just as a real relational database can).

◆ It can capture images and handwritten signatures.

◆ It has automatic date and time entry.

◆ You can specify match strings for text and note fields, as well as for date and number ranges and time records.

◆ The filtering tool works with Boolean logic, allowing for complex searches.

◆ You can sort any field in ascending or descending order by tapping on the field name.

◆ Reports can be run on various fields, calculating the minimum, maximum, average, sum, and more.

◆ Fields in any database can be searched for a particular word or expression, and the search feature includes a Global Find button.

◆ It has powerful viewing tools.

◆ It offers easy exporting.

◆ It has a Desktop tool (the HanDBase Desktop) that allows you to work on your Desktop databases and then transfer them to your Palm. Very cool.

## Getting Started with HanDBase

Let's say that you want to create a database for your famous book collection. First, don't forget to visit the HanDBase Web site for access to over 600 files of information in HanDBase form and other neat utilities and tools.

Then follow these steps:

1. Open HanDBase on your handheld.
2. Tap New.
3. Enter the name of the database.
4. Tap the Field 1 button.
5. For the field's name, type in **Last Name**.
6. Specify the type of field from the drop-down menu.
7. Tap OK.
8. Repeat steps 3 through 6, giving each new field a name that suits the purpose of your database.
9. Tap OK.
10. Open the database by selecting it, and click New to add a record.

## HanDBase: The Important Commands

Here is a table showing HanDBase commands.

| Menu | Command | Shortcut | What It Does |
|------|---------|----------|--------------|
| Prefs | Preferences | /R | Defines how you want the records to appear |
| Prefs | DB Properties | /D | Edits the basic structure of the database |
| Actions | Move Records To | /S | Moves records to a new location |
| Actions | Copy Records To | /F | Copies records to a new location |
| Actions | Export Records | /E | Exports records |
| Actions | Print Records | /P | Prints records |

| Menu | Command | Shortcut | What It Does |
|---|---|---|---|
| Actions | Beam Records | /B | Beams records |
| Actions | Delete Records | /D | Deletes a record |
| Actions | Run Report | /R | Begins report creation |
| Actions | Copy Template | /O | Copies a template of a database for use in a new database |
| Actions | Delete Database | /K | Deletes a database |
| Move | To Top | /T | Goes to the top of the database |
| Move | To Bottom | /B | Goes to the bottom of the database |
| Move | To Right | /I | Moves to the right |
| Move | To Left | /L | Moves to the left |
| Move | Page Right | /H | Moves one page to the right |
| Move | Page Left | /J | Moves one page to the left |
| Move | Move Up | /M | Moves up one screen in the database |
| Move | Move Down | /V | Moves down one screen in the database |
| Move | Page Up | /G | Moves up one page |
| Move | Page Down | /W | Moves down one page |
| Help | About | /A | Tells all about HanDBase |

# 12 Handy HanDBase Tool: dbPrint

Name of Program: dbPrint
E-Mail Address: support@www.nixdev.com
Web Address: http://www.nixdev.com
Version: 1.0
Type of Software: Shareware
Cost: $17.95

You've been using HanDBase (see previous app) for some time now and have become rather attached to this little marvel. Now that it's time to print out the database, however, you're stumped. You could use PalmPrint (see the section of this book titled "Getting the Most from Your Palm: Utilities and Tools"), but why not a dedicated HanDBase printing utility? That's exactly what dbPrint is.

dbPrint is a Windows-based utility that opens, formats, and prints HanDBase databases from your Desktop computer. You can simply open a HanDBase PDB file, change the formatting and appearance of the database as you see fit, and preview the printed document. You can then print the database or edit as you see fit. You can even use the Web Export feature that migrates your data to the Internet. This is one of those simple solutions to a potentially complex problem. Thank heavens for programmers!

If you want more, try these features:

◆ Full Windows printing/formatting

◆ Font selection with color and background colors

◆ Web HTML Export feature

◆ Print Preview with Zoom In and Zoom Out options

◆ Single-click column (field) sorting

◆ Column alignment options

◆ Column data formatting (dates, times, numbers, currencies)

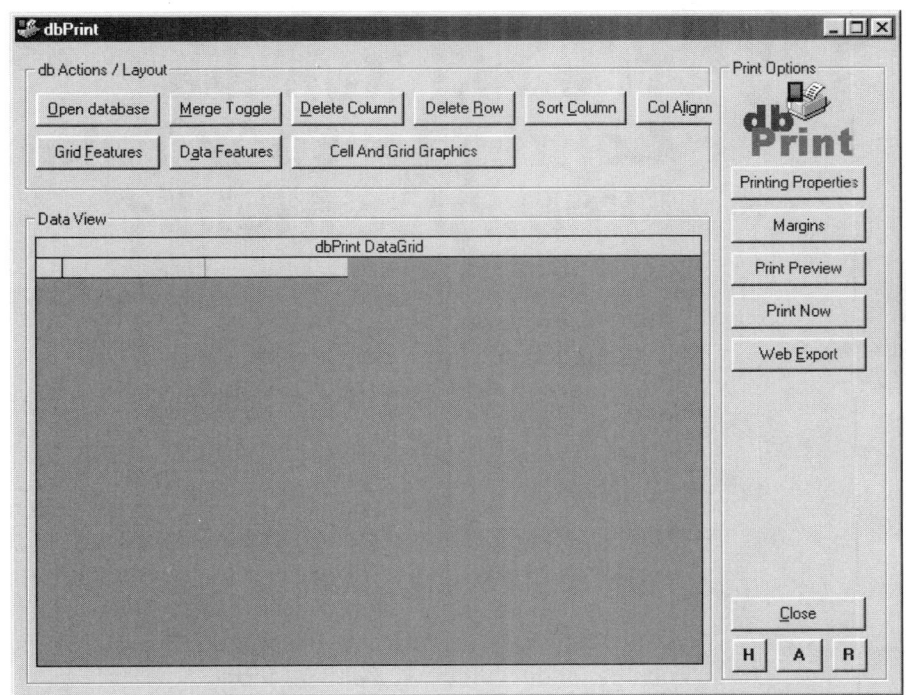

## Getting Started with dbPrint

To print a Palm file using dbPrint, follow these steps:

**1.** Open dbPrint on your Desktop.

**2.** Click the Open Database button. dbPrint will search through your directory for PDB files (the format that HanDBase can read).

**3.** Modify your database, as needed, using the commands shown in the dbPrint graphic above. You can set margins and printing properties, sort and align columns, and preview what you're going to print right from the Desktop application.

# 13 The Big Kahuna Comes to Your Palm: FileMaker Mobile

Name of Program: FileMaker Mobile
E-Mail Address: support@filemaker.com
Web Address: http://www.filemaker.com
Version: 1.0.1
Type of Software: Commercial
Cost: $49.95

In the personal computer world of database programs, there are two real players: Access and FileMaker. Access, a Microsoft product, is already available on personal digital assistants that run the Pocket PC operating system, but not for the Palm. FileMaker, a terrific Windows program, comes to the Palm in FileMaker Mobile.

Basically, you will create a database on your Windows or Mac computer and then download it to the FileMaker Mobile version that resides on your Palm. When you HotSync, the data on your Desktop computer and the Palm is synchronized and you are ready to go. (You must first tell the Desktop version of FileMaker which of your databases can be downloaded, but that's only a few mouse clicks.) If you or your employees have as any part of your job field-data collection, this is surely the way to go.

Other features include the following:

◆ You can select particular fields to download rather than downloading an entire database, so you take with you only what you need.

◆ The streamlined interface is very easy to use and understand.

◆ You can have your Mobile file overwrite the Desktop file and your Desktop file overwrite the Mobile file, or have them sync with one another when HotSynching.

◆ You can use FileMaker Mobile just as you would use FileMaker Pro: Enter and delete fields and add new records and new data as you see fit.

# Getting Started with FileMaker Mobile

Move a file from FileMaker (or FM) Pro to your Palm using FM Mobile by following these steps:

**1.** Locate and open the database you want to download to your Palm on the Desktop version of FileMaker. Of course, you'll need the full version of FileMaker to do this.

**2.** Using the Desktop version, click File ≻ Sharing.

**3.** In the File Sharing dialog box, click Single User and Mobile Companion for Palm OS.

**4.** Click Settings.

**5.** Click Specify Fields.

**6.** Select the fields you want to transfer to your Palm and click OK.

**7.** In the Mobile Settings dialog box, specify the records you want to transfer and click OK.

**8.** Click OK again, and then HotSync. Your FM database is now on your Palm. A small miracle, no?

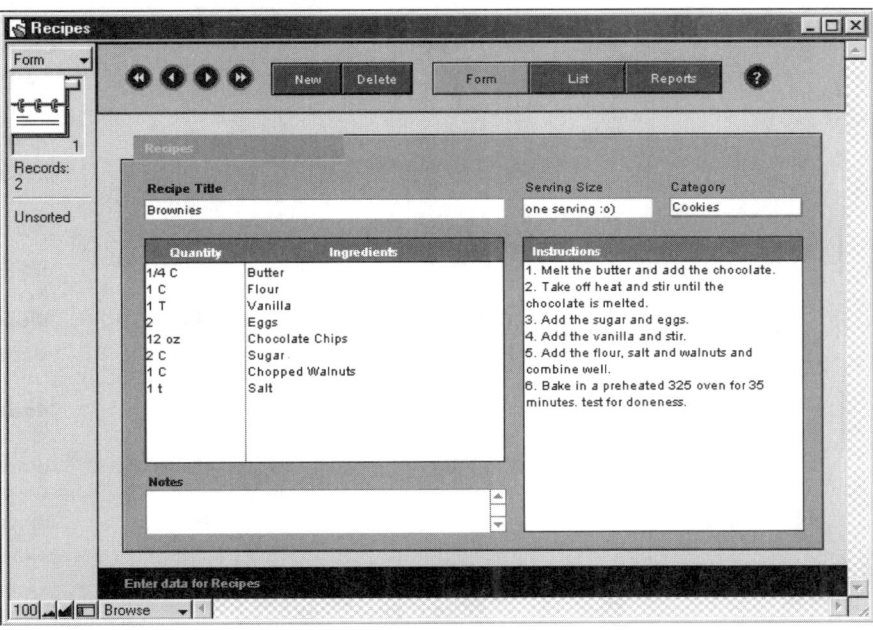

# FileMaker Mobile: The Important Commands

Here is a table showing FileMaker Mobile commands.

| Menu | Command | Shortcut | What It Does |
|---|---|---|---|
| Record | New Record | /N | Creates a new record |
| Record | Duplicate Record | /T | Duplicates a record |
| Record | Delete Record | /D | Deletes a record |
| Record | Delete All Records | None | Deletes all records |
| Record | Find Records | /F | Finds a record or records |
| Record | Show All Records | /I | Shows all records |
| Record | Sort Records | /S | Sorts records |
| Edit | Undo | /U | Undoes your last action |
| Edit | Cut | /X | Cuts selected text and saves it to the Clipboard |
| Edit | Copy | /C | Copies text and saves it to the Clipboard |
| Edit | Paste | /P | Pastes text from the Clipboard |
| Edit | Select All | None | Selects all entries on the screen |
| Edit | Keyboard | /K | Allows you to use the keyboard to enter information |
| Edit | Graffiti Help | /G | Displays graffiti strokes |
| Options | Font | None | Allows you to select a font |
| Options | Preferences | /R | Allows you to set preferences |
| Options | About FileMaker Mobile | None | Gives info about FileMaker Pro |

# 14 It's Right in This File: JFile

Name of Program: JFile
E-Mail Address: support@land-j.com
Web Address: http://www.land-j.com
Version: 4.1b2
Type of Software: Shareware
Cost: $24.95

If you've ever created a database, JFile will be a snap. And if you haven't, JFile is easy to learn and has clearly written documentation to back it up.

JFile offers a lot of flexibility for your Palm device. You can have up to 50 fields in a database—far more than even Superman might want! And JFile lets you define the fields the way you want. Besides allowing basic text, number, and date fields, it also allows pop-up lists and counters. It also gives you the option to create and modify automatic entries.

The demo version is pretty limited. It allows only one database, but one's enough to let you try your hand at database creation. JFile is also handy because dozens of databases have been set up for your use and are available for download. Good deal.

The following list includes some of the features of the latest JFile version:

◆ Scroll bars in most views for easy database navigation

◆ Lots of field types (including increment counters), options to create and modify the date and time, and multiple-item pop-up lists

◆ Categories in which databases may be grouped for easy selection

◆ Up to 50 categories per database

◆ Large font choices for easier viewing

◆ Read-only view of a record (similar to the Address Book)

◆ Printing of databases and records via the PalmPrint application (see the section on tools and utilities)

◆ Graphical method for sizing columns in the Database view

◆ Standard 4-digit years from the Date Picker

◆ Compatibility with launcher-type apps to launch a specific database

◆ Easy editing and viewing of text fields with large amounts of data

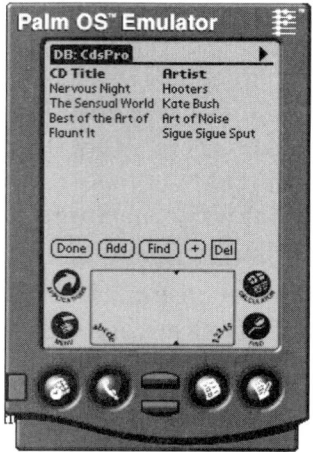

# Getting Started with JFile

To create a database using JFile, follow these steps:

1. After launching JFile, you will see the main screen, which provides a list of all JFile databases you have on your Palm device. If you've loaded the demo version and its accompanying sample database, you should have at least one database listed.

2. Tap the Eyeball icon at the left of the database to see it in read-only mode. Now you will see the list of records in the sample database.

3. Tap the arrow at the top of the screen to see the other fields in the database. Tap Done to return to the main screen.

4. Tap the name of the database. You will return to the Records screen, but this time you can do more than read it.

5. Tap Add to add a record.

6. Enter the information for the new record, which, in this case, is a new CD. Tap OK to return to the Records screen. Tap Done to return to the main screen.

7. If you're ready to create your own database, you'll first have to delete the CD database, because the demo version allows you to have only one database. To do this, tap Delete and then tap CdsPro, the name of the existing database. Tap OK to confirm the deletion.

8. Tap NewDB to create a new database and enter its title in the DB blank.

9. Enter the names of each field for your database. For this example, enter **Name**, **Birth Date**, and **Favorite**.

10. Notice that there is a String column to the right of the field blanks. If one of your fields, such as Name or Favorite, is a text field, do nothing.

   If the field, such as Birth Date, is something else, tap String next to the blank. Then choose the appropriate field type from the pop-up list.

11. Tap on the question mark (?) that appears to the right of the Date display to see more options. Select your preference, then tap OK.

12. Tap Done. Now you're ready to enter data.

13. Tap on the database name in the main screen. Tap Add, then enter the information.

## JFile: The Important Commands

Here is a table showing JFile commands.

| Menu | Command | Shortcut | What It Does |
|------|---------|----------|--------------|
| Options | App Prefs | /P | Lets you choose among various action and viewing options for all JFile databases |
| Options | Database Prefs | /B | Lets you choose among several options for handling a particular database |
| Tools | Sort Items | /S | Lets you sort records in the active database according to your specifications |
| Tools | Filter Records | /F | Lets you select items to view or not to view in a given database |

| Menu | Command | Shortcut | What It Does |
|------|---------|----------|--------------|
| Tools | Advanced Filter | /V | Provides more options for filtering a database (see the manual that comes with JFile for details) |
| Tools | Show All Records | /L | Shows all records in a database |
| Tools | Delete All Records | /D | Deletes all records in a database (after confirmation) |
| Tools | Print Records | /N | Prints records (with PalmPrint) |
| Tools | New Record | /R | Creates a new record |
| Goto | Go to Top of DB | /T | Jumps view to the top of the database |
| Goto | Go to Bottom of DB | /O | Jumps view to the end of the database |
| Goto | Go to First Field | /Y | Jumps view to the first field in the database |
| Goto | Go to Last Field | /Z | Jumps view to the last field in the database |

# 15 Keep It Simple and Smart: MobileDB

Name of Program: MobileDB/MobileDB Lite
E-Mail Address: sales@mobilegeneration.com
Web Address: http://www.mobilegeneration.com
Version: 2.1
Type of Software: Shareware/Freeware
Cost: $14.95/Free

You can find a database application that has more bells and whistles than MobileDB, but you aren't likely to find one that is easier to use. You also aren't likely to find one that has many more ready-to-use databases. You can download, for example, free databases that range from government and law to religion and history (wow! The Federalist Papers Database, anyone?), from radio stations and zip codes to Internet Provider Service telephone numbers. The standard MobileDB download alone comes with 23 databases. The list of databases is truly stupendous. Check them out at www.handmark.com/databases/.

And, at just $14.95 for the registered version, it's a bargain to boot. (MobileDB Lite is too light for most of us; it allows you to have only two databases at a time.) In addition, the companion MobileDB Desktop versions—available for Windows, Macs, and other systems—are free if you'd like to create your own databases on your Desktop with a touch of a MobileDB button and then HotSync them with your Palm. What a deal!

Here's a look at the features available in this very nice little application:

- ◆ View or edit up to 60 MobileDB databases on any Palm Computing Platform device.

- ◆ Beam databases to other MobileDB and MobileDB Lite users.

- ◆ Lock a database to hide it from the view of others using your Palm device.

- ◆ Clone a database or a record within a database.

- ◆ Utilize databases with up to 20 fields and 1,000 characters per field.

- ◆ Add, delete, or move fields within a database.

- ◆ Sort, filter, and search your databases.

- ◆ Include databases to be searched in the Palm Global Find command.

- ◆ Opt for single-handed navigation around the entire database using hard buttons.

- ◆ Choose to set Edit or View mode as the default for the selection of records.

◆ Use the many MobileDB tools, including MobileDB-PC, to create MobileDB databases on the Windows, Mac, or Unix operating system.

◆ Get huge support for MobileDB databases (hundreds are available for download now).

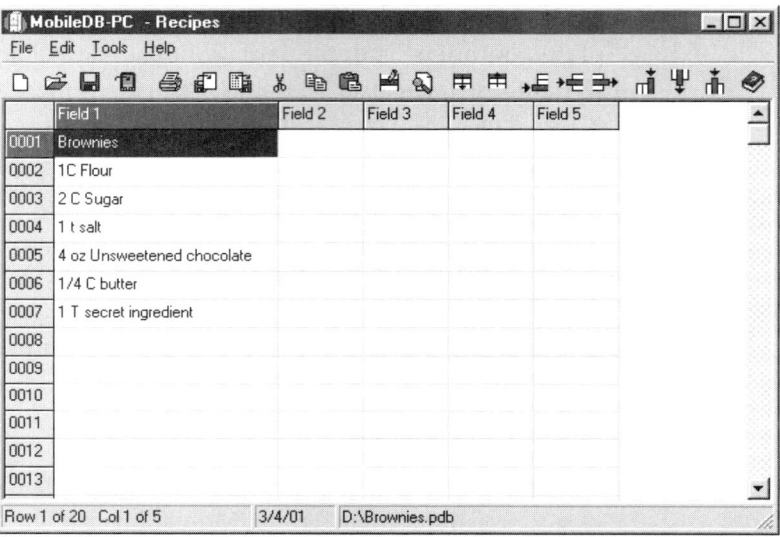

## Getting Started with MobileDB

To create a database using MobileDB, follow these steps:

**1.** When you install the unregistered version of MobileDB, go ahead and install a couple of the sample databases that come with the download. (The Food Values database is a good one for seeing the kinds of information and the size of database you can have on MobileDB.)

**2.** Then launch MobileDB, and the two databases you installed will appear on your screen.

**3.** Tap one of the databases, and it will immediately open to its main screen. You'll notice the scroll bars at the side of the screen and on the bottom-right corner.

**4.** Tap one of the records listed to open it. In the Record screen, you can edit or delete information by tapping on the appropriate button.

5. Tap Done to return to the main MobileDB screen.

6. Tap Delete, then tap one of the two databases on your screen. Confirm the deletion by tapping OK. Now you have room on MobileDB Lite to add a new database.

7. Tap New.

8. Enter the name of your new database. In this example, name yours **Library** for your personal books. Tap OK.

9. Enter the names of the fields. You can keep it simple and enter just three: **Title**, **Author**, and **Category**. Tap Done.

10. Now MobileDB presents the Records List screen for our new database. Tap New.

11. Enter a record and tap Done.

12. Tap New, enter another record, and tap Done. Repeat as many times as you'd like, and you've got a database!

13. You can use the commands listed below to work within your database.

## MobileDB: The Important Commands

Here is a table showing MobileDB commands.

| Menu | Command | Shortcut | What It Does |
|------|---------|----------|--------------|
| Database | Delete Database | /D | Deletes a database |
| Database | Rename Database | /N | Lets you give the current database a new name |
| Database | Beam Database | /I | Lets you beam the current database |
| Database | Clone Database | /+ | Lets you duplicate a database—records and all |
| Database | Modify Column Widths | /W | Lets you change widths of columns in the current database |

| Menu | Command | Shortcut | What It Does |
|------|---------|----------|--------------|
| Database | Modify Labels | /Y | Lets you alter labels on fields in the current database |
| Database | Change Password | /C | Lets you create or change the password to the current database |
| Database | Database Preferences | /P | Lets you select activity options for the current database |
| Record | Sort Records | /S | Lets you select first-, second-, and third-level sort options in the current database |
| Record | Filter Records | /L | Lets you view only records that meet your criteria |
| Record | Show All Records | /A | Shows all records |
| Record | Find Record | /F | Lets you search for records |
| Record | Repeat Find | /R | Repeats previous search |
| Record | Top of Database | /T | Jumps to the top of the database |
| Record | Bottom of Database | /B | Jumps to the bottom of the database |
| Options | MobileDB Preferences | /M | Lets you choose among various display options |

# 16 Create To Do Lists with Just a Tap of the Stylus: SuperList2

Name of Program: SuperList2
E-Mail Address: mfawcett@christianacare.org
Web Address: http://store.yahoo.com/pilotgearsw/tapsof.html
Version: 2.2a
Type of Software: Shareware
Cost: $12

Sure, you can use the Memo Pad or the To Do list on your Visor to make a list of the stuff you need at the grocery store. But does either of those tools come with more than 350 pre-entered supermarket items? Or allow you to create a simple list with nothing more than a tap of the stylus? Nope, and they're also not anywhere near as much fun as SuperList2.

With SuperList2, you can include up to 1,000 items (enough?) on a Master List, customize the Master List with new items (up to 20 characters per item), create a new one (for whomever might be doing the shopping), and enter new items using graffiti or the keyboard. And you can have up to 250 lists—that's a lot of Saturdays!

But why stop at creating a shopping list for the supermarket? You can create Master Lists for other stores and even create sets of weekly tasks that need to be done intermittently.

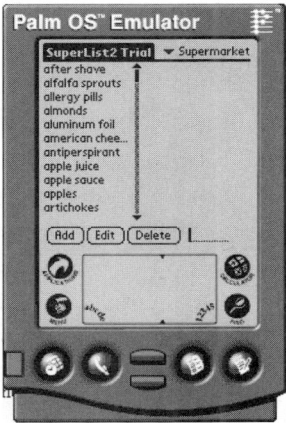

## Getting Started with SuperList2

Shop 'til you drop with SuperList2. Follow these steps to create your own list:

1. Click the item you want on the Master List (on the left side of the screen).

2. Tap on the right side of the screen to create your own list and to add the item to it.

3. To add your own item, tap the Add button and enter the item you want to add.

4. Tap the Save button.

## SuperList2: The Important Commands

Here is a table showing SuperList2 commands.

| Menu | Command | Shortcut | What It Does |
|------|---------|----------|--------------|
| Items | New | /N | Creates a new item for the Master List |
| Items | Delete | /D | Deletes an item from the Master List |
| Items | Edit | /E | Edits an item |
| Items | Clear | /L | Clears a list |
| Items | Grab All | /R | Copies all items in a list |
| Items | Select | /I | Selects an item |
| Items | Deselect | /J | Deselects an item |
| Lists | New | /W | Creates a new list |
| Lists | Delete | /H | Deletes a list |
| Lists | Rename | /F | Renames a list |
| Lists | Spawn | /Q | Copies a list based on another list |
| Lists | Reindex | /Z | Reindexes a list |
| Edit | Copy | /C | Copies an item |

| Menu | Command | Shortcut | What It Does |
|---|---|---|---|
| Edit | Keyboard | /K | Enters information using the keyboard |
| Edit | Graffiti Help | /G | Enters information using graffiti |
| Options | Instructions | /T | Gives instructions on how to use SuperList2 |
| Options | Preferences | /B | Sets preferences for SuperList2 |
| Options | About | /Y | Tells all about SuperList2 |
| Options | Register | /O | Registers SuperList2 |

# 1,234,567:
# Calculate Anything and Everything

There's more than one way to perform calculations, and Palm OS software creators have come up with a bunch. The software selections in this section go from the basic (but still an improvement over the plain-vanilla Palm-provided calculator) to beyond the comprehension of ordinary human beings. Some of these applications really put the computing in your handheld computer. Oh, sure, they can add and subtract, multiply and divide, figure percentages, and all that. But they can also let you write your own equations, figure amortizations, convert measures, and plan that trip to Mars so you can use the VPN application you'll learn about in the connectivity section. Most of them have more capabilities than any one person will ever need. What's great, though, is that there is sure to be one that's exactly what you need. And you'll be able to leave your scientific (or financial or engineering) calculator at home, because it's already on your Palm device.

# 17  Programmable Computing for a Song: APCalc

Name of Program: APCalc
E-Mail Address: ipscone@halcyon.com
Web Address: http://www.halcyon.com/ipscone/apcalc
Version: 3.1
Type of Software: Shareware
Cost: $13.75

If you want to do some fancy calculations at a very reasonable cost, try Advanced Programmable Calculator, or APCalc to its loyal users. For a lot less money than some other snazzy calculators, it gives you a ton of functions and it is easy to use.

In addition to providing normal calculator functions, APCalc lets you create your own custom calculators and programs. You will save a specific set of commands (such as computing the volume of a cylinder), enter the important data (such as height, etc.), and APCalc does all the figuring for you. You can group programs into a User Function Key Group—of which you can have nine—to allow you to transform APCalc quickly from a scientific calculator to a financial calculator to one that figures conversions of various kinds.

APCalc can handle subroutines, variables, conditional branching (labels), looping, comparison (==, !=, <, >), scientific functions, financial functions (N, I, PV, FV, PMT), graphing without programming, base conversion (2–36), 64-bit floating point, degree/radian modes, programmability, store and recall functions, input prompting, output labels, internal program database, and more. Whew!

If you know what all those things are, APCalc is just for you. You can even save expressions and execute them as a sequence of expressions. But the pocket protector is extra.

Here's the lineup of some of the many features:

- 27 scientific functions
- 62 functions
- 11 graphing functions
- 5 financial functions
- Statistical functions
- Auto-prompting variables
- Importing and exporting to Memo Pad (very handy)
- 108 programs/subroutines
- 108 user-definable function keys
- 64 program steps
- 100 user registers
- History stack (last 32)
- Graphing without programming
- Repeating any multiple instruction line so looping can be performed on a multiple line instruction

## Getting Started with APCalc

Follow these steps to create your own custom program with APCalc:

**1.** To create a program, tap the QEd button on the main screen. Tap any line to begin editing it.

**2.** Enter the expression you want to use, such as the one shown in the graphic below to compute the hypotenuse of a triangle.

**3.** Tap Done when the expression is complete.

**4.** Select Save As from the menu to name and save the new program.

To load and run the program you have created, follow these steps:

**1.** Tap the Group Key Button for that program or run the program when currently loaded by tapping R/S from the main calculator screen.

**2.** Tap Done.

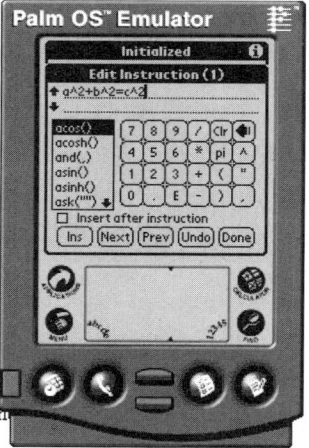

**N O T E**   See the Web site for information on limits for unregistered users.

# APCalc: The Important Commands

Here are the commands for APCalc.

| Menu | Command | Shortcut | What It Does |
|------|---------|----------|--------------|
| Program | Load/Import | /L | Lets you load or import a program for execution or editing |
| Program | Save | None | Saves changes to an existing program |
| Program | Save As | None | Saves new program |
| Program | Run | /R | Runs or stops a loaded program |
| Edit | Undo | /U | Undoes your last action |
| Edit | Cut | /X | Cuts selected text and saves it to the Clipboard |
| Edit | Copy | /C | Copies text and saves it to the Clipboard |
| Edit | Paste | /P | Pastes text from the Clipboard |
| Edit | Select All | /S | Selects all entries on the screen |
| Edit | Keyboard | /K | Allows you to use the keyboard to enter information |
| Edit | Graffiti Help | /G | Displays graffiti strokes |
| Edit | Edit Key Groups | None | Lets you change the User Key Group names |
| Info | Preferences | /I | Lets you set various display and activity preferences |

# 18   Put Your Equations in Writing: MathPad

Name of Program: MathPad
E-Mail Address: rhuebner@probe.net
Web Address: http://www.radiks.net/~rhuebner/index.html
Version: 1.5
Type of Software: Shareware
Cost: $11.95

Here's a simple and inexpensive calculator application that allows you to solve and store your equations. MathPad uses standard algebraic syntax, and it works like the standard Memo Pad, except that if you write down an equation and tap the Solve button, MathPad computes the answer and fills it in for you. These equations can be simple math expressions, such as 2 + 2 =, or algebraic expressions using variables.

MathPad provides the following:

◆ Operators for exponentiation

◆ Bitwise operators, including and, or, not, and xor

◆ Integer or modulo division

◆ Comparisons

◆ Boolean logic

MathPad also comes with functions for trigonometry (including inverse and hyperbolics), logarithms, and date manipulation, and it also allows you to annotate variables.

**NOTE**   If you are always wondering "what if…?" MathPad has a feature you should test out. With this feature, you supply the values for the known variables in your equation and solve for a single remaining unknown variable without having to reorganize the equation to isolate the unknown. This allows you to easily solve equations that would ordinarily be a pain to redo and solve. This is great for figuring monthly car or mortgage payments, for example, because you need only to have the formula and input the data.

Once you've finished a calculation, MathPad stores your equation or formula in a list similar to Memo Pad's. Thus, you can build a custom library of frequently used equations for quick reference, whether they're engineering equations (such as those for mass and stress), mortgage calculations (such as monthly payments), or drug dosage calculations. And if you write your formulas as text rather than entering them into a calculator, you can copy and paste them into other applications. Then you can beam them to your colleagues and show everyone how smart you are.

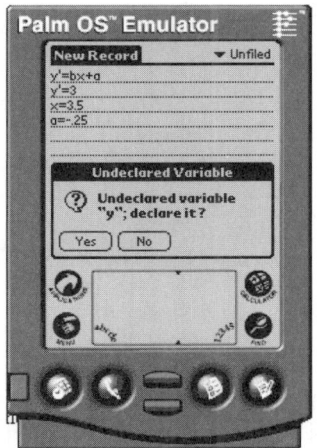

## Getting Started with MathPad

Want to solve $e=mc^2$? Here's how to get started:

**1.** Tap New.

**2.** For this example, start with a simple calculation. Using graffiti or the keyboard, enter this equation: **4 + 6 =**.

**3.** Tap Solve, and MathPad completes the calculation.

**4.** Tap Done.

Your completed equation is now listed on the opening screen. Back on the MathPad screen, your calculation is added to your equation list, and it is now stored so that you can beam it to a colleague or copy and paste it into another file, such as a spreadsheet.

# MathPad: The Important Commands

Use MathPad with these different menu options.

| Menu | Command | Shortcut | What It Does |
|------|---------|----------|--------------|
| Edit | Undo | /U | Undoes your last action |
| Edit | Cut | /X | Cuts selected text and saves it to the Clipboard |
| Edit | Copy | /C | Copies text and saves it to the Clipboard |
| Edit | Paste | /P | Pastes text from the Clipboard |
| Edit | Select All | /S | Selects all entries on the screen |
| Edit | Keyboard | /K | Allows you to use the keyboard to enter information |
| Edit | Graffiti | /G | Displays graffiti strokes |
| Options | Clear Input Variables | /I | Clears the variables you entered |
| Options | Undo Last Solve | /L | Undoes last computation |
| Options | Go to Top of Record | /A | Goes to the top of the record displayed |
| Options | Go to Bottom of Record | /Z | Goes to the bottom of the record displayed |

# 19 A Calculator Where You Need It: PopUp Calculator

Name of Program: PopUp Calculator
E-Mail Address: benc@benc.hr
Web Address: http://www.benc.hr/
Version: 1.0.1
Type of Software: Shareware
Cost: $9.95

What a great little program this is! With PopUp Calculator, you can figure your expenses while running your expense program, or calculate the unit cost of an item while making a note in Memo Pad. In fact, you can do any number of calculations—and here's the key—without having to cycle to the built-in calculator, back to the applications window, and then back to the program where you want to record the result. PopUp Calculator is a Hack-Master extension, so you can conveniently pop it open without having to close out of the application you're currently running. (For information about HackMaster and X-Master, see the section titled "Getting the Most from Your Palm: Utilities and Tools.")

PopUp Calculator not only lets you perform a calculation while another application is running, it lets you copy (and paste) directly from (and to) the PopUp Calculator's window. How handy can you get? What's more, you can drag the calculator anywhere you want on your Palm device's screen to allow you to see information that you might want for your calculations. In case you're worried, yes, it does do more than add and subtract. You can also choose to do exponential and trigonometric functions from pop-up lists.

## Getting Started with PopUp Calculator

Follow these steps to X-Master your way to calculator fame:

**1.** Start up X-Master. Tap on the check box next to PopUp Calculator to activate it. (You can choose other activation options from X-Master's PopUp Calc Setup screen.)

**2.** Tap the Home button on your Palm device.

**3.** Start another program (for example, the built-in To Do List).

**4.** Drag your stylus from the silk-screened Calculator button to the Find button.

**5.** Up pops PopUp Calculator. Do your calculation by entering your numbers either by tapping the buttons on PopUp Calculator or using graffiti.

**6.** To exit, either use the Space keystroke or tap anywhere outside the PopUp Calculator screen.

## PopUp Calculator: The Important Commands

You can start using PopUp Calculator quickly. You only need to know one command (which follows) to use all its features.

| Menu | Command | Shortcut | What It Does |
|------|---------|----------|--------------|
| Options | Toggle Window Size | /T | Lets you change size of the PopUpCalc window |

# 20 Worksheets for Every Occasion: powerOne Personal

Name of Program: powerOne Personal
E-Mail Address: support@infinitysw.com
Web Address: http://www.infinitysw.com
Version: 1.1
Type of Software: Freeware
Cost: Free

Here's a basic but versatile calculator that's a big improvement over the standard one that comes with your Palm device. Its developers evidently think so, too, since they've made it so that powerOne Personal automatically becomes your Palm's default calculator, or the calculator that shows up when you touch the silk-screened Calculator button. (Don't worry; the excellent documentation that comes with powerOne tells you how to make the change if you don't want your handheld set up that way.)

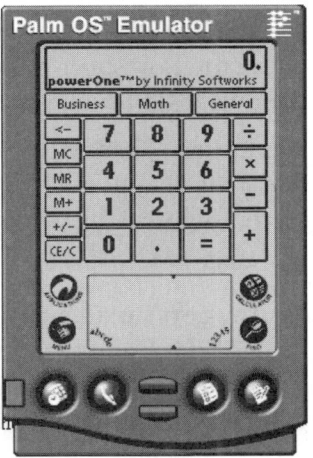

Besides the main calculator keypad that displays when you start up powerOne Personal, the application also has three buttons just under the calculator's virtual screen that let you use powerOne Personal's built-in worksheets. The Business button gives you spreadsheet-like worksheets that you can use for markups, discounts, sales tax, and other types of pricing calculations. The General button gives you worksheets for calculating restaurant tips and totals (and for splitting them among diners), for figuring date differences, and for viewing a log of all prior calculations. The Math button gives you a list of more complex calculations such as square root, x-squared, and reciprocals.

## Getting Started with powerOne Personal

Follow these steps to start using powerOne Personal.

1. Double-click `powerOne_Personal.exe` on your desktop computer. It loads a copy of the manual and an Uninstall utility. Then use the Install tool to place powerOne on your handheld.

2. Once you've started powerOne, enter one number either by tapping the buttons on the calculator keypad or using the graffiti pad.

3. Tap an operator button, such as the plus sign. Enter another number and tap the equals sign. Simple.

4. Tap the Business or General button to bring up a worksheet list. Select the worksheet you want. For this example, go to Markup under the Business button.

5. Tap the triangle next to Method to see a list of possible markup methods. (The default method is Discount.) Tap the zero next to Orig. Price. A new calculator keypad will pop up. Enter the original price.

6. Tap Save.

7. Tap the next variable; in this case it's Percent%. Enter a number and tap CPT (for Compute) on the right side of the screen beside the New Price: Indicator field. There's your marked-up price. You can also enter the new price and compute the discount percent.

## powerOne Calculator: The Important Commands

Here are the important commands for the powerOne calculator.

| Menu | Command | Shortcut | What It Does |
|------|---------|----------|--------------|
| Edit | Copy | /C | Copies text and saves it to the Clipboard |
| Edit | Paste | /P | Pastes text from the Clipboard |
| Edit | Graffiti Help | /G | Displays graffiti strokes |
| Options | Error Help | /E | Displays a list of possible reasons for getting an error message |
| Options | Keystroke Help | /O | Displays list of graffiti strokes that correspond to calculator buttons |

# 21 More Than Its Name: Yet Another Unit Converter

Name of Program: Yet Another Unit Converter
E-Mail Address: mariusm@yahoo.com
Web Address: http://www.blueneptune.com/~maznliz/marius/palm.shtml
Version: 1.2.2a
Type of Software: Freeware
Cost: Free

The creator of Yet Another Unit Converter (YAUC) acknowledges, with its name, the existence of a lot of other conversion calculators. But this one is special because it's free, it's easy, and it really covers the waterfront (or leagues or knots…).

To use this calculator, pick a conversion category, tell it what kind of unit you're starting with and what you want it converted to, and YAUC converts it in a flash. If you want to use your calculation in another application, YAUC lets you copy your conversions to the Clipboard for pasting.

Here is a list of the conversion categories:

- Acceleration
- Angle
- Angular Acceleration
- Angular Velocity
- Area
- Capacitance
- Charge
- Current
- Density
- Dynamic Viscosity
- Energy
- Flow (Mass)
- Flow (Volume)
- Force
- Frequency
- Fuel Economy
- Illuminance
- Inductance
- Kinematic Viscosity
- Length
- Luminance
- Magnetic Flux
- Magnetic Flux Density
- Mass
- Paper Density
- Power
- Pressure
- SI Prefixes
- Solid Angle
- Specific Heat
- Temperature
- Thermal Conductivity
- Time
- Torque
- Velocity (Speed)
- Voltage
- Volume
- Yarn Density

Yarn Density? Maybe it isn't important to you, but if it is, you've got to love this program.

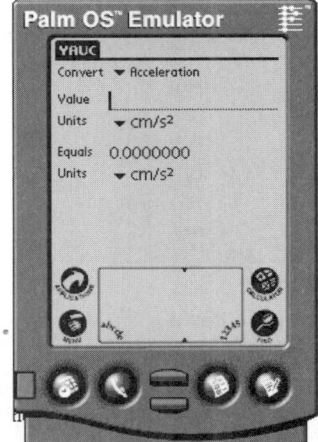

## Getting Started with Yet Another Unit Converter

You can go from Fahrenheit to Celsius and back again. To do so, follow these steps:

**1.** When you start up Yet Another Unit Converter, it presents you with its only screen. Choose the kind of conversion you want to make from the pop-up list next to the Convert arrow.

**2.** Enter a value in the first blank.

**3.** Tap the first Units pop-up list to select the kind of unit you want to convert *from*.

**4.** Select the kind of unit you want to convert *to* from the second Units pop-up list. Almost instantaneously, YAUC gives you the answer.

## Yet Another Unit Converter: The Important Commands

Want to know what a micron of pressure equals in kilopascals? The following table shows you what you need to know to figure it out with YAUC.

| Menu | Command | Shortcut | What It Does |
|------|---------|----------|--------------|
| Edit | Undo | /U | Undoes your last action |
| Edit | Cut | /X | Cuts selected text and saves it to the Clipboard |
| Edit | Copy | /C | Copies text and saves it to the Clipboard |
| Edit | Paste | /P | Pastes text from the Clipboard |
| Edit | Keyboard | /K | Allows you to use the keyboard to enter information |
| Edit | Graffiti Help | /G | Displays graffiti strokes |
| Units | Swap | /S | Switches your to value (your conversion results) to the initial value blank and vice versa |
| Units | International | None | Gives British spellings in units lists (e.g., metre) |
| Units | USA | None | Gives American spellings in units lists (e.g., meter) |

# 22 A Dollar Down, a Dollar a Day: FCPlus Professional

Name of Program: FCPlus Professional
E-Mail Address: support@infinitysw.com
Web Address: http://www.infinitysw.com/
Version: 2.2
Type of Software: Shareware
Cost: $39.95

Even if you can't own a Mercedes automobile, you can own what is, according to a well-known computing magazine, the Mercedes of calculators. FCPlus Professional is a powerful business calculator that allows you to compute annuities, loans and leases, amortization, and complex and simple interest. You can also quickly calculate markups and markdowns, profit margin, and percent change. And if you're a fan of mathematical functions, you'll be glad to find such functions as power, square root, reciprocal, natural log, square, exponential, and factorial included.

Here are some favorite features:

◆ 400 functions for business, finance, statistics, and mathematics

◆ Business computations including percent change, percent total, markups, markdowns, and profit margin

◆ Conversion worksheets including currency, area, length, temperature, volume, and mass

◆ Either RPN or standard input modes

◆ 12 distinct decimal-place settings to format up to 14-digit numbers

◆ Extensive manual and online help

◆ History of calculations for review

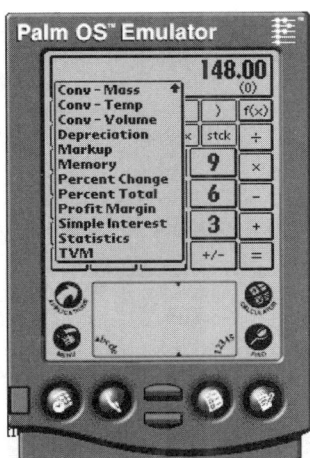

## Getting Started with FCPlus Professional

FCPlus Pro does more things than you can imagine and is very flexible above and beyond even complex calculations. Here's an example of how you can use the worksheet function to compute percent change:

**1.** On the main calculator, tap Wkst.

**2.** On the menu that appears, tap Percent Change.

**3.** Tap Old:0.00 and enter the Old value using the calculator keypad or the numeric writing area; then tap Save and tap CPT.

**4.** Tap New:0.00 and enter the New value using the calculator keypad or the numeric writing area; then tap Save.

**5.** Tap CPT next to Change %, and there it is.

## FCPlus Professional: The Important Commands

Here are the important FCPlus Professional commands.

| Menu | Command | Shortcut | What It Does |
|---|---|---|---|
| Stack | Drop | /0 | Throws out the selected value |
| Stack | Duplicate | /1 | Duplicates a selected item |
| Stack | Move | /2 | Moves an item to the Main view |
| Stack | Rotate | /3 | Moves the list in a clockwise direction |
| Stack | Rotate Reverse | /4 | Moves the list in a counter-clockwise direction |
| Stack | Swap | /5 | Swaps a value |
| Edit | Copy | /C | Copies selected text and saves it to the Clipboard |
| Edit | Paste | /P | Pastes text from the Clipboard |
| Edit | Graffiti Help | /G | Gives help with graffiti |

| Menu | Command | Shortcut | What It Does |
|------|---------|----------|--------------|
| Options | Clear All | /A | Allows you to select a font |
| Options | Clear History | /H | Allows you to set preferences |
| Options | Clear Memory | /Y | Clears the register memory |
| Options | About FCPlus Professional | None | Tells all about FCPlus Professional |
| Options | Error Help | /E | Gives information about error messages |
| Options | Keystroke Help | /O | Gives information about using keystrokes to access FCPlus Pro functions |
| Options | Back Up Options | /B | Backs up application and data |
| Options | Preferences | /R | Sets preferences |

# 23 Asleep in Sydney?: CityTime 3.0

Name of Program: CityTime 3.0
E-Mail Address: citytime@codecity.com
Web Address: http://www.codecity.com.au/
Version: 3.1
Type of Software: Shareware
Cost: $14.95

Say you're in Chicago and you have to call your honey in Sydney, but you still can't remember what time it is there while you're having breakfast in Chicago. You can use CityTime to set the time in your home city and calculate the time in four other cities on your Palm screen. And, if you have trouble with the A.M./P.M. thing, you can actually see if it's daytime or nighttime on your Palm (the section of the map that is dark indicates that

it's nighttime there). For instant information, you can simply tap the map and find out the day and time for the pop-up location. If you like your new color Palm, you'll love applications like this one!

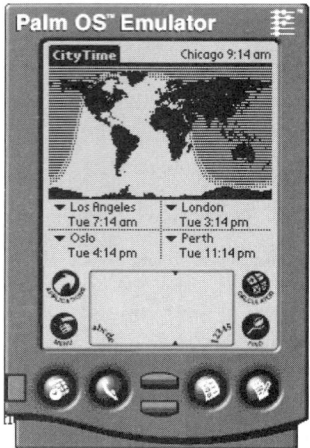

## Getting Started with CityTime

Be sure that you don't wake up anyone in Hong Kong (or anywhere else!) as you follow these steps to determine the time in two cities.

**1.** Tap the Menu button in the lower-left corner of the Palm screen.

**2.** Tap Select Home City on the Options menu.

**3.** Tap the Home City menu and specify another location. The time and date of the city you specify will appear on the opening screen.

**N O T E**  What if you live in Dodge City, Kansas, and it's not on the CityTime list? You can easily enter a new city by choosing the Edit Cities option on the Options menu and defining the new city and its current time.

## CityTime: The Important Commands

Use these commands to make sure your call to Hawaii or Amsterdam gets there when you meant for it to!

| Menu | Command | Shortcut | What It Does |
|------|---------|----------|--------------|
| Options | Help | None | Gets CityTime help |
| Options | Select Home City | /H | Selects the home city |
| Options | Edit Cities | /E | Edits and adds cities |
| Options | Register | None | Registers CityTime |
| Options | About CityTime | None | Gives information about CityTime |
| Utilities | Preferences | /R | Sets preferences |
| Utilities | Change Location | /L | Changes the current city location |
| Utilities | Time Calculator | /T | Finds out a particular time in a particular city |
| Utilities | Sun Rise/Set | /S | Calculates the time for sunrise and sunset in a particular city (and the phase of the moon, by the way) |
| Utilities | Distance/Time | /D | Calculates the distance between cities (and you can even set the speed of your trip!) |

# Does Anyone Really Know What Time It Is?: Clocks and Calendars

If you want a lot more than the time of day from your Palm device, you'll want to check out these time-keeping applications. As a group, they are simple, straightforward, and easy to use, and they'll let you do a lot more than check the time. For example, they'll measure lapsed time and cumulative time, count down time, allow you to time laps at athletic events, and save your timed events. They'll wake you up, let you snooze, and alert you with bells, lights, and words. In short, they offer many, many ways to help you handle time.

Two of the applications covered in this section aren't clocks per se, but they do provide help in keeping track of time-related events. DST Panel keeps track of daylight saving time and automatically resets your Palm device's clock for you. Meanwhile, DayNotez fills the same need as a journal page in your old paper calendar. You can take notes and keep them with your calendar, so you'll always know who said what to whom and when—among many other things. Time marches on, but with these applications, you'll at least know where it's going.

## 24 It's an Alarming Reminder: Clock+

Name of Program: Clock+
E-Mail Address: info@bitwareoz.com
Web Address: http://www.bitwareoz.com
Version: 3.41
Type of Software: Shareware
Cost: $14.95

Clock+ is simple, straightforward, and does what it needs to do. First off, it shows the time in nice BIG numbers, which is what we all need on a handheld clock. Second, it lets you set innumerable alarms and reminders.

You can also customize each of your alarms in several ways. For instance, you can select your alarm's sound from an array of sounds—from your basic alarm to a bird to Bach's Minuet in G Major. You can also choose how many times that alarm sound plays once it goes off, how often it will repeat when you hit Snooze, and how loudly it will sound. (My favorite is the Ascending feature, which makes the alarm sound louder each successive time it goes off.) Also, it has an Alarm+Backlight feature so you can use your Palm device as an alarm clock in the dark.

Clock+ also has a simple-to-use timer, which continues to run even when you leave the Clock+ application to use other Palm applications. The timer also gives you the choice of accumulating or counting down the time. And Clock+ understands that whipping out your stylus is sometimes inconvenient, such as when you want to hit Snooze. No problem. Clock+ has a big Snooze button you can tap with your fingertip. Same thing goes for the timer; you can start and stop it with a tap of your fingertip or with a pencil eraser.

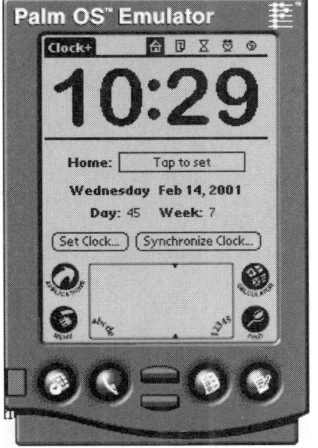

Here's a list of some of its hit features:

◆ Displays the current time with large, easy-to-read digits

◆ Supports all international date and time formats

◆ Displays the local time for four selected locations anywhere in the world and adjusts automatically for daylight saving

◆ Includes a database of over 300 countries/time zones (Yikes!) and nearly 1,000 cities

◆ Creates up to eight custom cities/aliases

◆ Sets an unlimited number of named alarms with flexible Repeat options

◆ Maintains accuracy in all timer and alarm events, even if the device is turned off

◆ Prompts to change device clock when daylight saving starts/ends

◆ Includes a selection of additional MIDI alarm sounds (OS 3.*x*)

## Getting Started with Clock+

Get started with Clock+ by following these steps.

**1.** Tap OK to clear the About screen.

**2.** Tap the box next to Home and select your home time zone from the list that appears. (The right column shows the number of hours that the chosen location's time zone differs from Greenwich mean time.)

**3.** Tap Set. (Now if you tap the Home box to see the location list again, the numbers next to the locations will tell you how many hours the times in those locations differ from the time in your home location.)

**4.** Tap Set Clock if the clock doesn't show the current time.

**5.** Tap the Page icon at the top of the screen to look at a Month view of the calendar.

**6.** Tap the Hourglass icon to start a timer.

**7.** Tap the Alarm Clock icon to set an alarm.

**8.** Tap the Globe icon to set up to four other clock displays, following the same procedures as setting your home clock.

## Clock+: The Important Commands

Use these commands to get started with Clock+.

| Menu | Command | Shortcut | What It Does |
|------|---------|----------|--------------|
| Record | List Events | /L | Opens a list of alarms |
| Record | Delete Snoozes | /Z | Deletes all upcoming snoozes |
| Record | Delete All Events | /D | Deletes all alarms, snoozes, and reminders |

| Menu | Command | Shortcut | What It Does |
|------|---------|----------|--------------|
| Edit | Undo | /U | Undoes your last action |
| Edit | Cut | /X | Cuts selected text and saves it to the Clipboard |
| Edit | Copy | /C | Copies text and saves it to the Clipboard |
| Edit | Paste | /P | Pastes text from the Clipboard |
| Edit | Select All | /S | Selects all entries on the screen |
| Edit | Keyboard | /K | Allows you to use the keyboard to enter information |
| Edit | Graffiti Help | /G | Displays graffiti strokes |
| Options | Help | /H | Shows a list of tips for operating Clock+ |
| Options | Preferences | /R | Lets you choose among various display options |

# 25  Less Is More: ClockPro

Name of Program: ClockPro
E-Mail Address: info@mapletop.com
Web Address: http://www.mapletop.com/
Version: 4.05
Type of Software: Shareware
Cost: $12 (includes a $10 registration fee plus a $2 fee for orders placed over the phone)

Clock, alarm, and timer are the three basic functions of ClockPro, and you can customize them to fit your individual needs. The timer, for instance,

understands that you may want to time splits while your daughter runs laps around the track.

It also lets you see as much or as little accessory information as you may want or need, and it provides a distinct and unusual Palm display. Its basic arrangement provides nice, big numbers for your clock, alarm, or timer and a collection of empty boxes and shapes. Each of these boxes and shapes has a use—a sound indicator, for instance. You must tap a box or shape to use it, though, because ClockPro makes it visible only when you want it to be.

In other words, it gives you all the functionality you could want but eliminates the visual distractions that are common on many clock applications.

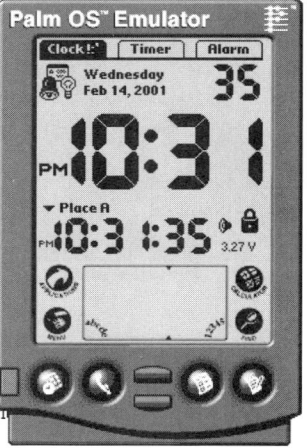

# Getting Started with ClockPro

Follow these steps to see it REALLY B-I-G with ClockPro:

1. The first time you launch ClockPro, your opening screen will be, appropriately enough, the Clock screen. Tap the tabs at the top of the screen to see the Timer and Alarm screens, then return to the Clock screen to start.

2. Tap one of the shapes in the upper-left corner of the screen. For example, if you'd like your clock to chime on the hour, tap on the bell shape. Tap on the lightbulb if you want your Palm device to flash at

the hour. And tap on the rectangle, which represents a screen, if you want your handheld to display the alarm information. Notice that symbols appear next to the Clock field when you add one of these options, and the corresponding shape fills in with a picture.

**3.** Tap on the Clock tab and make any desired changes as to the frequency and type of chime. You can also choose to preset three other locations to determine the corresponding time differences. Tap OK.

**4.** Tap the other shapes to reveal the date, the elapsing seconds, the time in your preset locations, and the time on the timer or alarm you're running elsewhere on ClockPro.

**5.** Tap the Timer tab. Tap it again to set your preferences for timer alerts. (Tap the Information icon [*i*] for more information.) Tap OK.

**6.** Tap the Alarm tab twice. Set your alarm preferences.

## ClockPro: The Important Commands

This table gives commands for using ClockPro.

| Menu | Command | Shortcut | What It Does |
|---|---|---|---|
| Options | Clock | /C | Opens the **Clock** Preferences screen |
| Options | Timer | /T | Opens the **Timer** Preferences screen |
| Options | Alarm | /A | Sets the alarm |
| Options | Notification | /N | Lets you choose general preferences, such as always using sound for the notification of alarms, chimes, and so forth |
| Options | System | /S | Lets you change the device's time and date settings |
| Help | Info | /I | Gives general tips on using ClockPro |

# 26 All in a Day's Work: DayNotez

Name of Program: DayNotez
E-Mail Address: support@natara.com
Web Address: http://www.natara.com
Version: 1.2.1
Type of Software: Commercial
Cost: $14.95

DayNotez is for you if you use your calendar not only for keeping appointments, but also for keeping notes. You can record what's decided in a meeting, note who volunteers for what committee, or keep track of anything else you'd like to record (the annoying phone calls from your least favorite vendor, for example, or each time you ask the executive committee to approve your conference).

DayNotez provides many versatile features that make its calendar/journal handier than the paper variety. You can conduct a search within DayNotez to find that note about an idea you had for the New Year's party, for instance. You can then convert your note into a To Do item, or turn it into a memo. And you can categorize your notes any way you'd like, because you can add your own categories to the basic Business, Personal, and Unfilled categories.

Adding to its utility is the Desktop version, which is available only to Windows users (it works on all versions). The developers have also thoughtfully included the necessary code to make DayNotez compatible with printer drivers and the stowaway keyboard. This all adds up to a very handy journal and calendar.

There are more features than you'll even have time for:

◆ Four views of your notes (single, daily, by list, and monthly calendar)

◆ Categories for organizing and filtering your entries

◆ Multiple entries per day

◆ Time-stamped entries with auto-rounding preferences

◆ Support for private entries

◆ Option to beam an entry to a friend (e.g., "How about dinner at 8?")

◆ Options to import and export memos and to create To Do's

◆ Stowaway portable keyboard support

◆ Ability to work with products offered by the Teal group, a major supplier of Palm applications

◆ DOC format for exporting

◆ A Details screen that includes the number of days since an entry was made

## Getting Started with DayNotez

Relate your notes to your dates by following these steps:

**1.** After launch, tap New to start a new date-related note.

**2.** Using graffiti or the keyboard, enter the information you want to remember.

**3.** Tap Details if you want to change the time or date from the current time and date. Tap OK.

**4.** Tap the triangle next to Unfiled and select a category for your note.

**5.** Tap OK. The main screen now lists your note, along with the time, rounded to the nearest hour, and the category.

**6.** Try out the different views by tapping each icon. For example, the icon of the square with the single dot in the left corner of the screen represents the Day view, which is the default. The middle icon—the one with the lines—shows your notes in a chronological list and provides a Week view, and the third view is the Month view.

## DayNotez: The Important Commands

These commands appear on the Notes menu in Calendar view.

| Menu | Command | Shortcut | What It Does |
| --- | --- | --- | --- |
| Record | Delete | /D | Deletes the note that's on-screen |
| Record | Export to Memo | /E | Creates a new Memo Pad memo from the note displayed |
| Record | Create To Do | /O | Creates a new To Do item using either the text selected or, if no text is selected, the entire note |
| Record | Beam | /M | Beams displayed note to another device that has DayNotez |
| Edit | Undo | /U | Undoes your last action |
| Edit | Cut | /X | Cuts selected text and saves it to the Clipboard |
| Edit | Copy | /C | Copies text and saves it to the Clipboard |
| Edit | Paste | /P | Pastes text from the Clipboard |
| Edit | Select All | /S | Selects all entries on the screen |
| Edit | Insert Date | /I | Opens date-selection screen and then pastes the selected date into your note |
| Edit | Keyboard | /K | Allows you to use the keyboard to enter information |
| Edit | Graffiti Help | /G | Displays graffiti strokes |
| View | Go to Top | /T | Shows the top of the displayed note |
| View | Got to Bottom | /B | Shows the bottom of the displayed note |

| Menu | Command | Shortcut | What It Does |
|------|---------|----------|--------------|
| Options | Preferences | None | Lets you choose among various options for display and actions |
| Options | Purge | /R | Lets you purge notes before a date of your choice |
| Options | Phone Lookup | /L | Looks up the name under the insertion point |

# 27 Time Marches On: DST Panel

Name of Program: DST Panel
E-Mail Address: cocos.nucifera@gmx.net
Web Address: http://www.geocities.com/SiliconValley/Cable/5206/
Version: 1.04
Type of Software: Freeware
Cost: Free

Love it or hate it, daylight saving time is here to stay—until it changes back to standard time, of course. DST Panel makes the time change easier by eliminating your need to remember when daylight saving time comes and goes.

**NOTE**   You may have heard recently on the evening news that consideration is being given to extending daylight saving time because it would save energy. Should this happen, DST Panel will allow you to adjust to the proper time on your Palm.

This application resides in your Palm device's Preferences panel (instead of in the Programs panel), so you never have to look at it once you've got it set up. Then, every April and October (or is it March and November?), your

Palm device will automatically adjust to the proper time. Not a big deal, but every worry-reduction app like this one translates to a little stress reduction, and that's what our Palm devices are all about, right?

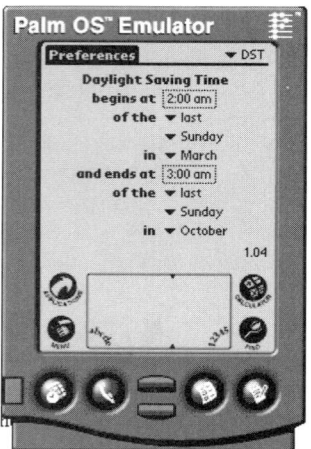

## Getting Started with DST Panel

Sleep in that extra hour and still know what time it is. Here's how:

**1.** After you install (choose dstpanel_en.prc for the English version, dstpanel_de.prc for the German version), tap the Prefs application on your handheld's Home or Applications screen.

**2.** Tap the arrow in the upper-right corner of the screen to get a pop-up menu. Select DST.

**3.** Review the settings and change any as needed to conform to the daylight saving time rules in your local area. (If you're pretty sure your area follows the typical pattern for the United States, select Defaults for USA from the Options menu.)

**4.** When you're done, tap the Applications or Home button to return to your Palm device's main screen.

**5.** Never worry again about changing to or from daylight saving time.

## DST Panel: The Important Commands

Use these commands with DST Panel.

| Menu | Command | Shortcut | What It Does |
|------|---------|----------|--------------|
| Options | Defaults for Europe | /E | Sets the daylight defaults for the European norm |
| Options | Defaults for USA | /U | Sets the daylight defaults for the U.S. norm |

# 28 Keep Track Down to the Second: TikTok

Name of Program: TikTok
E-Mail Address: TikTok@MikeMcCollister.com
Web Address: http://MikeMcCollister.com/palm/
Version: 2.07
Type of Software: Freeware
Cost: Free

You've got to love TikTok, and not just because of its amusing name. Why? It's easy to understand, it does just what it needs to do, and it does it well. If you need to time that long-distance call to Timbuktu, it's no problem with TikTok. Maybe you're wondering just how much time each day that you spend sitting at stoplights. TikTok will add it up. (Are you sure you really want to know?)

Or maybe you need a timer that works the other way around. TikTok can, for example, count down the 15 minutes you've allotted for your e-mail and then alert you when your time is up. What's more, TikTok not only runs timers for you when your Palm device is on or off, it also gives you the option to name the timer and save the results.

You say you ran a mile in 3 minutes and 54 seconds? Now your Palm can back you up (although that doesn't keep people from being skeptical; after all, you can edit the Time field of a timer that isn't running).

**WARNING**  The Tools menu has lots of handy commands to start, stop, and clear timers, but you should use these with caution because TikTok doesn't ask twice. When they're gone (or stopped or started), they're gone.

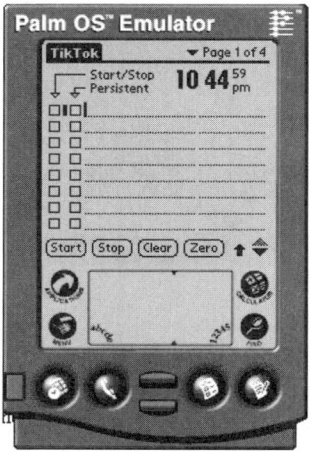

# Getting Started with TikTok

Make sure those brownies bake for just the right amount of time. Use these steps to get started using TikTok:

**1.** Tap a square in the left column (under Start/Stop) to start the clock.

**2.** Tap the same square to stop the clock. You've got the essence of TikTok!

**3.** Let's get fancy: In a blank in the right column, enter **-5:00**. Tap its Start/Stop box. TikTok is now running a timer for you. It will sound an alarm when it hits zero, show a screen advising you that the alarm has gone off, and reset the completed timer to the amount of time it counted down.

# TikTok: The Important Commands

This table of commands will help you with TikTok.

| Menu | Command | Shortcut | What It Does |
|------|---------|----------|--------------|
| Tools | Start All | /T | Starts all existing timers |
| Tools | Stop All | /O | Stops all running timers |
| Tools | Clear Focused | /L | Clears your focus marker (the black line between two boxes) |
| Tools | Clear Stopped | None | Clears all lines that have stopped timers |
| Tools | Clear All | None | Clears all timers |
| Tools | Zero Focused | /Z | Leaves text but zeros out the timer on the line with the focus marker |
| Tools | Zero Stopped | None | Zeros out all stopped timers |
| Tools | Zero All | None | Zeros out all timers |
| Alarm | 1 Minute | /1 | Creates and starts timer counting down 1 minute |
| Alarm | 1 Hour | /H | Creates and starts timer counting down 1 hour |
| Alarm | 1 Day | /D | Creates and starts an alarm that counts down 24 hours |
| Options | Preferences | /R | Lets you set various display and alarm preferences |
| Options | Get Info | /I | Provides a few pointers on using TikTok |

# 29 Get Yourself Together: DataViz WhatzUp 2.0

Name of Program: WhatzUp 2.0
E-Mail Address: support@dataviz.com
Web Address: http://www.dataviz.com
Version: 2.0
Type of Software: Shareware
Cost: $9.95

It's not a clock, but it sure is a cool and convenient way to keep track of things that happen on a schedule. WhatzUp helps you to organize daily appointments and tasks in one place and provides you with the option to view them for a particular day, week, or month. This all appears in one view, so there's no more switching screens.

WhatzUp is simple in its elegance, and that's what makes it powerful. For example, just for your To Do List, you can assign the priority, choose a category, include a note symbol, add a due date, and much more. This application is definitely a must. As an added bonus, it comes as part of DataViz's Desktop To Go utility. Check them all out at the DataViz Web site.

## Getting Started with WhatzUp

What more can we say? This program is so easy to use that there's not much more to do than to install it and get going. To get started, tap the WhatzUp icon on your Palm to combine and display today's Calendar and To Do List.

## WhatzUp: The Important Commands

Use these commands with WhatzUp.

| Menu | Command | Shortcut | What It Does |
|------|---------|----------|--------------|
| Options | Appointments | /A | Sets Appointment options |
| Options | To Do's | /T | Sets To Do options |
| Options | General | /R | Sets general options |
| Info | About DataViz WhatzUp | None | Gives information about WhatzUp |
| Info | Register | None | Tells how to register WhatzUp |

# 30  I Could've Sworn It Was on My Palm: DesktopReminder

Name of Program: DesktopReminder
E-Mail Address: info@linkesoft.com
Web Address: http://linkesoft.com/
Version: 1.3
Type of Software: Shareware
Cost: $15

This is so obvious that it's amazing someone hasn't thought of it earlier. You're at your desk working away while your Palm is tucked away, and the big meeting with your boss is about to occur. Your Palm is going nuts (tucked away in your briefcase). Its alarm is going off; it's trying to let you know, but you're hard at work on the next report and don't have a clue.

DesktopReminder reminds you of appointments stored in your Palm calendar. But it has a special feature: It will also remind you of all appointments in a pop-up window on your Desktop PC. Now that's worth the price of admission alone. This Desktop tool also has loads of options for customizing DesktopReminder. For example, you can choose for a beep (or any other sounds you have recorded, for that matter) to remind you at the right time, choose to have the message appear in red on-screen, show private entries and untimed appointments, and exclude certain categories of To Do's.

 **WARNING** DesktopReminder will not work if you synchronize your appointments with a third-party organizer software, such as Outlook.

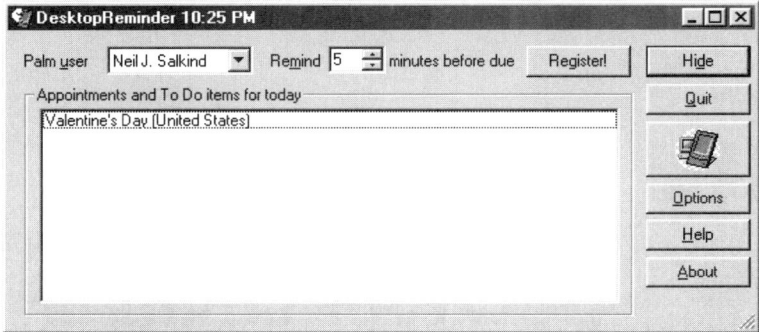

## Getting Started with DesktopReminder

Since DesktopReminder is a Windows Desktop program, just download it and install it. Then, each appointment that you enter in your Palm calendar will show up on DesktopReminder as it is due. You're on remote control and autopilot. There's nothing more to do than work away and, of course, be sure you enter your appointments in your Palm!

# Worth a Thousand Words: Writing and Language Utilities

When you get right down to it, a lot of the time you spend using your Palm device is spent entering words. You use words to enter your To Do items, your appointments, and even, in part, your Address Book entries. And as you might expect, the number one frustration with using hand-helds is in entering words. Wouldn't it be grand if the language interaction with your Palm device could be just a little easier?

Guess what? It can be! With the nice selection of language-related applications that are available, you'll find data entry, editing, and document reading a lot less painful. The applications in this section include an editor, an application that replaces graffiti, an alternative keyboard for text and number entry, and three different document readers. The document readers serve essentially the same purposes, but each has its special features, so you'll want to try out all of them to see which is best for you.

## 31 Read It Now: iSilo

Name of Program: iSilo and iSiloWeb
E-Mail Address: email@isilo.com
Web Address: http://www.iSilo.com
Version: 2.58
Type of Software: Shareware
Cost: $12.50

One of the nicest features of iSilo isn't evident when you start up the application and just read a sample document; it's evident when you need to convert formats so you can read a document on your Palm. iSilo is a document converter for Windows and Macintosh that switches HTML documents and other formats into a format that you can read on your Palm device. Best of all, it's a one-step conversion and installation process. Using the Windows 95/98/NT or Mac converter, you just need to specify the document to convert, and the next time you HotSync, the document automatically downloads to your Palm organizer. Very nice indeed.

In addition, many Palm OS developers are now making documents already in the iSilo format. There's a ton available at www.aportis.com/library.

**N O T E**   iSilo also makes a freeware version (iSoloFree), but the $12.50 you'd spend for the shareware version lets you see images, choose varied text styles, use hyperlinks, copy text, use bookmarks, and get free upgrades. It seems like a very reasonable price for all these added features.

Here's a shortened version of the developer's extensive list of features:

◆ It occupies only 81K of memory and does not require the installation of any additional font databases.

◆ It uses a document-storage format that saves 20 percent more memory than the DOC format.

◆ It doubles the speed for document access and display. One clear area where this helps is in the search engine.

◆ It can create richly formatted (HTML) documents, including varied type styles and lines that make document viewing and information absorption easier.

◆ It includes embedded hyperlinks so that the reader can easily jump to related content.

◆ It allows you to view images embedded in the document.

◆ It enables you to read AportisDoc documents (see later in this section for info about this application) directly without the need for a separate application.

◆ You can use bold, italic, underline, strikethrough, standard font, large font, bulleted lists, numbered lists, and left, right, and center text alignment.

◆ It offers scroll bars for scrolling up and down lines and screens and for quickly moving to any location.

◆ It allows on-screen scrolling.

◆ You can jump to the top, to the bottom, or (get this) to a percentage of the screen.

◆ You can jump to any page, to the first or last page, or to the previous or next page.

◆ You can beam documents from one device to another.

◆ You can convert HTML-formatted, plain-text, and Word documents.

◆ BMP, GIF, and JPG formats in HTML documents convert automatically with scaling, dithering, and contrast enhancements.

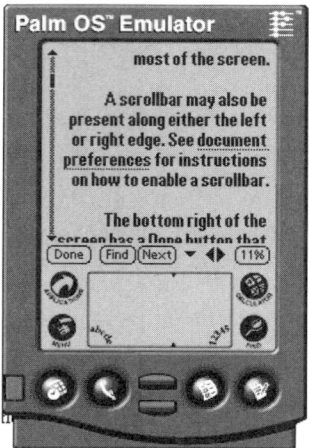

## Getting Started with iSilo

Any DOC file (in the AportisDoc format) can be synched so you can read it using iSilo. The really cool part of iSilo is using iSiloWeb, which allows you to convert documents.

**1.** Install iSilo and an iSilo document, such as the iSilo Manual. Then launch iSilo and tap OK to leave the introductory screen.

**2.** The first iSilo screen shows a list of iSilo documents you have on your Palm device. A triangle for a pop-up list is at the bottom left of the screen, and the word Open should appear next to the triangle. If not, tap the triangle and select Open from the pop-up screen.

**3.** Tap the document you want to read and start reading.

**4.** Tap the bottom of the screen to move the text up.

**5.** You may encounter underlined items, such as those you'd see on Web pages. These are indeed links to other spots in the document. Tap one to jump to that content.

**6.** Tap on the sideways triangle/arrow that now appears next to the % button to return to the link.

**7.** Notice that the arrow has changed direction. Tap it again, and it will take you back to your previous spot. Cool.

**8.** Tap Done when you've finished reading, and you'll return to the iSilo documents list.

iSilo organizes HTML files into channels. The easiest way to create a list of HTML files in a channel is by dragging them from the actual browser you use to the iSiloWeb window. To use iSiloWeb (a Windows-based application), follow these steps:

**1.** Download `iSiloWeb.exe` from `www.iSilo.com`.

**2.** Unzip the application.

**3.** Double-click the Windows-based iSiloWeb application to open it.

**4.** You can cut and paste a URL into the iSiloWeb application or even drag a URL (by dragging the small Explorer or Netscape icon to the immediate left of the URL in the browser) into the iSiloWeb window.

**5.** Click the Convert icon in the iSiloWeb window.

**6.** Then HotSync, and the HTML file will appear on your Palm.

## iSilo: The Important Commands

These commands speed up your navigation in iSilo.

| Menu | Command | Shortcut | What It Does |
|---|---|---|---|
| Commands | Copy Text | /C | Copies selected text |
| Commands | Preferences | /P | Lets you choose among several display and action options |
| Commands | Details | /D | Provides information and options for the book you're actively reading |

| Menu | Command | Shortcut | What It Does |
|------|---------|----------|--------------|
| Marks | Mark Location | /M | Adds an unnamed marker at the current location |
| Marks | Jump to Mark | /J | Jumps to the unnamed marker |
| Marks | Add Bookmark | /B | Creates a named bookmark |
| Marks | Edit Bookmarks | /E | Lets you organize your bookmarks |

# 32 Speed Typing by Stylus: Keyboard Hack

Name of Program: Keyboard Hack
E-Mail Address: horace@palmgadget.com
Web Address: http://palmgadget.com
Version: 2.8
Type of Software: Shareware
Cost: $5.95

If you're willing to trade for smaller Palm OS keyboard keys in order to have more of them on your screen, you'll like Keyboard Hack. Keyboard Hack, a Hack extension, replaces the standard Palm OS keyboard with a 69-character keyboard that combines alpha and numeric keys. It's that simple! It allows you to enter keys much faster than the standard keyboard, because many of the characters that are often needed (such as numbers and punctuation points) are readily available on Keyboard Hack.

Once installed, just tap on the Graffiti screen, and up pops the expanded shrunken keyboard. No more switching!

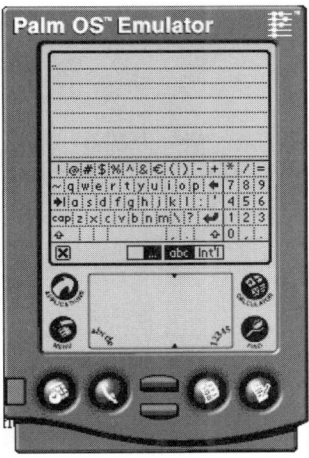

## Getting Started with Keyboard Hack

You can avoid having to shift from one keyboard to another by using Keyboard Hack:

**1.** If you don't already have it, install HackMaster or X-Master, and then install Keyboard Hack.

**2.** Launch the Hack Handler, and check the box next to Keyboard Hack to activate it.

**3.** Tap the Configure button to change any of the standard Keyboard Hack settings. Tap OK when you're done.

**4.** Return to the main Home/Applications screen by tapping the silk-screened Home button on your Palm device, or press the To Do or Memo Pad hardware button.

**5.** If you returned to the main screen, launch an application by tapping on it.

**6.** Tap in the Graffiti ABC area to start your new keyboard.

**7.** Start entering text. With the computer keyboard display, entering text will be easier, and your entry displays at the top of the screen.

**8.** Tap the X in the lower left of the screen to return to your application.

## Keyboard Hack: The Important Commands

Use these commands to move text in Keyboard Hack.

| Menu | Command | Shortcut | What It Does |
|------|---------|----------|--------------|
| Edit | Undo | /U | Undoes your last action |
| Edit | Cut | /X | Cuts selected text and saves it to the Clipboard |
| Edit | Copy | /C | Copies text and saves it to the Clipboard |
| Edit | Paste | /P | Pastes text from the Clipboard |
| Edit | Select All | /S | Selects all entries on the screen |

# 33   A Book in Hand: Palm Reader

Name of Program: Palm Reader (was Peanut Reader)
E-Mail Address: info@peanutpress.com
Web Address: http://www.peanutpress.com
Version: 3.1
Type of Software: Freeware
Cost: Free

Palm Reader turns your Palm device into your own e-book reader. You'll just need to install a book as well as the reader, and start reading. (This program was called Peanut Reader, but its maker, peanutpress, was recently acquired by Palm and is now Palm Digital Media.)

The developers have included several options to make the reading easier. For instance, you can choose between two text sizes, and you can choose to have the text displayed sideways, or even upside down, on your handheld. Also, the Palm's Up and Down hardware buttons make leafing through the pages easy, and you can insert bookmarks or make notes about your reading as you go.

What's more, you can view a list of all your bookmarks or annotations, and you can jump to a specific page with a flick of your stylus. A set of admittedly tiny icons at the bottom of the screen lets you do various menu-driven functions, such as making annotations, from the display screen.

Books for the Palm Reader can be found at the Web site listed on the previous page, and the huge collection includes both free and commercial readings. Among the commercial entries are *Star Wars: Death Maul*, *Timeline*, *When We Were Orphans*, and John Le Carre's new book, *Single & Single*. You can even check out the findings from the *United States of America v. Microsoft Corporation* case (see the following illustration for the opening page). And now that the newest models of the Palm (the m500 and m505) will come with Palm Reader already installed, this is likely to become an increasingly useful resource.

**WARNING**    Going to Tahiti and planning to take Stephen King's newest novel *Dreamcatcher*? Don't get too excited until you check the memory requirements of what you want to download (668KB in this case). Tap the Menu icon on your Palm, then tap the App menu and the info item to see how much free menu is available.

Palm Digital Media offers a variety of books across a wide range of topics:

- Action/Adventure
- Biography/Memoir
- Business and Technology
- Business Magazines
- Classics
- Entertainment
- Espionage and Thrillers
- Family and Parenting
- Fantasy
- Fiction and Literature
- Gay/Lesbian
- Handheld Computing Magazine (Tap)
- History
- Horror
- Humor
- Investing and Money

- ◆ Law
- ◆ Mind, Spirit, and Self-Help
- ◆ Modern Library
- ◆ Mystery and Detectives
- ◆ Mystery Magazines
- ◆ Nonfiction
- ◆ Poetry
- ◆ Politics
- ◆ Romance
- ◆ Science Fiction
- ◆ Science Fiction Magazines
- ◆ Sports and Athletics
- ◆ Star Trek Books
- ◆ True Crime
- ◆ Western
- ◆ Young Adult

## Getting Started with Palm Reader

More books than you can imagine are available using this reader. Learn how to use it by following these steps:

1. When you install Palm Reader, you will also want to install a Palm Digital Media book. Two come with the download.

2. The first Palm Reader screen you see gives you the option of going straight to the application or reading Help. Tap OK (although you're welcome to read the Help Guide first).

**3.** Tap the book you're interested in reading to select it. Tap Open.

**4.** Now you're on the first page of your e-book.

**5.** To go to the next page, tap in the bottom half of your screen with the stylus, or press the Down button.

**6.** To go to the preceding page, tap on the top half of the screen, or press the Up button.

## Palm Reader: The Important Commands

Palm Reader has an extensive set of menu commands and options.

| Menu | Command | Shortcut | What It Does |
|------|---------|----------|--------------|
| Book | Open | /O | Opens a book |
| Book | Delete | /D | Deletes a book |
| Book | Beam | /B | Beams a book |
| Go | Find | /F | Searches for text |
| Go | Find Again | /L | Searches for the next instance of your previous search item |
| Go | Bookmarks | /M | Lists all bookmarks for current book |
| Go | Add Bookmark | /A | Creates a bookmark for current location |
| Go | Annotations | /T | Lists all annotations for current book |
| Go | Add Annotations | /N | Lets you create a note about the text |
| Go | Go to Page | /J | Opens book to a page you specify |

| Menu | Command | Shortcut | What It Does |
| --- | --- | --- | --- |
| Go | Go to Chapter | /H | Opens book to the first page of a chapter you specify |
| Go | Go to Beginning | /B | Opens book to its first page |
| Go | Go to End | /E | Opens book to its last page |
| Go | Back | /K | Returns you to the previous location in the book |
| Options | Preferences | /R | Lets you choose among various display and action options |
| Options | Screen Preferences | /Y | Lets you view text sideways or upside down on your Palm device |
| Options | Font Small | /1 | Sets display type to small font |
| Options | Font Large | /2 | Sets display type to large font |
| Options | Invert Screen | /Z | Changes screen to white text on dark screen or vice versa |
| Options | Start AutoScroll | None | Makes text begin to scroll up your screen, as for scanning |
| Options | AutoScroll Options | None | Lets you select the Auto-Scroll method |
| Options | Book Info | /I | Gives you details, such as title and book length, about current book |

# 34 Recognizing Your ABC's: simpliWrite

Name of Program: simpliWrite
E-Mail Address: support@artcomp.com
Web Address: http://www.artcomp.com
Version: 1.0 demo
Type of Software: Commercial (with a five day free trial)
Cost: $19.95 (introductory price)

This Palm application builds on your first-grade, lowercase ABC's. It's perfect for the user who just can't get the hang of the graffiti language and finds the keyboard inconvenient.

The developers of simpliWrite bill their application as character-recognition software. Although it doesn't recognize the way you, specifically, write, it does recognize the standard lowercase printed letters. You no longer need to switch back and forth between uppercase and lowercase letters, as in graffiti.

Although it probably will take some getting used to (I could never seem to get Y's right), simpliWrite is intuitive and easy to use. For instance, you make two-stroke letters, most particularly T's and F's, with (ta-da!) two strokes. Fortunately, its user manual is thorough and easy to follow.

**NOTE**  As you write, your "pen" strokes appear briefly on the screen, which can help you see whether or not you're making stray strokes that might yield an alternate letter. Plus, the Graffiti Help menu item that appears in many applications will now give you simpliWrite help.

simpliWrite has some nice additional features. For example, it automatically assumes you'll want a capital letter after a period. Also, you can set it to enter a space automatically when you pause at the end of a word.

Here are some other features you may like:

◆ It offers compatibility with all Palm command shortcuts.

◆ You can use the writing area of the Palm (bottom part of screen) in the way you are used to.

◆ It supports English, German, French, Italian, Spanish, Portuguese, and Dutch and includes accented characters, punctuation, and digits. It allows you to write accented characters as you do on paper.

◆ It recognizes and adjusts to your own writing speed.

◆ It allows easy switching to punctuation and uppercase characters.

# Getting Started with simpliWrite

Don't yet have graffiti down to a science? Join the rest of us and get better at it with simpliWrite. Here's how to use it:

**1.** Launch simpliWrite.

**2.** In the opening screen, tap on the square next to Activate simpliWrite.

**3.** Press the Memo hardware button so you can try simpliWrite.

**4.** Write letters in the left part of the entry area and numbers in the right, just as you would in graffiti. Use standard, printed lowercase letters.

**5.** Your writing appears in the lower portion of the screen, and as soon as you complete a letter, it disappears. The character indicator at the bottom right of your screen lets you know whether the next letter you enter will be lowercase, uppercase, or a punctuation mark.

**6.** Tap Done.

**7.** Try simpliWrite in other applications, too.

**8.** If you want to try out the options, return to the Applications screen and relaunch simpliWrite. Choose any options you like under the pop-up menus next to Language and Ink Display, or tap Advanced for more options.

# 35 Read All about It: TealDoc

Name of Program: TealDoc
E-Mail Address: business@tealpoint.com
Web Address: http://www.tealpoint.com
Version: 3.61
Type of Software: Shareware
Cost: $16.95

Here's a nice, usable document reader at a reasonable price. TealDoc makes it easy to scroll through documents of all kinds (including graphics, as you see in the following screen shot), add bookmarks, and search for a word or part of a word, and it gives you plenty of operational and display options. TealDoc's sophisticated navigation system lets you go through documents line by line, page by page, bookmark by bookmark, manually, or automatically. What's more, it supports color Palm devices.

TealDoc also has a companion printing application, TealPrint ($19.95), that will let you print your TealDoc documents straight to many printers.

TealDoc's features are numerous:

◆ Support for embedded images

◆ Link buttons for going within a document or between documents

◆ Selectable fonts

◆ Convenient forward and backward searching

◆ Advanced search options

◆ Configurable display

◆ Multispeed autoscroll

◆ Function for creating private documents

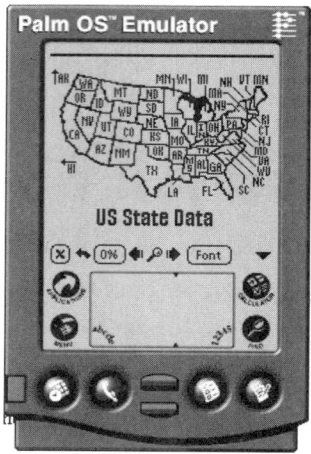

# Getting Started with TealDoc

This is another excellent reader that has many documents available for reading. Follow these steps to use it:

**1.** Be sure to install at least one TealDoc document along with the Teal-Doc application. The opening window will list the TealDoc books or documents available to you.

**2.** The Open box should be highlighted at the bottom of the screen. If it isn't, tap on it to highlight it.

**3.** Tap the document you want to read in the list.

**4.** Once the document is open, you can tap the bottom half of the screen to move the document up one line. (You can change the amount scrolled in the Preferences screen.) Tap and hold to get continuous scrolling.

**5.** Tap (or tap and hold) the top half of the screen to move the document down.

**6.** Tap the arrow at the bottom right of your screen. A list of preset bookmarks will pop up. To add your own, select New Bookmark.

**7.** Enter a name for your bookmark, then tap OK. Now, any time you want to return to that spot, you can just pick that bookmark from the pop-up list.

**8.** Select a bookmark from the pop-up list. You're automatically taken to that location.

**9.** Tap the angled left arrow at the bottom left of the screen. Now you're back where you were before using the bookmark.

**10.** See the button showing the percent sign and a number? The number there indicates your location within the overall document. For instance, "10%" means that you've gone 10 percent of the way through the document.

**11.** Tap the % button. Up pops a scroll bar to provide another means of going through the document. You can scroll a page at a time by tapping to the right or left of the dark bar, or you can tap and drag the dark bar to move you swiftly through the document.

**12.** Tap the % button again to hide the scroll bar.

**13.** Tap the Magnifying Glass icon to search for an item. Enter what you want to search for in the blank. (You can check any of the four boxes on the screen to restrict your search; see the user's manual for details.) Tap OK.

**14.** Tap the right arrow beside the magnifying glass to search forward in the document for the same term.

**15.** Tap the left arrow to search backward in the document for the same term.

**16.** Had enough for now? Tap the X at the bottom left of the screen to close the document and return to the TealDoc list.

## TealDoc: **The Important Commands**

Here are the reading, scrolling, and navigation commands in TealDoc.

| Menu | Command | Shortcut | What It Does |
|------|---------|----------|--------------|
| Doc | Find | /F | Opens Find screen to search for an item you specify |
| Doc | Find Next | /N | Searches forward for the next occurrence of the specified Find item |
| Doc | Find Last | /L | Searches backward for the previous occurrence of the specified Find item |
| Doc | Preferences | /P | Lets you choose among various display and function options |
| Doc | Details | /E | Lets you change or view the setting details of the current document |
| Doc | Delete | /Z | Lets you delete the current document from your Palm device |
| Doc | Close | /X | Closes current document |
| View | Go Up Page | /U | Scrolls a page up |
| View | Go Down Page | /D | Scrolls a page down |
| View | Got to Top | /T | Jumps to top of document |
| View | Go to Bottom | /B | Jumps to bottom of document |
| View | Copy | /C | Copies selected text |
| View | Show Font Panel | None | Opens Select Font window |
| View | Show Scroll Panel | None | Opens scroll bar |
| Marks | Add New Bookmark | /1 | Lets you add a bookmark |
| Marks | Delete Bookmark | /2 | Lets you delete a bookmark |

| Menu | Command | Shortcut | What It Does |
|---|---|---|---|
| Marks | Delete All Bookmarks | /3 | Lets you delete all bookmarks |
| Marks | Rename Bookmark | /4 | Lets you rename a bookmark |
| Marks | Scan for Bookmarks | /5 | Scrolls from one bookmark to the next |
| Marks | Custom Scan | /6 | Lets you choose options for scanning document |
| Special | AutoScroll Go | /G | Starts scrolling automatically through the document |
| Special | AutoScroll Stop | /S | Stops automatic scrolling |
| Special | Help | /H | Provides Tips screen |

# 36 Read E-Books on Your Palm: AportisDoc

Name of Program: AportisDoc
E-Mail Address: custcare@aportis.com
Web Address: http://www.aportis.com
Version: 2.21
Type of Software: Shareware
Cost: $30

There's too much to say about AportisDoc; it may even be the de facto industry standard for displaying and interchanging electronic text and books of any size. AportisDoc contains full search capabilities and allows the customization and personalization of your Palm reading efforts. You can read documents in an extra large font or even on the full screen—a great help when the available light is not that great. And this very cool application can even act as a teleprompter for your next presentation. You just set the speed and AportisDoc will automatically scroll the text for you.

You'll soon be able to get PDF files on your Palm using the AportisDoc PDF Converter. And, until AportisDoc Professional is available, you can create AportisDoc documents using MakeDoc. With this utility, text (.txt) and HTML files can easily be transformed into the AportisDoc format.

## Getting Started with AportisDoc

To read a document using this reader, you have to install the reader files (ApotisDoc.prc and AdocReference.pdb) and then install whatever document you want to read on your Palm. Here are some of the basics:

1. Double-tap in the List screen on the doc you want to read.

2. Tap on the screen to scroll to the next page or press the Up and Down button on your Palm. You can even set the prompter to scroll automatically for you.

3. Tap the Done button when you've finished reading a document. Even if you go to another document, AportisDoc will save your place.

Go to the Aportis e-book library (at www.aportis.com/library/index.html) for just about anything and everything you could need. It's H-U-G-E.

## AportisDoc: The Important Commands

You can manage and move through your text with these actions in AportisDoc.

| Menu | Command | Shortcut | What It Does |
| --- | --- | --- | --- |
| Options | About AportisDoc | /Q | Gives info about AportisDoc |
| Options | Preferences | /Z | Allows you to set preferences for how you want text to appear |
| Options | Copy | /C | Copies text |
| Options | Details | /I | Gives details about the document itself |
| Options | Beam | /B | Beams a document |

| Menu | Command | Shortcut | What It Does |
|------|---------|----------|--------------|
| Options | Close | /W | Closes the current document |
| Go | Find | /F | Finds text |
| Go | Find Again | /O | Finds the same text again |
| Go | Go to Bookmark | /M | Goes to a defined bookmark |
| Go | Add Bookmark | /R | Creates a bookmark |
| Go | Delete Bookmark | // | Deletes a bookmark |
| Go | AutoBookmark | /Y | Enters text in a dialog box and bookmarks it throughout the document |
| Go | To Top | /< | Goes to the top of the document |
| Go | To Bottom | /> | Goes to the bottom of the document |
| Display | Start Prompter | /T | Starts the prompter |
| Display | Stop Prompter | /H | Stops the prompter |
| Display | Set Up Prompter | /N | Selects the time you want the prompter to go to a new page or line |
| Display | Larger Text Window | /+ | Increases text size |
| Display | Smaller Text Window | /- | Decreases text size |
| Display | Regular Font | /1 | Uses a regular font |
| Display | Big Font | /2 | Uses a large font |
| Display | Bold Font | /3 | Uses a bold font |
| Display | Monospaced | /4 | Uses a proportional font |
| Display | Screen Width | /E | Sets the screen width |

# 37 A Language That's Easier Than Graffiti: Thumbscript

Name of Program: Thumbscript
E-Mail Address: info@thumbscript.com
Web Address: http://www.thumbscript.com
Version: 1.1
Type of Software: Freeware
Cost: Free

A few years ago, a clever physician noticed that the buttons on most Palm devices are similar to those on a phone and other communication devices. He saw these models as visual keypads, and he created an entire alphabet out of the patterns that you could create with your thumb. Based on the nine keys on your phone or, in the case of the Palm, an array of nine dots on your screen, you can enter any character as if you were using graffiti or the keyboard.

Thumbscript works as follows. Think of the keypad you use as a simple drawing tablet consisting of nine dots to represent a numeric keypad. You use that drawing tablet to construct letters. You press the start key (indicated by a dot) at the beginning of the letter and then the stop key at the end of the letter. In this way, each character is defined by a two-stroke key sequence. All letters are drawn from one of the outer buttons to the center and back to an outer button, and all letters are drawn from top to bottom. If start and stop are on the same line, then you draw from left to right. The vowels *a*, *e*, *i*, *o*, and *u* are drawn with a straight line through the center. For example, to enter the letter *a*, press the 7 key and then the 9 key. Any character including letters and numerals can be drawn with the same two strokes. And if you want to be really cool, you can even use Thumbscript to send e-mail. No kidding! See the Web site for more.

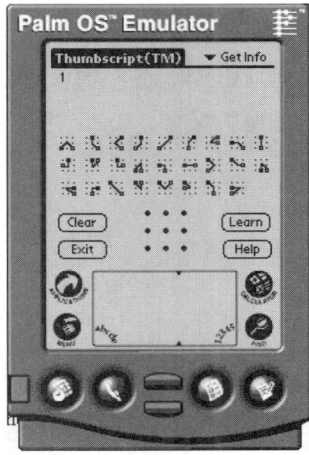

The complete kit that you download from www.thumbscript.com includes the following:

◆ A speedometer for continuous monitoring of your input speed in standard WPM

◆ Wide Writing so you can use the full screen as an input area

◆ Instructions

◆ Quick Trainer

◆ A beamable Palm demo

◆ A Desktop demo you can use with your browser

◆ A formal white paper (for techies) on Thumbscript

# Getting Started with Thumbscript

A really nice alternative to graffiti and the keyboard, Thumbscript is a whole new way of entering text that can be used by anyone. It's so simple all you need to do is download and start Thumbscript, then simply use the nine buttons on the full screen to form the characters you want to enter as text.

# 38 Spell-Check on Your Palm: SpellMan

Name of Program: SpellMan
E-Mail Address: info@standalone.com
Web Address: http://www.standalone.com
Version: v.1.15b1
Type of Software: Commercial (with thirty-day free trial)
Cost: $15 (with free upgrade)

No matter how you write—using your stylus and graffiti, the keyboard, or Thumbscript—it's likely that you will make spelling (and not just typing) errors. SpellMan does just what it says. It checks the spelling of a Palm document and provides you with alternatives. And it's simple to use.

**WARNING**  SpellMan is definitely cool, but it's also *big*. If you want to load all the dictionaries, you're talking about half the amount of space available on a Palm V (close to a megabyte). So choose your words (and space) carefully.

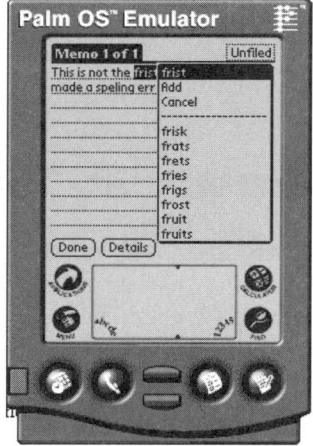

# Getting Started with SpellMan

To spell-check a section of text, go to the beginning of the text and double-tap the first word that you would like to check. SpellMan will continue to check the rest of your document until you tap Cancel or until SpellMan runs out of misspelled words. Before you use SpellMan, you have to install the files containing the library of 100,000 available words (Word List a-m.pdb and Word List n-z.pdb).

In addition to the spell checker, SpellMan is very flexible and can be personalized by tapping on the SpellMan icon. For example, you can have SpellMan do the following:

◆ Capitalize any word that SpellMan cannot find in its dictionary

◆ Beep if it finds an unknown word

◆ Look up an unknown word and give you the option to change it

◆ Ignore capitalized words when it checks for spelling errors

◆ Ignore any nonstandard words

# SpellMan: The Important Commands

SpellMan doesn't use much in the way of menu items.

| Menu | Command | What It Does |
|------|---------|--------------|
| Options | Enter Password | Enters the password sent when registered |
| Options | About SpellMan | Gives info about SpellMan |

# Get Smart: Education and Learning

That little handheld computer you have stores and organizes a lot of information, as you well know. But it also has interactive capabilities far beyond what most applications ever tap into. This section explores some education-related applications that take interactivity a lot further. For instance, you can hone your mental math skills or work to increase your reading speed with applications that will help you and track your progress. Also, two applications in this section can help you keep track of your classes and assignments, which is critical to success in school.

Other applications will help you to increase your language skills and even keep a beat. It's always satisfying to continue learning, and just think how smart you'll be when you finish this section.

# 39 Tracking Work and More: A+ StudentAid

Name of Program: A+ StudentAid
E-Mail Address: manuni02@hotmail.com
Web Address: http://www.zdnet.com/downloads/pilotsoftware and search for A+ StudentAid
Version: 1.54
Type of Software: Shareware
Cost: $7

Since you're so smart, you probably don't need any directions on how to use this handy application. It's a good thing, too, because it doesn't seem to come with any. Still, A+ StudentAid is easy to use and seems to do what needs to be done. It lets you enter a list of classes and record homework, projects, and test assignments on separate tabs.

In addition, there's a Schedule tab that provides a grid so that you can enter your class schedule and view it at a glance. The main feature, though, is that A+ gives you an easy way to keep track of your assignments and their due dates. That means you're going to have to work harder to forget to study. (An A+ would be nice, though, wouldn't it?)

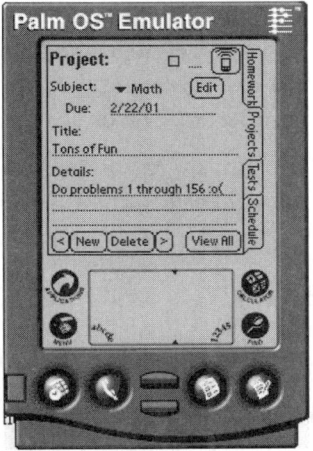

# Getting Started with A+ StudentAid

Turn in those assignments on time! Here's how…

1. Tap on the Edit button next to the Subject field in the Homework screen.

2. Using graffiti or the keyboard, enter the name of a subject. Tap New. Enter another subject. Repeat until all of your subjects are entered.

3. Tap on the Homework tab. Tap the arrow next to Subject, and you'll notice that all of your subjects are now available to you in this pop-up list. Choose a subject from the pop-up list.

4. Enter your homework assignment and any details about it. A+ Student Aid automatically saves it for you.

5. Tap the Projects tab. Enter project information just as you would a homework assignment in the Homework tab. The only difference is that a Due Date field is added when you use the Projects tab. Once you tap Due, a Date Picker will pop up.

6. Tap the Tests tab and enter your test information.

7. After you've entered several assignments, you might want to tap on the View All button to reveal a list of all your assignments. Tap on one and the full Assignment Entry screen—complete with details—opens for you.

8. When you've completed an assignment, you can delete it simply by tapping Delete in the Assignment Entry screen. Or you might prefer to tap the box at the top right to indicate that an assignment has been completed. The check mark will appear in the View All screen.

9. You can share your assignments with a friend by tapping the Beam icon at the top right.

## A+ StudentAid: The Important Commands

Here are the basic commands for A+ StudentAid.

| Menu | Command | Shortcut | What It Does |
|------|---------|----------|--------------|
| Edit | Undo | /U | Undoes your last action |
| Edit | Cut | /X | Cuts selected text and saves it to the Clipboard |
| Edit | Copy | /C | Copies text and saves it to the Clipboard |
| Edit | Paste | /P | Pastes text from the Clipboard |
| Edit | Select All | /S | Selects all entries on the screen |
| Edit | Keyboard | /K | Allows you to use the keyboard to enter information |
| Edit | Graffiti Help | /G | Displays graffiti strokes |

# 40 Conjugate *That*: eVerbe and eVerbo

Name of Program: eVerbe and eVerbo
E-Mail Address: info@floodlight.net
Web Address: http://www.floodlight.net
Version: 1.0 and 1.1
Type of Software: Shareware
Cost: $19.95

These very simple applications perform what is, for most language students, one of the most difficult tasks of learning a new language: conjugating verbs. (Some of us have a hard enough time of it in our native language.) eVerbe covers all the French verbs, and eVerbo handles the Spanish.

Although novices could use these applications, they go beyond the simple and straightforward present and past tenses. *Plus-que-parfait du subjonctif*, anyone? It's covered (in eVerbe). *Futuro perfecto?* Got it (in eVerbo). The only tricky thing about these apps is remembering to use all the appropriate diacritics. Without those accents and cedillas, verbs just aren't the same.

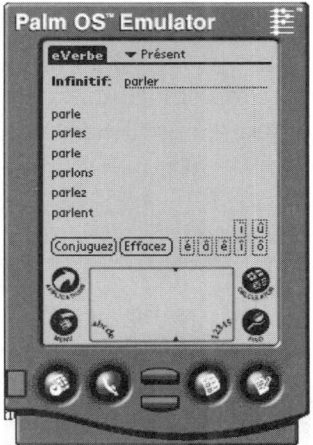

## Getting Started with eVerbe

Here's how to get going with eVerbe.

1. eVerbe and eVerbo are pretty simple. After you launch either application, you will see eVerbe's (or eVerbo's) only screen. This screen will display the last verb conjugated. Tap Effacez (or Borre) to erase the current entry.

2. Enter the exact infinitive of the verb you want to conjugate. You can use graffiti or the keyboard. Accents and other diacritical marks are important, so you might want to use the Int'l part of the keyboard.

3. Select the desired tense from the pop-up menu in the on-screen title bar.

**4.** Tap Conjuguez/Conjugue.

**5.** *Voilà!* Your verb is conjugated.

**6.** To see the same verb in another tense, just select the tense from the pop-up menu. *Bravo!*

# 41 The Head of the Class: Four.Zero

Name of Program: Four.Zero
E-Mail Address: `info@handmark.com`
Web Address: `http://www.handmark.com/products/fourzero`
Version: 3.11
Type of Software: Shareware
Cost: $14.99

Four.Zero is a comprehensive coursework tracker for your Palm device. It lets you enter your assignments, as well as the assignments' corresponding grades, textbooks, class meeting times, places, and instructor information. Just think of it: You can enter any grades you want, and then show your parents or spouse how well you're doing in school.

Four.Zero has a very nice feature that will add, either optionally or automatically, your assignments to the Palm To Do and/or Date Book, leaving you one less excuse for not doing your work.

The developers have clearly put a lot of thought and improvements into this application. Here are its features:

◆ Tracks class details, grades, and coursework information for up to 15 classes

◆ Offers one-tap access to instructor information, including phone numbers, office hours, e-mail, etc.

◆ Offers one-tap access to class information, including time, location, department, section, and Web page

- ◆ Tracks coursework details, including type, due date, and score, and allows you to enter notes about assignments

- ◆ Offers a view of the coursework due today, this week, by a specific date, by coursework type, or by class

- ◆ Offers a view of all the coursework entered or of just the uncompleted coursework

- ◆ Defines grading policies for each class

- ◆ Defines an overall grade point average (GPA) policy for GPA calculation

- ◆ Supports weighting your coursework either by coursework type or by each individual coursework item

- ◆ Supports the option to specify the allowable number of dropped coursework items

- ◆ Exports coursework to the standard Palm Date Book

- ◆ Exports coursework to the standard Palm To Do List

- ◆ Offers a view of the current class grade or the overall term GPA

- ◆ Offers a function that performs "what if" scenarios to predict grades through the end of the term

- ◆ Imports Four.Zero data into a Microsoft Excel spreadsheet to keep a hard copy of the details from each term

- ◆ Supports the left-hand option to move the scroll bar to the left side of the screen

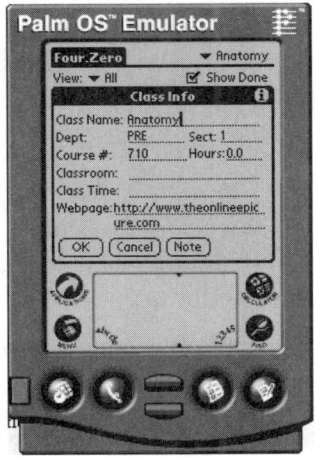

# Getting Started with Four.Zero

Here's the ground zero on Four.Zero.

1. Upon launching, tap Try the Demo. You'll notice that the opening screen is pretty blank.

2. Start entering your classes by selecting New from the Class menu.

3. In the Add Class screen, enter as much of the requested information as you wish, using the keyboard or graffiti. Tap OK.

4. To add another class, you can again select New from the Class menu or tap the arrow to get the pop-up box at the top-right corner of your screen and choose Add Class.

5. Enter the requested information and tap OK.

6. When you've entered all your classes, you're ready to record homework and other information.

7. Pick a class from the pop-up menu in the title bar.

8. Tap New. Enter an assignment on the Name line.

9. Tap the Due box and pick the due date.

10. Add any details you need in the Details line.

11. Tap the triangle next to the Textbook field, then select Edit Textbooks. Enter the name of a textbook, then choose Add to add another one. Tap OK when you're done, then select the book needed for the assignment, if appropriate.

12. You can tap the To Do button to add the assignment to your Palm device's To Do List, and tap Date Book to add it to your Date Book. Tap OK.

13. You're now in Class view, where all assignments for this class appear in the upper-left pop-up window.

14. You'll see two new icons in this screen. Tap the one that looks like a document to review or change the basic class information, such as the classroom.

    Tap the Apple icon to record the teacher's name, office information, telephone, etc. Tap OK.

Later, when you start getting test scores and paper grades, you can record them in Four.Zero so that it can figure your GPA.

# Four.Zero: The Important Commands

Here are the significant Four.Zero commands.

| Menu | Command | Shortcut | What It Does |
|------|---------|----------|--------------|
| Class | New | /N | Adds a new class to your records |
| Class | Sort | /O | Changes the order in which classes appear in the All Classes listing |
| Class | Delete | /D | Deletes a class |
| Class | Add Coursework | /A | Adds an assignment |
| Class | Coursework Types | /E | Adds to the pop-up list of assignment types |
| Class | Instructor | /I | Opens the Instructor Information screen for the current course |
| Class | Textbooks | /T | Opens the Textbook Entry screen for the current course |
| Class | Grading Policy | /Y | Lets you designate scores and their letter-grade equivalents |
| Class | Class Info | /F | Opens the Class Info screen |
| Options | GPA Setup | /4 | Lets you set grade-point equivalents for letter grades |
| Options | Report Card | /Z | Summarizes grades from classes |
| Options | What If | /W | Lets you test various grade outcomes |
| Options | Preferences | /R | Lets you choose among several activity and display options |

# 42 Keep to the Beat: Gachin Gachin

Name of Program: Gachin Gachin
E-Mail Address: fujima@shore.net
Web Address: http://odin.prohosting.com/fujima
Version: 2.3
Type of Software: Freeware
Cost: Free

Nothing complicated about a metronome, right? You just set the tick-tick-tick or beep-beep-beep to the number of beats per minute that you want. But why buy a metronome when you have your Palm device? Gachin Gachin does the job and does it with more options than many metronomes. For instance, you can choose your sound type (or choose none at all), and you can set it to count the beats per measure. It isn't rocket science, but it's convenient, simple, and free. That's music to my ears.

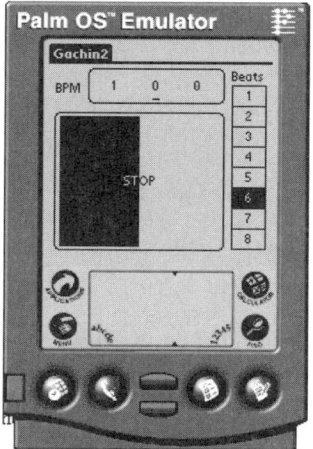

## Getting Started with Gachin Gachin

Follow these steps to use Gachin Gachin.

**1.** Gachin Gachin's only screen appears upon launch. In this screen, you can set the number of beats per minute in the BPM area. Use graffiti, the up-arrow and down-arrow buttons, or tap on the numbers.

**2.** If you want to keep track of measures, not just beats, select the number of beats per measure in the right column. (Leave it at 1 if you don't want the measures counted.)

**3.** Tap Start. Your Palm device will display the beat and, if you selected beats per measure, the beat number will cycle in the Beats column.

**4.** When you're done, tap Stop.

## Gachin Gachin: The Important Command

There's only one menu item to know about in Gachin Gachin.

| Menu | Command | Shortcut | What It Does |
|------|---------|----------|--------------|
| Options | Preferences | None | Lets you set sound level, sound type, and other options |

# 43 Go Figure: Mental Arithmetic

 Name of Program: Mental Arithmetic
E-Mail Address: mental@bubbling.com
Web Address: http://www.bubbling.com
Version: 1.21
Type of Software: Shareware
Cost: $25

If you've become so dependent on your calculator that you can no longer even figure a tip in your head, maybe you ought to try Mental Arithmetic. It takes you through a progression of increasingly difficult addition, subtraction,

multiplication, and division problems and gives you a score that takes your calculating speed into account. Practice really does make perfect.

Don't let that description worry you, though. If you need a strategy for solving a problem in your head, Mental Arithmetic offers tips at every step. What's more, Mental Arithmetic keeps track of your scores and your speed and lets you know how you're doing. Pretty soon, you'll be able to impress your friends by figuring sales tax in your head or even the coefficient needed for a lunar landing. The program icon on your Palm is the same as the one for Superman. You'll be a genius!

## Getting Started with Mental Arithmetic

Here's how to get started with Mental Arithmetic.

1. After tapping OK to leave the Registration screen, you will see a Welcome screen, which alerts you that you will be asked questions to determine where you need work on your math skills. Tap OK.

2. Next you'll see the intro window to Level One. Tap Enter to continue.

3. You'll be asked a math question. Answer by tapping on the number pad or using graffiti. Tap Enter. The word Correct or Incorrect will appear at the bottom left of the screen.

4. Continue answering and tapping Enter until you come to the end of Level One. If you need help answering a question, tap Help and then Show to get tips on solving the problem.

**5.** Once you've completed a level and scored perfectly, you can tap Continue to go to the next level.

Otherwise, you'll see the Some Wrong screen. Tap Show if you want to see strategy tips, or tap Skip if you want to see the practice questions first.

**6.** At the end of a level, you have the option of going to the next level or tapping Scores to see how you've done. Tap the Information icon (*i*) on the Scores screen for a full explanation of these numbers.

**7.** Tap Done to leave the Information screen, then tap OK to leave Scores.

**8.** When you're ready to leave Mental Arithmetic, just go to the Palm Home/Applications screen or to another application.

## Mental Arithmetic: The Important Commands

The commands you need to know for Mental Arithmetic are these.

| Menu | Command | Shortcut | What It Does |
|------|---------|----------|--------------|
| Options | Scores | /S | Shows your scores |
| Options | Introduction | None | Gives brief overview of the application |
| Options | Reset | None | Erases all records of your scores |

# 44 Why Not Read Faster: Read@Speed

Name of Program: Read@Speed
E-Mail Address: support@palmprimed.com
Web Address: http://www.palmprimed.com
Version: 1.0
Type of Software: Shareware
Cost: $15

Read@Speed provides a tool for handheld users who'd like to increase their reading speed. It's easy to use, and various operational options let you use it in the way that works best for your particular needs.

First, Read@Speed offers a quick test to gauge your current reading speed. Then, you set the application to present text to you at a reading rate of your choice. You can choose to see the text line by line or page by page, and you can choose to read silently or add a tone to keep you on pace. You can even set up a metronome to beep at a given rate to correspond to a book you're reading.

The developer cautions that Read@Speed isn't a full-scale speed-reading program. It's an awfully good start, though, and a nice way to make your Palm device work for you.

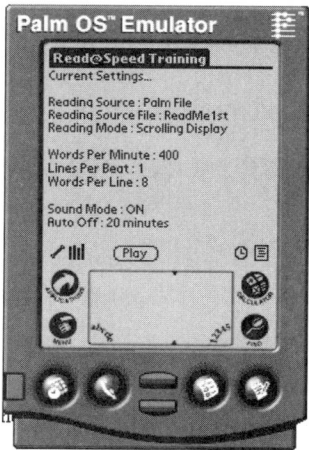

## Getting Started with Read@Speed

Here's how to get started with Read@Speed (cool name, no?).

1. After the Registration screen, the first screen that you'll see upon launch shows the current settings for Read@Speed. These settings include a reading speed of 400 words per minute, which is pretty fast. To try it out and see how you measure up, tap Play to begin.

2. Whoa! Too fast for me! If it's too fast for you, tap Stop to take you back to the Settings screen.

3. To test yourself, tap the Clock icon on the bottom right of the screen.

**4.** Read the instructions, then tap Play. When you've finished reading a full page, tap Done. (You can read more than one full page. Just make sure you tap Done when you've completely finished reading the last page.)

**5.** When you tap Done, a pop-up screen will tell you your reading speed in WPM (words per minute). If your results qualify you for the Hall of Fame, tap No (for now) when asked if you want to enter your name. If you didn't qualify, tap OK.

**6.** Tap the Page icon in the lower-right corner to see the Hall of Fame. You might want to tap Reset, which will clear all the names and speeds so that *your* top ten speeds and dates will be recorded. Tap OK.

**7.** Now that you know your speed, you can set up Read@Speed to boost your reading rate. Tap the first icon on the bottom left (called the Spanner icon). Now you will see the Settings screen.

**8.** Tap the number next to Words Per Minute for a pop-up screen of options. Select the same number as your current speed, or the closest one to it.

**9.** If you didn't like using the sounds, uncheck the Sound Settings box by tapping on it. For now, leave the other settings as they are.

**10.** Tap the Calibration icon (which looks like a bar graph) next to the Words Per Minute number. For accuracy, you'll need to calibrate each time you change the speed setting. Tap Calibrate and tap Done.

**11.** Now you're back in the main screen. Tap Play, and the currently selected document will be presented at the speed designated. As you learn, you can increase your speed setting and choose different reading files from the Settings screen.

## Read@Speed: The Important Commands

Here are the Read@Speed commands you'll want to be familiar with.

| Menu | Command | Shortcut | What It Does |
| --- | --- | --- | --- |
| Options | Settings | None | Takes you to the Settings screen |
| Options | Calibrate | None | Takes you to the Calibration screen |

| Menu | Command | Shortcut | What It Does |
|------|---------|----------|--------------|
| Test | Speed | None | Takes you to the opening Test screen |
| Test | Results | None | Opens the Read@Speed Hall of Fame |
| Help | Introduction | None | Explains different reading modes |
| Help | Manual | None | Describes the Read@Speed user's manual and gives the Web address for it |
| Help | Tips | None | Provides tips on using Read@Speed |

# 45 It's Greek to Me: Dictionary

Name of Program: Dictionary
E-Mail Address: support@evolutionary.net
Web Address: http://www.evolutionary.net
Version: 2.3
Type of Software: Shareware
Cost: $18

Dictionary is a great idea for a translation application to use on your Palm device, but its usefulness is limited by the thoroughness of the language databases you use. Although there's a cost for the shareware download, there are more than 60 free language dictionaries. Good deal!

The unregistered version has a limited-sized database of words. In the registered version, you can add words and phrases that you want to remember to the dictionary, which is great for studying vocabulary. So give it a try; it just might speak your language.

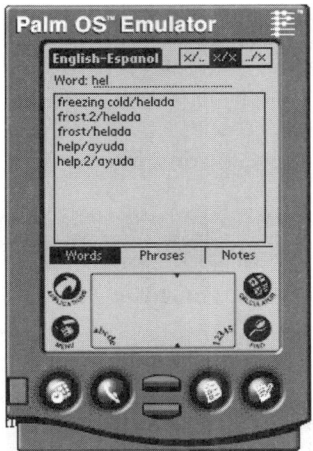

# Getting Started with Translation Dictionary

Here are the steps to begin using Translation Dictionary.

**1.** Install a language database as well as the Translation Dictionary application. Tap the Dictionary icon to launch.

**2.** Start entering a word, and Translation Dictionary will start listing possibilities.

**3.** If more possibilities exist than will fit on your screen, an arrow will appear on the top or bottom right of the translation square. Tap on the arrow to see more.

**4.** If you want to see only one language, tap on one of the boxes at the upper right. Tapping the middle, default setting (x/x) shows the entered word, any variations of that word, and the translations. Tapping the x/.. box shows only the first language named in the title bar, and tapping the ../x box shows only the second language shown in the title box.

**5.** Tap on Phrases to search phrases in the database (which may not be active in all databases).

**6.** Tap on Notes to read language notes, such as pronunciation tips (which may not be active in all databases).

# Translation Dictionary: The Important Commands

Translation Dictionary lets you manage your databases and their contents with these commands.

| Menu | Command | Shortcut | What It Does |
| --- | --- | --- | --- |
| Options | Modules | None | Lets you delete or load language databases into Translation Dictionary |
| Options | Clear Search Field | None | Deletes previous translation entry |
| Options | New Entry | None | Lets you add to the database (not available in unregistered version) |
| Options | Backup | None | Lets you back up your database when you synchronize with your Desktop |
| Options | Random Word | /R | Displays a word randomly chosen from the database |
| Edit | Cut | None | Cuts selected text and saves it to the Clipboard |
| Edit | Copy | None | Copies selected text and saves it to the Clipboard |
| Edit | Paste | None | Pastes text from the Clipboard into Translation Dictionary |

# 46 Where Is That Test?: Teacher's P.E.T.

Name of Program: Teacher's P.E.T.
E-Mail Address: tim@coffeepotsoftware.com
Web Address: http://www.coffeepotsoftware.com
Version: 1.63
Type of Software: Shareware
Cost: $19.99

Teacher's P.E.T. (for Teacher's Portable Educators Toolkit) is the toolset for teachers on the go. It keeps track of grading, attendance, contact info, and more, and allows you to maintain information for up to 10 different classes.

Other features include the following:

◆ You can print your records and such using PalmPrint.

◆ A Modes feature allows for faster and easier grading!

◆ You can back up files using the Memo Pad application.

◆ You can easily recalculate grades.

◆ You can give all students the same grade (and contribute to your own dismissal).

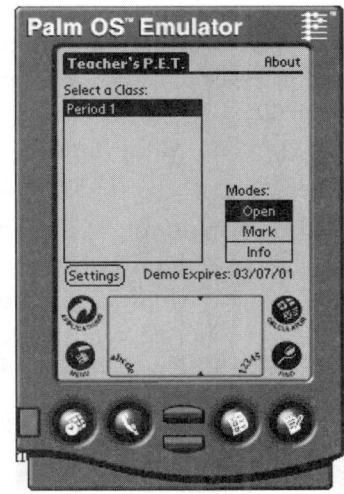

## Getting Started with Teacher's P.E.T.

Here's how to get started with Teacher's P.E.T.

1. Once you tap and open P.E.T., you have to first designate the settings you want to use and then you can select to work with classes, assignments, students, or categories.

2. Tap Students.

3. Enter the name of a student.

4. Enter the student's phone number.

5. Using the drop-down menu, enter the class the student is enrolled in.

6. Enter the student's ID.

7. Tap on the Notes button to enter additional information.

8. Tap Done to finish with the Students module, or tap New to enter information about another student.

# 47 Beam Me the Test, Scotty: ReviewMaster

Name of Program: ReviewMaster
E-Mail Address: brant@thereviewmaster.com
Web Address: http://www.thereviewmaster.com
Version: 2.0
Type of Software: Shareware
Cost: $14.95

Your Palm is, no doubt, a huge amount of fun, and you probably use it in some very productive ways as well. If you're a teacher, trainer, or have anything to do with multiple-choice or true-false quizzes, then ReviewMaster is the killer application you've been waiting for. You can create a test using the Windows application, then transfer the test to your Palm, and use the ReviewMaster Palm version to read and use the test. And if this isn't enough, ReviewMaster allows you to combine different types of tests, such as multiple-guess and true-false, and it also grades the test for you. What a way to do things!

To make things even sweeter for the user, there is a library of tests available and ready to be downloaded in the following categories:

- ◆ Certification Tests, such as A+, insurance, real estate, private pilot, commercial driver, and more

- ◆ Standardized Tests, such as the SAT and the ACT

- ◆ Trivia Quizzes, just for fun

- ◆ Humor, just for more fun (after all, who can have enough?)

- ◆ Miscellaneous, containing any other test that doesn't fit easily into any of the above categories

**Question #1.** "This day will be long remembered. It has seen the end of Kenobi, it will soon see the end of ...."?

**a.** Skywalker?

**b.** The Empire?

**c.** Obviously not… it's the Rebellion!

This is just one of the many gems you can find at the Web site, or you can create your own. This is a hugely useful application and one that companies are personalizing for their internal use, complete with the company logo on the screen. You can even sell the tests that you create using the program (as long as they don't violate any copyright laws). Just think of it: "OK students, line up with your Palms while I beam today's quiz to you." Yikes!

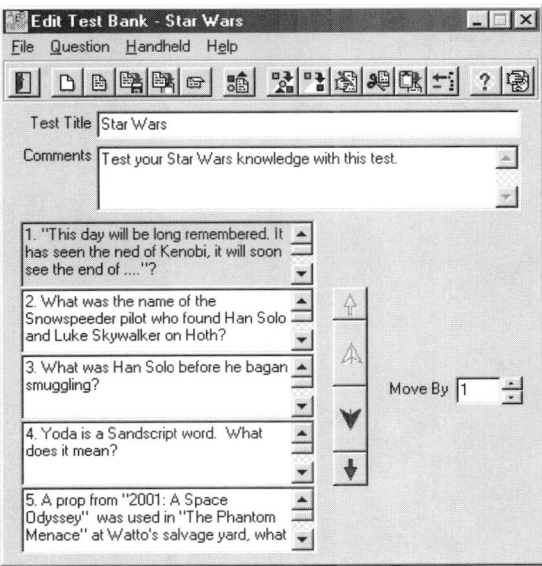

## Getting Started with ReviewMaster

Here's how to get started with ReviewMaster.

1. On your Windows computer, install and open ReviewMaster program and create the type of test and the specific items you want to use.

2. Save the test (and be sure you see where it is being saved).

3. Click Handheld and then click Select Tests for Handheld.

4. Click Add.

5. Find the test you want to transfer.

6. Double-click the test's name and then click Add.

7. Click Close.

8. The next time you HotSync, the test contents will appear in the ReviewMaster file ready to be used.

# Health and Fitness

A pocket companion can be mighty helpful when you're trying to maintain a healthy lifestyle. By keeping track of your exercise, diet, and other health-related activities, you can gauge your progress and stay on track. Many Palm applications are ready and able to do just that. The ones in this section range from very simple (a body-fat calculator) to fairly complex (a nutrition analyzer). They can help you develop good habits, like regular exercise, or reduce bad habits, like smoking. So get going! When it comes to good health, right now is always the best time to start.

## 48

# One to Use before the Road: Blood Alcohol Calculator

Name of Program: Blood Alcohol Calculator
E-Mail Address: tomdo98@aol.com
Web Address: http://hotfiles.zdnet.com/cgi-bin/texis/swlib/
hotfiles/info.html?fcode=001EE0&b=zdpalm
Type of Software: Freeware
Cost: Free

Let's face it; few people who have had a drink—or several—are good judges of their own level of sobriety. Blood Alcohol Calculator gives an independent estimate of your blood-alcohol content based on sex, body weight, and number of drinks. Then it compares the estimate of your blood-alcohol content with your state's legal limit.

Maybe better than using it to determine whether you should drive home or not, you can use it to plan your evening, as in deciding whether or not it's okay to have a glass of wine or an after-dinner drink before you go home.

The developer includes a disclaimer so that you, too, understand that this easy little application isn't necessarily accurate. Still, it provides a good estimate, and that's a reasonable place to start.

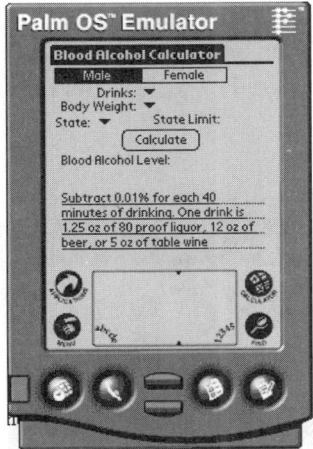

# Getting Started with Blood Alcohol Calculator

Here's how to get started with Blood Alcohol Calculator.

**1.** Install both files that come in the Blood Alcohol Calculator folder, then launch from the BACCalc icon.

**2.** First, you will see a disclaimer to let you know that this app doesn't guarantee accuracy. Read it, then tap Start.

**3.** Choose Male or Female, as appropriate, as the first variable in estimating your blood-alcohol content.

**4.** Tap the arrow next to Drinks and select from the pop-up list the number of drinks you have consumed. The text at the bottom of the screen defines what counts as a drink.

**5.** Tap the arrow next to Body Weight and select your weight or the closest to it.

**6.** Tap the arrow next to State and select your state from the pop-up list. Blood Alcohol Calculator displays your state's legal limit on the blood-alcohol content for drivers.

**7.** Tap Calculate. Blood Alcohol Calculator now estimates and shows your blood-alcohol level, and states whether or not that level is under the legal limit.

**8.** If the alcohol has been consumed over more than 40 minutes' time, then you can subtract from the level 0.01% for each 40-minute time period to get a closer estimate of your blood-alcohol content.

# 49  A Truer Measure of Weight: BFC

Name of Program: BFC
E-Mail Address: questions@palmtrainer.com
Web Address: http://palm-trainer.com/bfcinfo.htm
Version: 1.1
Type of Software: Commercial
Cost: $9.95

This app offers a quick and easy way to calculate body-fat percentages. Using BFC (as in Body Fat Calculator) and a pair of calipers, you can get an accurate body-fat measure. You just measure the thickness of skin folds in three specified locations, then record them in BFC. And if you're on a fitness program, these measurements that you record in BFC help you get a better idea of how you're doing by looking at body fat rather than at weight. One big fault with the program, however, is that it doesn't tell you what units to use.

BFC can calculate the following:

◆ 3 Site Total, which is the sum of the three skin-fold measurements. (As you continue to use BFC—and stick to your fitness program—you can see how your three-site total decreases.)

◆ Body Fat %, which is your percentage of body fat.

◆ Lean Weight, which is your lean weight (the total amount of non-fat body weight) in pounds.

◆ Fat Weight, which is your fat weight (the total weight of fat) in pounds. (Just in case you didn't know, chocolate contains the good unsaturated fats.)

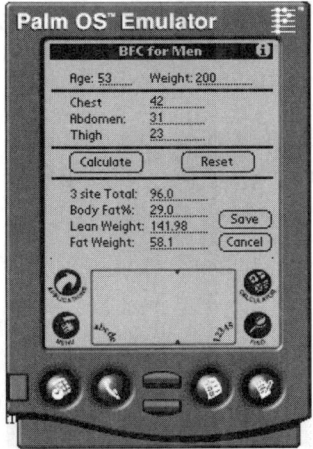

# Getting Started with BFC

How to get your accurate body-fat count:

**1.** Launch the application and tap on Women or Men, as appropriate.

**2.** Tap New on the next screen.

**3.** Enter the requested data for age and weight.

**4.** Tap the Information icon (*i*) at the top right of the screen, or tap the silk-screened Menu button, and read the descriptions of where you should measure the skin folds. (Measurements include triceps, far-right abdominals, and thigh for women and chest, abdomen, and thigh for men.) Enter the three skin-fold measurements requested.

**5.** Tap Calculate, and BFC will display the body-fat percentage, along with lean and fat weights.

**6.** Tap Save to record the calculation.

**7.** Enter your name and tap Yes.

## BFC: The Important Commands

Here's what you need to use BFC.

| Menu | Command | What It Does |
|------|---------|--------------|
| Description | Chest | Describes the chest measurement |
| Description | Abdomen | Describes the abdominal measurement |
| Description | Thigh | Describes the thigh measurement |
| Description | Calipers | Explains the use of calipers |
| Description | Triceps | Describes the triceps measurement |
| Description | Far-Right Abdominals | Describes the far-right abdominals measurement |

# 50 Track Those Smokes: CigTrack

Name of Program: CigTrack
E-Mail Address: david@hogan.net
Web Address: http://www.leedsalabama.com/dhc/cigtrack.htm
Version: 1.7
Type of Software: Shareware
Cost: $5

Anybody who smokes knows that quitting ain't easy. CigTrack is intended to give you a little help along the way. Use CigTrack to log every cigarette you smoke, and at the end of the day or week, you can look back and identify patterns in your smoking habits. Then you can use this log to help you create techniques for avoiding those situations. Also, just keeping track of your smoking habits can be very helpful in reducing or cutting back, because it helps you to eliminate those smokes you grab without thinking.

## Getting Started with CigTrack

Here's how to start using CigTrack.

**1.** Launch CigTrack, and you'll come to the main screen, LightUp.

**2.** On the LightUp screen, you'll record every cigarette you smoke. Enter a time you lit up in the first blank.

**3.** Tap the arrow next to Activity When Lit, and select the appropriate activity. If you don't see your specific activity on the list, select See Notes.

**4.** Answer the question "Did you fight by changing activity...?" by tapping the Yes or No block.

**5.** Optionally, you can enter your feelings (such as "I was stressed") or describe the situation that wasn't on the Activity list (such as Coffee Break).

**6.** Tap New to record another cigarette, or tap List to look at the smokes you've recorded up to now.

## CigTrack: The Important Commands

These CigTrack commands make it easier to enter and change data.

| Menu | Command | Shortcut | What It Does |
|------|---------|----------|--------------|
| Edit | Undo | /U | Undoes your last action |
| Edit | Cut | /X | Cuts selected text and saves it to the Clipboard |
| Edit | Copy | /C | Copies text and saves it to the Clipboard |
| Edit | Paste | /P | Pastes text from the Clipboard |
| Edit | Select All | /S | Selects all entries on the screen |
| Edit | Keyboard | /K | Allows you to use the keyboard to enter information |
| Edit | Graffiti Help | /G | Displays graffiti strokes |

# 51 Track a Woman's Cycle: FloChart

Name of Program: FloChart
E-Mail Address: mike@thenar.com
Web Address: http://www.thenar.com/chart
Version: 1.11
Type of Software: Shareware
Cost: $15

If you are a woman, you will find that FloChart provides an easy way to keep track of your menstrual cycles, and it is also helpful in answering any related questions from your doctor. Each month, you simply enter the date your period starts, and FloChart automatically refigures your average cycle length. Based on that computation, it estimates your next period and ovulation date. In addition, FloChart keeps your cycle history, including the dates and the length of each cycle, which you can consult with a tap of the stylus.

The ovulation estimate can also be handy for couples who are trying to conceive, but the built-in tips warn that using this estimate to avoid contraception is a *very bad* idea. A good idea that the developer has instituted, though, is donating $1 of every registration fee to the Susan G. Komen Breast Cancer Foundation.

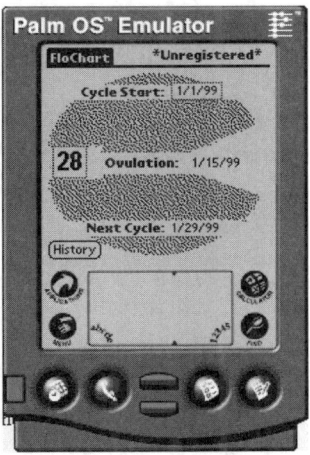

## Getting Started with FloChart

Use these steps to benefit from FloChart.

1. When you start up FloChart, you will see the main FloChart screen, which is a graphic representing your menstrual cycle. Tap the date next to Cycle Start. Record the date on which your most recent period began.

2. The default sets your cycle at 28 days. The first time you use FloChart, then, it will estimate your next period based on a 28-day cycle.

3. You can change that default by tapping the big 28 on the left side of the screen and entering your cycle length. A better option, though, is to wait and record your next period, and FloChart will calculate the cycle length and adjust the average length with each new cycle.

**4.** Tap History to see your cycle over time.

**5.** If you make a mistake when entering your period date, tap History, tap the incorrect date, then tap Delete, and reenter the correct date. (A flaw in the program: If you change an incorrect date months after the fact, your average cycle doesn't compute properly.)

**6.** FloChart will also alert you to your probable ovulation date, which is noted on the right side of the screen.

## FloChart: The Important Commands

The FloChart menu commands are few and simple.

| Menu | Command | Shortcut | What It Does |
| --- | --- | --- | --- |
| Options | Preferences | /P | Makes records private or locks cycle length |
| Options | Help | /H | Gives you tips on using FloChart |

# 52 Make a Splash: SwimLog

E-Mail Address: info@fitnesslogs.com
Web Address: http://www.fitnesslogs.com/swim
Version: 1.0
Type of Software: Shareware
Cost: $12

A gazillion swimmers can't be wrong. Swimming is fun, healthy, and one of the most popular sports for both fitness and competition. But at the end of that long workout, how do you keep track of all those yards and meters? And how do you total them and see everything from your speed to your recorded heart rate? SwimLog can help you do those and other things:

◆ Records all workout data

◆ Specifies pool length in yards or meters

◆ Enters up to 20-lap or length splits

◆ Records swimming stroke, number of laps, and elapsed time

◆ Creates a list of your specific racing events

◆ Computes your pace (very handy)

◆ Calculates total swimming distance and average pace for the previous four weeks, months, or the entire year

◆ Allows notes of up to 255 characters with each entry

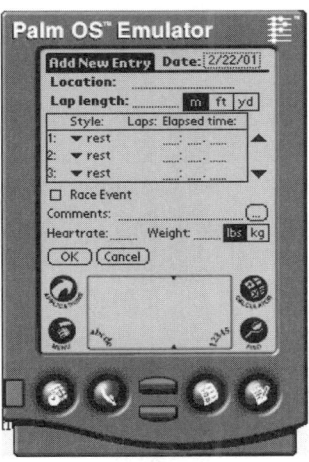

## Getting Started with SwimLog

Swim like a fish with SwimLog—here's how.

**1.** Tap New.

**2.** Enter the location of the meet or event.

**3.** Enter the length and metric (meters, feet, or yards).

**4.** Select the style of stroke from the drop-down menu.

**5.** Enter the number of laps and elapsed time.

**6.** Optionally, you can enter additional information such as heart rate.

**7.** Tap OK and you will see a summary for all the swimming you've completed (and entered) in the current year and past years of events you have entered.

## SwimLog: The Important Commands

Here are the significant SwimLog commands.

| Menu | Command | Shortcut | What It Does |
|------|---------|----------|--------------|
| Edit | Undo | /U | Undoes your last action |
| Edit | Cut | /X | Cuts selected text and saves it to the Clipboard |
| Edit | Copy | /C | Copies text and saves it to the Clipboard |
| Edit | Paste | /P | Pastes text from the Clipboard |
| Edit | Set Category | None | Allows you to assign a swim to a certain category |
| Edit | Keyboard | /K | Allows you to use the keyboard to enter information |

# 53 Recording Every Step: Runner's Log

Name of Program: Runner's Log
E-Mail Address: marty@fitnesslogs.com
Web Address: http://www.fitnesslogs.com/runnerslog
Version: 2.3
Type of Software: Shareware
Cost: $10

Runner's Log is a nice application for keeping track of your running routine or other exercise regime. Entries are easy and quick, and Runner's Log can keep track of all your workouts.

Once you use it for a while, its utility becomes more apparent, as it will remember the routes you take, calculate the calories you consume, and accumulate your mileage over time. It even provides features for noting weather conditions, heart rate, and more. You can also choose what information you want to see at a glance, from a simple single-line log of outings to a grid presentation that shows lots of data for each run.

Here are the Runner's Log features:

◆ Calculates total miles or time logged for the present week, month, and year

◆ Accepts distance input as either miles or kilometers, and displays in and converts to either format

◆ Calculates your pace in either minutes/mile or minutes/kilometer

◆ Has three attractive log formats to show you varying amounts of data

◆ Memorizes your most recent running locations so you don't have to reenter them

◆ Computes approximate calories burned for any workout, as well as total calories burned over a period of time

At $10, it's an economical piece of shareware. The only complaint runners have about it is that it lacks a shoe tracker. Maybe it will include one in a future upgrade.

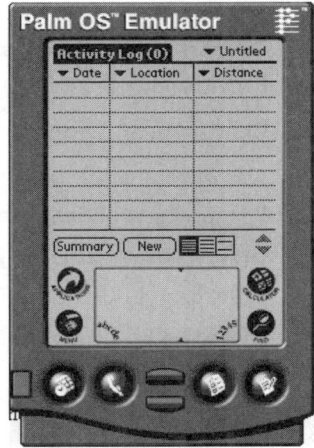

# Getting Started with Runner's Log

Here's how to get started running and logging those miles!

1. When you start up Runner's Log, you'll first see the Activity Log screen; the first time you run it, there will be a little zero in parentheses next to the screen name. As you enter your activities, Runner's Log will show the actual number of entries instead of that zero.

2. Tap New. Today's date automatically appears as the date in the Log Entry screen. If you need to change it, simply tap in the Date box and choose the correct date from the pop-up calendar.

3. Enter a location or route. A nice feature is that Runner's Log will remember that location, and next time it will be available on the Location pop-up list.

4. Enter the number of miles or kilometers. It's preset to miles, but you may choose kilometers by tapping km.

5. Enter your time in hours, minutes, and seconds.

6. Select Conditions from the two pop-up menus and add any comments you wish to make.

7. You can choose to assign the run to a category. If you need to create a category, tap the Category arrow and choose Edit Categories from the pop-up menu. Tap New and enter a new category name. Tap OK.

8. Tap More if you wish to enter your heart rate and weight, and tap the appropriate box if the run was a Race Event. Tap OK.

9. Tap OK again, and you're back at the Activity Log.

10. Tap Summary. You'll see a summary of your logged activities for the week, month, year, last year, and total, plus an account of your last activity.

11. Tap View Log. Back at the Activity Log, you can choose different options under any or all the columns, and you'll see the new information about your activities displayed.

## Runner's Log: The Important Commands

Here are the commands that let you keep up your Runner's Log.

| Menu | Command | Shortcut | What It Does |
| --- | --- | --- | --- |
| Options | New Log Entry | /N | Opens new Log Entry screen |
| Options | Duplicate a Log Entry | /D | Duplicates a log entry |
| Options | Activity List | None | Lets you select options for calculating pace and calorie consumption |
| Options | Preferences | None | Lets you choose among several display options |
| Options | Export Data to Memo | None | Opens Export Options screen for setting up export |

# 54 Work Out Your Workout Records: The Athlete's Diary

Name of Program: The Athlete's Diary
E-Mail Address: sales@stevenscreek.com
Web Address: http://www.stevenscreek.com/palm/tad.shtml
Version: 1.09
Type of Software: Commercial
Cost: $39.95

Stevens Creek Software, which makes the popular Desktop app of the same name, offers up this Palm version. It records the critical time, distance, and route information athletes like to keep track of, and it computes pace automatically. The Athlete's Diary also keeps track of your training over time, so you can look at a week's work or more. The developers have recognized the

Palm's data entry challenges by building in two mechanisms for automatic entry.

First, its AutoFill feature lets you store entire records. When you store one, you just leave the parts blank that you know will change. For instance, you might store a record that shows the distance, sport type, and a standard route. Then you would just need to enter your time each time you recall that stored record.

Second, it provides for keywords. For instance, you might create a keyword for each pair of shoes you use, or you might use the ready-made Weight keyword.

You don't need both the Desktop and handheld versions, but if you want both, the company does offer a price break on the pair.

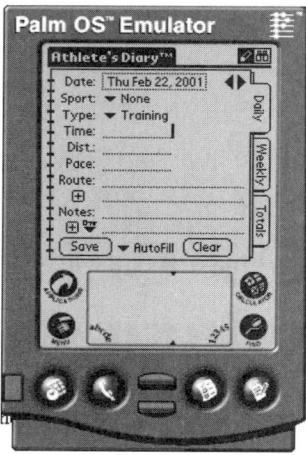

## Getting Started with The Athlete's Diary

Get started with The Athlete's Diary.

**1.** Starting up The Athlete's Diary opens the Daily Record screen. Tap on the triangle next to Sport and select the activity you want to record. (Select Edit Sports if you want to add another sport.)

**2.** Tap on the triangle next to Type and select whether your activity was for training, intervals, or a race.

**3.** Enter your time in the blank.

**4.** Enter the distance covered. If your distance is in a measure other than miles, tap the arrow next to Miles and select the appropriate measure from the pop-up list.

**5.** Record your route. If your route description runs longer than the two lines available, tapping on the plus sign will show you a screen that allows the whole message.

**6.** Record any other notes you might have. Tap on the Key icon under the Notes label if you wish to use a keyword. (Choose Edit Keywords if you want to add more to the short list that's available.)

**7.** Tap Save.

**8.** Repeat these steps for each workout. Then tap the Weekly and Totals tabs to see your workout history.

## The Athlete's Diary: The Important Commands

The Athlete's Diary provides these commands.

| Menu | Command | Shortcut | What It Does |
|---|---|---|---|
| Options | Purge Records | None | Lets you delete old records |
| Edit | Undo | /U | Undoes your last action |
| Edit | Cut | /X | Cuts selected text and saves it to the Clipboard |
| Edit | Copy | /C | Copies text and saves it to the Clipboard |
| Edit | Paste | /P | Pastes text from the Clipboard |
| Edit | Select All | /S | Selects all entries on the screen |
| Edit | Keyboard | /K | Allows you to use the keyboard to enter information |
| Edit | Graffiti Help | /G | Displays graffiti strokes |

# 55 Please, Just One More Cookie?: Nutrition Minder

Name of Program: Nutrition Minder (also called NutritionDB)
E-Mail Address: None
Web Address: `http://south.dynip.com/~wilper/software.html`
Version: 1.1
Type of Software: Shareware
Cost: $20

Don't know whether that apple is a better snack for you than that big fat fudge brownie staring you in the eye? Well, you don't need Nutrition Minder to tell you; clearly, it's the brownie. But, if you are counting calories, then this neat little HanDBase program is just what the doctor (or nutritionist) ordered.

This application offers over 8,000 foods to choose from and includes an easy-to-use Find engine. Each food description includes the following information:

Serving size

Calories

Calories from fat

Fat

Saturated fat

Cholesterol

Sodium

Protein

Dietary fiber

Vitamin A

Vitamin C

Calcium

Iron

Now, please pass that plain buttermilk biscuit with (only!) 548 calories.

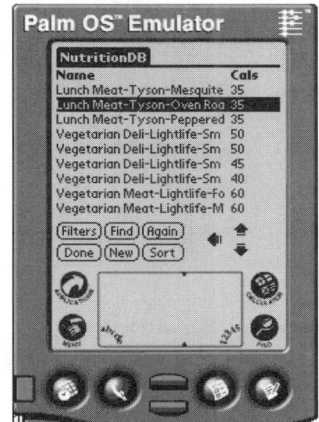

## Getting Started with Nutrition Minder

Here's how to get started with Nutrition Minder.

**1.** Be sure you have HanDBase installed.

**2.** Scroll through the list of foods to find the number of calories and serving size.

Or tap the Find button, enter the food for which you want the same information, and then tap Go.

**3.** Want to add a food? Just tap the New button and add the food, the average serving size, and the amount of calories.

## Nutrition Minder: The Important Commands

Nutrition Minder has quite a few commands to manage your database.

| Menu | Command | Shortcut | What It Does |
| --- | --- | --- | --- |
| **Prefs** | **Preferences** | **/R** | **Lets you set preferences** |
| **Prefs** | **DB Properties** | **/D** | **Reports the properties of the database you are working with** |

| Menu | Command | Shortcut | What It Does |
|------|---------|----------|--------------|
| Actions | Move Records To | /S | Moves a record or records |
| Actions | Copy Records To | /C | Copies a record or records |
| Actions | Export Records | /E | Exports records to another application |
| Actions | Print Records | /P | Prints records (Note: you need InPrint or PalmPrint installed) |
| Actions | Beam Records | /Z | Beams a record or records |
| Actions | Delete Records | /X | Deletes a record or records |
| Actions | Run Report | /U | Creates a database report |
| Actions | Copy Template | /O | Copies the template for a database to another setting |
| Actions | Delete Database | /K | Deletes an entire database |
| Move | To Top | /T | Moves to the top of a database |
| Move | To Bottom | /B | Moves to the bottom of a database |
| Move | To Right | /I | Moves to the right in a database |
| Move | To Left | /L | Moves to the left in a database |
| Move | Page Right | /H | Moves one page to the right |
| Move | Page Left | /K | Moves one page to the left |
| Move | Move Up | /M | Moves up a line |
| Move | Move Down | /V | Moves down a line |
| Move | Page Up | /G | Moves up a page |
| Move | Page Down | /W | Moves down a page |
| Help | About | /A | Gives information about Nutrition Minder |

# 56 Count Those Calories: MHM-Mobile Health Management

Name of Program: MHM-Mobile Health Management
E-Mail Address: subslef@ev1.net or subsmhm@msn.com
Web Address: http://stores.yahoo.com/pilotgearsw/ipinpatas.html
Version: 3.01
Type of Software: Commercial
Cost: $39.95

You'd think there would be a ton of applications out there to help people lose weight, but there aren't. The nutrition applications out there are limited in number and often not very helpful. MHM-Mobile Health Management (also promoted as MHM-Mobile Nutritionist) seems to be an exception. It provides detailed nutritional information about a raft of foods, and it lets you calculate and store the details of your intake.

If you aren't ready to spend 40 bucks for a product that remains a little mysterious, you might want to contact the developer to find out more. Another option would be to try one of the free or low-cost databases that run on JFile, thinkDB, or HanDBase. Check your favorite Palm software Web site, or see the Web pages and descriptions associated with those applications elsewhere in this book.

## Getting Started with MHM-Mobile Health Management

Here's how to start and use MHM.

1. Indicate in the opening window which five nutritional values you want MHM to track by tapping the square next to any or all of them. Tap OK.

2. Tap Foods in the Food Entry screen. MHM presents a serious list of foods to choose from. You can narrow the list by tapping the pop-up menu triangle next to Source.

3. Tap on the food item you want to add to your eating record. (The selection is limited if you haven't registered.)

4. The Nutritional Info window will show the nutritional values for your food choice. You can change the number of servings if other than one. Tap Count Values to add it to your nutrition history.

5. After MHM presents the total for your selection, tap More to add another item. Repeat the selection process until you've entered all your meal items, then tap Done.

6. The main screen presents a summary of each meal. Because it won't all fit on one screen, you can tap on Tap to See Protein/Calories to see the rest of the food values for your meal.

## MHM-Mobile Health Management: The Important Commands

The most important and basic commands for MHM follow.

| Menu | Command | Shortcut | What It Does |
|---|---|---|---|
| Records | Go to First | /F | Selects the first record in your list |
| Records | Go to Prev | /R | Selects the previous record in your list |
| Records | Go to Next | /T | Selects the next record in your list |
| Records | Go to Last | /L | Selects the last record in your list |
| Records | Create | /N | Creates a new record in your list |
| Records | Delete | /D | Deletes selected record from your list |
| Edit | Undo | /U | Undoes your last action |
| Edit | Cut | /X | Cuts selected text and saves it to the Clipboard |
| Edit | Copy | /C | Copies text and saves it to the Clipboard |
| Edit | Paste | /P | Pastes text from the Clipboard |
| Edit | Select All | /S | Selects all entries on the screen |
| Edit | Keyboard | /K | Allows you to use the keyboard to enter information |
| Edit | Graffiti Help | /G | Displays graffiti strokes |

# Just Plain Fun: Who Would Have Thought Your Palm Could Do *This!*

We all know our Palm devices are for serious business, but all work and no play makes Palm a dull device! As you might imagine, anyone who can create terrifically useful applications for a computer with so little memory also likes to break free sometimes and just be a bit crazy.

This section offers a sampling of some of the plain cool apps. They range from the oh-so-human (Zounds) to the divine (BibleReader). They cover the two-legged relatives (My Roots) and the four-legged variety (Pet Assistant). They let you play tunes (Audio Player) or record your golf scores (GolfUtil) and even keep your own pet (DigiPet).

More than *just* cool, huh?

## 57 If Your Palm Could Talk: Palm Audio Player

Name of Program: Palm Audio Player
E-Mail Address: info@netmite.com
Web Address: http://www.netmite.com
Version: 1.1.2
Type of Software: Shareware
Cost: $9.95

Palm Audio Player doesn't sound like your personal CD player humming tunes into your headset, but it still gives you tunes, and that's a pretty good deal from a handheld that's mainly for giving information!

The basic download comes with two sample files (elton.wav.pdb and snow.wav.pdb) that you can try out. If you like the results but not those particular files, you can go to the Netmite Web site and convert your PC audio files to PDB files that you can run on your Palm device. You can also go to www.netmite.com/palmaudiofiles.htm for lots of files to download.

Palm Audio Player features include the following:

◆ It offers the ability to listen to a Palm Audio Player file while doing other work on your Palm device.

- It has support for WAV and AU audio files of any file size.

- It has a volume control.

- The memory requirements are small, consuming just 39KB.

- It runs on most Palm devices, from Palm M100 to Handspring Platinum and Prism.

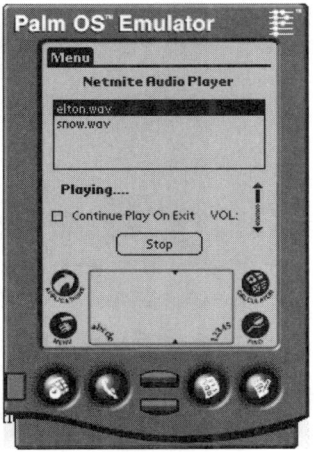

# Getting Started with Palm Audio Player

Using Palm Audio Player is simple.

**1.** Install both Palm Audio Player and the sample audio files.

**2.** When you launch Palm Audio Player, you will see a list of available files to hear. Select a file by tapping it.

**3.** Tap the Play button.

**4.** Adjust the volume by dragging the dark bar between the arrows up or down.

**5.** If you want to listen to the tunes while doing other things on your Palm device, check the box next to Continue Play on Exit, and then get on with your work!

## Palm Audio Player: The Important Commands

There are only two Palm Audio Player commands.

| Menu | Command | Shortcut | What It Does |
|------|---------|----------|--------------|
| File | Delete | None | Lets you delete selected file |
| File | Exit | None | Takes you back to the Home/Applications screen |

# 58 Taking the Word on the Road: BibleReader

Name of Program: BibleReader
E-Mail Address: support@olivetree.com
Web Address: http://www.olivetree.com/handheld/Palm/PalmBible.html
Version: 3.3 b16
Type of Software: Freeware
Cost: Free

If you've been praying for a handy way to carry your Bible, say "Hallelujah." Some people never travel; some people don't have a Bible. But this application is for you if you do both. Now you can pack your Bible on your Palm device. With BibleReader, you can pack the whole Bible or just parts of it on your handheld.

You aren't limited to one particular Bible translation. You can choose from numerous versions, some free and some with fees. The King James Version, for instance, is free, but the Revised Standard Edition has a fee. It's also available in several languages from the BibleReader Web site.

## Getting Started with BibleReader

Follow these steps to get started with BibleReader.

**1.** When you launch BibleReader, it automatically opens to the first page of the first Bible you installed on your handheld.

2. If that's where you want to be, start reading! Press on the up-arrow and down-arrow buttons to scroll through the text. One click moves the text a verse at a time. The title bar shows the exact passage that first appears on your screen.

3. You can search the text for a specific word or phrase. To begin your search, tap the Magnifying Glass icon.

4. Tap Clear to eliminate the current search terms. Use the keyboard to enter the word or phrase you want to look for. For this example, let's search for a passage about love.

5. BibleReader will seek an exact match of what you've entered, unless you tap on one of the other four boxes in the center of the screen. For this example, you can tap Ignore Case, because it doesn't matter whether "love" is capitalized. (When searching for a phrase, All Words will seek only passages that contain all the words in your phrase, and Any Word will seek passages that contain one or more words in your phrase.)

6. You can specify in which books BibleReader will look. Enter the starting and ending book names; Range 1 is the first area where the search will begin. If you want the application to look elsewhere, enter the other ranges in the other blanks. (If you leave the blanks empty, they all default to Genesis.) Tap Find First.

7. Once BibleReader finds the first instance of "love," you can tap the Magnifying Glass icon with the plus sign next to it to find the next instance.

8. If you want to be able to recall the passage, tap the Check Mark icon in the upper-right corner to create a bookmark for the location.

## BibleReader: The Important Commands

The important commands for BibleReader are:

| Menu | Command | Shortcut | What It Does |
|------|---------|----------|--------------|
| Bible | Open a Bible | /O | Gives you a list of available Bibles to open |
| OT | VerseChooser | /V | Opens a screen that allows you to pick Old Testament verses quickly |

| Menu | Command | Shortcut | What It Does |
| --- | --- | --- | --- |
| OT | Genesis | /G | Opens Genesis, if available |
| OT | Exodus | /E | Opens Exodus, if available |
| OT | Joshua | None | Opens Joshua, if available |
| OT | 1 Samuel | None | Opens 1 Samuel, if available |
| OT | Ezra | None | Opens Ezra, if available |
| OT | Psalms | /S | Opens Psalms, if available |
| OT | Isaiah | None | Opens Isaiah, if available |
| OT | Daniel | /D | Opens Daniel, if available |
| OT | Malachi | None | Opens Malachi, if available |
| NT | VerseChooser | /U | Opens a screen that allows you to pick New Testament verses quickly |
| NT | Matthew | /M | Opens Matthew, if available |
| NT | Mark | None | Opens Mark, if available |
| NT | Luke | None | Opens Luke, if available |
| NT | John | None | Opens John, if available |
| NT | Acts | /A | Opens Acts, if available |
| NT | Romans | /R | Opens Romans, if available |
| NT | Galatians | None | Opens Galatians, if available |
| NT | Ephesians | None | Opens Ephesians, if available |
| NT | Philippians | None | Opens Philippians, if available |
| NT | Colossians | None | Opens Colossians, if available |
| NT | Hebrews | /H | Opens Hebrews, if available |
| NT | Revelation | None | Opens Revelation, if available |

| Menu | Command | Shortcut | What It Does |
|------|---------|----------|--------------|
| Edit | Copy | /C | Copies selected text to the Clipboard |
| Edit | Paste | /P | Pastes selected text from the Clipboard |
| Edit | Find | /F | Opens Find screen |
| Edit | Find Next | /N | Finds next instance of item last sought |
| Edit | Preferences | None | Lets you choose among several display and function options |

# 59 Keeping the Scores: GolfUtil

Name of Program: GolfUtil
E-Mail Address: ed@witkowski-design.com
Web Address: http://www.witkowski-design.com
Version: 3.2
Type of Software: Shareware
Cost: $10

Forget the little bits of cardboard and the stubby pencils. You can now use your Palm device to keep track of your golf game. GolfUtil does more than simply keep score. It lets you accumulate scores to see how you're improving (or not) over time. It even lets you record details, such as how many putts you take on any given hole. In fact, if you're so inclined, you could build a whole database of your golf scores and back up the files in the Backup folder of your Palm Desktop.

GolfUtil can admittedly be a bit of a pain the first time you play a course, because you'll need to set up the par, distance, and handicap for each hole. But then, if golf were easy, you wouldn't want to play it, now would you? And if things get really rough out there, you can use your Palm as a divot replacement.

**164** JUST PLAIN FUN: WHO WOULD HAVE THOUGHT YOUR PALM COULD DO THIS!

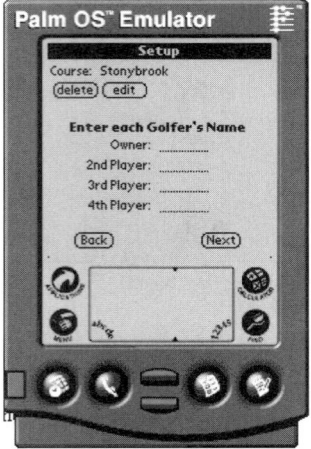

## Getting Started with GolfUtil

Get started with GolfUtil as follows:

1. Launch GolfUtil and click Continue to move past the Registration Reminder box.

2. Unless you happen to be playing at Stonybrook, tap Add in the Select Your Course screen.

3. Enter the course name in the Golf Course Layout screen.

4. Select the par from the Par pop-up arrow for each hole. Enter the distance in yards from the tee to the hole.

5. Tap the button in the Handicap column, and select the hole's handicap from the pop-up Handicap Picker screen.

6. Tap the large arrow at the bottom left of the screen to move to the next holes.

7. When you're finished with the course, tap Done.

8. Tap OK to pass the Prevent Data Loss screen.

9. Select your course by tapping on it.

10. In the Setup screen, enter your name (as Owner) and the names of other players.

11. Tap Next, and you're ready to keep score. Tee off!

12. As each player takes his or her turn, record the scores using pop-ups.

13. If you want details on your play, tap ADV (for advanced) under your score. Record the number of putts, whether you hit the fairway, and other details as you wish. When you're done, tap Continue to return to the Score Card screen.

14. When you're finished with the first hole, tap Next Hole.

15. Record the scores on each hole.

16. As you go along, you can tap Score to see the cumulative total for the players and how their scores compare to par.

17. Tap Continue to return to the Score Card, or tap End to finish the game before the 18th hole.

18. Tap Yes or No to save the data or not.

19. If you tap Yes, tap OK to pass the Backup Reminder screen.

20. Back at the main screen, tap History to see scores over time.

# 60 Supporting the Family Tree: My Roots

Name of Program: My Roots
E-Mail Address: sales@tapperware.com
Web Address: http://www.tapperware.com/MyRoots
Version: 1.64
Type of Software: Shareware
Cost: $17.95

My Roots makes your Palm device the next best thing to having a laptop computer at a library or family reunion when you're learning new information about your relatives. With My Roots, you can import and export data between your handheld and your Desktop computer, and you can flag any records that have new information. In addition, My Roots has various sorting and searching functions that make finding, changing, and deleting information a snap. In addition, the documentation is thorough and easy to read, which is important in a relatively complex application like this one.

My Roots also lets you make connections quickly and easily. Look at these features:

◆ One-tap navigation from a person to parents, children, and related events (two taps to get to a sibling)

◆ Import from an existing GED file (PC and Macintosh)

◆ Export data to a new GED file (PC and Macintosh)

◆ Sort the people in your family tree by name, year of birth, or year of death

◆ Specify up to three filters to view a subset of your data

◆ View a graphical representation of your family tree (both ancestors and descendants)

◆ Ability to keep several databases

◆ Create separate notes for each person and event

◆ Find Person function for quickly locating an individual

◆ Automatically create categories for major surnames, which are retained across import/export

◆ Display Soundex code for any surname (handy for using phonetic spelling for finding relatives)

◆ Tracking of changes for easy update of desktop data

◆ 38 built-in event types in 5 categories and the ability to create 50 custom event types

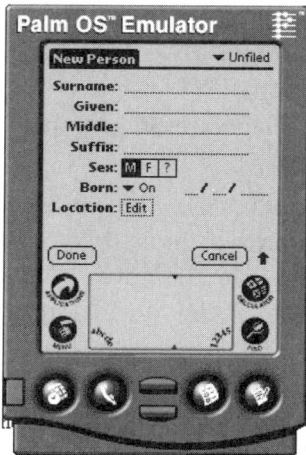

# Getting Started with My Roots

Here's how to get started with My Roots.

1. The first screen you see upon launch is an empty My Roots database list. Tap New to start. You'll see the New Person screen.

2. Enter the person's last name (surname), first name (given), and middle name (middle) in the appropriate blanks, plus any suffix, such as Jr., in the Suffix line.

3. From the boxes next to Sex, select M for male, F for female, or ? for unknown.

4. Next to Born, enter the date of birth, making sure to use a four-digit birth year. If you aren't positive of the birth date, tap the arrow to select an option besides Born On (the default) from the pop-up menu next to Born.

5. Tap Edit in the square next to Location. Enter the place of birth (if known) in the Born Event Location screen. Tap Done, then tap Done again.

6. The name you entered now appears in the My Roots screen. Enter another name or two, including at least one parent (either father or mother) of the first person.

7. Select a name from the My Roots screen by tapping on it, and you'll see a Details screen pertaining to that person. Tap Select next to Father.

8. Select the person's father from the screen that appears. Tap Done.

9. After you've made several entries, the links start making sense. If a person has one or more siblings, tap the arrow next to Siblings, and the names of the siblings appear. Select a name from the siblings list, and My Roots displays that person's details. You can also tap on the Mother Name or Father Name to see that person's details.

10. Open a person's Details screen by tapping on his or her name and tap Event. Select an event, such as Died or Marriage.

11. Enter the details in the Edit Event screen. Tap Done.

## My Roots: The Important Commands

These are the significant commands for My Roots.

| Menu | Command | Shortcut | What It Does |
|------|---------|----------|--------------|
| Record | Show Ancestors | /A | Shows the antecedents of the person whose record is active |
| Record | Show Descendants | /D | Shows the descendants of the person whose record is active |
| Record | Mark As Changed | /M | Creates a marker in an export file to identify a person whose record has changed |
| Record | Delete Person | None | Deletes the person whose record is active |
| Record | Create Category | None | Automatically creates a category with the last name of the person whose record is active and adds up to 15 more people with that name in the category |

# 61 Caring for Coco: Pet Assistant

Name of Program: Pet Assistant
E-Mail Address: palmfriend@hotmail.com
Web Address: http://hotfiles.zdnet.com/cgi-bin/texis/swlib/hot-files/info.html?fcode=001FDN&b=zdpalm
Version: 1.0
Type of Software: Commercial
Cost: $5

From all indications, this is the best pet application around, and for $5, you're not out much. The demo version of this application, however, won't let you do anything but see how it works. In other words, it won't let you enter even one of your own pets. Also, the developer evidently doesn't have a Web site, although the instruction document is pretty thorough.

That said, the application itself is dandy and seems to solve a lot of the problems with other pet applications. It allows records for several pets, and it links a pet's basic information (date of birth, weight, etc.) to its medical information.

For particularly doting pet lovers, it also provides an Events database, where you can keep track of, if you're so inclined, your pet's birthday parties, trips to the kennel, obedience school graduation, or what have you.

So, download it, take a look at it, and, if you're pleased, go ahead and fork over the $5 to PalmGear to get a usable version.

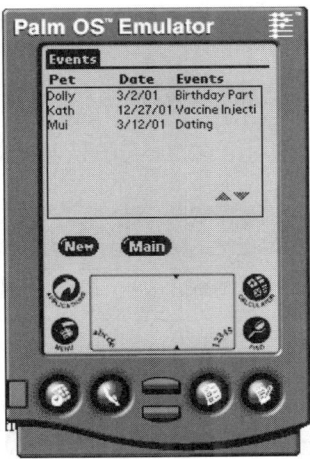

## Getting Started with Pet Assistant

How to take care of that favorite pet!

1. The opening screen presents the four databases that make up this application. Tap Pet to enter your pet's information.

2. Tap New. Enter one pet's information in the blanks shown. For the ID#, enter the number your veterinarian assigns to your pet, its

license number, or, if applicable, the number on its identification chip. Tap OK and then tap Main. (Although the screen specifies height and weight in metric terms, you can enter inches and pounds instead since no computations are based on these fields; just remember what units you used.)

**3.** Tap Sergeon [sic]. Enter the vet's name in the Surgeon line and the clinic's name in the Veterinary line. Enter other information as needed, then tap OK.

**4.** Tap Medical. Select a type of pet from the list, and enter the date and time of your visit to the vet from the pop-up pickers. Also enter the symptom and any notes. Then enter the fee in the Amount line. Tap OK and then tap Main.

**5.** Tap Events and then tap New to enter a new event. Select the pet from the pop-up list, and enter any pet-related events you want to remember. Tap OK.

## Pet Assistant: The Important Commands

Pet Assistant gives you these commands for entering data.

| Menu | Command | Shortcut | What It Does |
|------|---------|----------|--------------|
| Edit | Undo | /U | Undoes your last action |
| Edit | Cut | /X | Cuts selected text and saves it to the Clipboard |
| Edit | Copy | /C | Copies text and saves it to the Clipboard |
| Edit | Paste | /P | Pastes text from the Clipboard |
| Edit | Select All | /S | Selects all entries on the screen |
| Edit | Keyboard | /K | Allows you to use the keyboard to enter information |
| Edit | Graffiti Help | /G | Displays graffiti strokes |

# 62 For a Cool Summer Evening: Star Pilot

Name of Program: Star Pilot
E-Mail Address: sp@star-pilot.com
Web Address: http://www.star-pilot.com
Version: 3.01
Type of Software: Shareware
Cost: $29.95

Star Pilot sounds like it ought to be a game, but it's a serious—and seriously cool—star-watching application. And, it may be the best all-around application in this book. Not only does it display a star map for any location and any time, but it also gives you information about any sky object you tap on. When you register, you'll also be able to search for stars or constellations, and the found objects will flash on the screen to help you identify them.

The unregistered version is awesome, and the registered version is stellar (heh, heh). It includes these features:

◆ 753 stars in the shareware database (1,480 in the registered database!)

◆ All 90 constellations

◆ All 110 Messier objects are plotted

◆ Plot stars in black and white, gray, or color

◆ Choose from preprogrammed cities, or enter your own latitude and longitude for precise results

◆ Zoom factor can be set on any portion of the sky

◆ Display constellation lines in either the main screen or the Zoom window in three different gray shades

◆ Identify any star on the display with a single tap

◆ Map displays either the Pilot's date and time or another specified date and time

**172** JUST PLAIN FUN: WHO WOULD HAVE THOUGHT YOUR PALM COULD DO THIS!

◆ See what your night sky looks like in City or Rural mode, or specify your own magnitude range

◆ Specify which objects you wish to see displayed

◆ Customize the symbols used for each planet

◆ Specify how often you wish the display to be redrawn

◆ Find any star in the sky by name (registered version only)

◆ Find any constellation in the sky by name (registered version only)

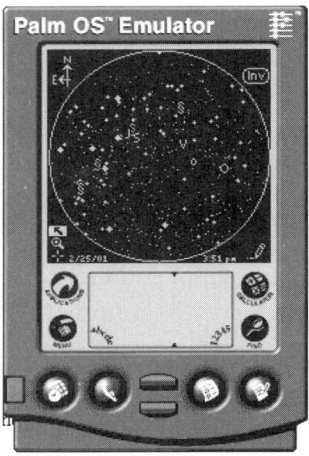

## Getting Started with Star Pilot

Here's how to get started exploring the stars.

**1.** Make sure you install all the necessary files (`sp3.prc`, `spdb3.pdb`, and `MathLib.prc`, which you may already have), as well as the Location Manager files (`locmgr.prc` and `llmgr.prc`).

**2.** Launch Star Pilot. You will see either an initial set-up location screen or the main screen as it fills with stars. Either way, the first thing you need to do is to tell it where you are.

**3.** If you got the set-up location screen, select the city closest to you from the pop-up menu labeled City, or enter your exact longitude and latitude in the designated spaces. Also enter your Greenwich mean time offset (the number of hours' difference between your time and GMT). If you're in daylight saving time, tap in the check box next to DST.

4. If you started with the main screen, tap the silk-screened Menus button, then select Location from the Options screen or enter **/L** on the graffiti pad.

5. Find the nearest city in the Choose Location box, and select it. Tap OK.

6. Now you're in the main screen, and it shows the stars at your location at this moment. (Yes, they're out there, even if they're obscured by daylight.) The dots are stars, and the letters are planets.

7. If you hold your handheld over your head with the top of the screen pointed north and the screen so that you can see it, Star Pilot's display will replicate the stars that you see overhead and to the horizon.

8. Now you can use some of the tools. The Arrow icon is preselected, so try it first. Tap the stylus on the screen, and the location will be identified in the upper-right corner of the screen.

9. Select the Magnifying Glass icon. Tap on a location in the sky. You will see a zoomed-in area of the sky where you tapped. When you're done, tap Close.

10. Select the Crosshair icon and tap on a star or planet. The Object Information screen will pop up and identify the object by name, type, and (unless it's a planet!) constellation it belongs to, as well as give other information including distance. Tap Close when you're done.

11. To update the view (those stars just keep moving along) and redraw the sky, tap the Pencil icon in the lower-right corner. Note the time display next to the pencil; it gives the last time the view was updated.

12. If you think you'd like a different view, tap the Inv button (for invert) and see dark stars on a light background.

## Star Pilot: The Important Commands

The important commands while using Star Pilot:

| Menu | Command | Shortcut | What It Does |
| --- | --- | --- | --- |
| Actions | Change Date & Time | /T | Sets the date and time for a star display |
| Actions | Find Star | /F | Searches for a specific star |

| Menu | Command | Shortcut | What It Does |
|------|---------|----------|--------------|
| Actions | Find Constellation | /C | Searches for a specific constellation |
| Options | General | /G | Lets you choose operation options |
| Options | Location | /L | Lets you set your location |
| Options | Magnitudes | /M | Lets you set minimum and maximum star magnitudes to display and choose rural or city display |
| Options | Objects | /O | Lets you choose from several display options |
| Options | Planets | /P | Lets you choose which planets you want displayed |
| Options | Zoom | /Z | Lets you choose the amount of zoom and whether to have constellation lines displayed on zooms |

# 63 Frothy Raw-Boned Flap-Dragon: Zounds

Name of Program: Zounds
E-Mail Address: surfTao@yahoo.com
Web Address: http://www.geocities.com/surftao/zounds/zounds.htm
Version: 1.0.1
Type of Software: Freeware
Cost: Free

I don't care what anyone says. I think this is an essential application for your Palm device. In this modern world, we've become far too lazy and unimaginative in our insults.

Zounds revives the art of the colorful insult. You have probably seen a version of this application online or perhaps in a magazine. If you haven't, this insult generator takes two pejorative adjectives found in Shakespeare's works and puts them in front of a Shakespearean pejorative noun. You've got to admit that "you sottish fly-bitten pumpion" is ever so much more interesting than "you jerk." Besides, it might confuse the insultee, making the insult all the more fun.

(If anybody asks, remember that "zounds" rhymes with "wounds," not "sounds." You must maintain the eloquent front, or you'll look like a purpled shag-eared minnow.)

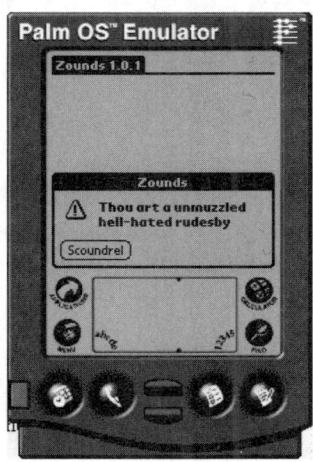

## Getting Started with Zounds

Zounds is this easy! Here's how to get started.

1. Launch Zounds.

2. Tap Knave.

3. Read insult, preferably aloud.

4. Laugh.

5. Tap Scoundrel.

6. Repeat steps 1–5 until you're tired, or until you're a roguish paper-faced pantaloon.

## Zounds: The Important Commands

Just one menu command for Zounds:

| Menu | Command | Shortcut | What It Does |
|------|---------|----------|--------------|
| Alack! Sufi | Accost Me, Knave | /A | Generates an insult |

# 64 How about a No-Mess Pet?: DigiPet

Name of Program: DigiPet
E-Mail Address: shuji@umap.net
Web Address: http://www.wakuwaku.ne.jp/shuji
Version: 0.95
Type of Software: Freeware
Cost: Free

Not only does this pet not need to be talked to or fed, but it costs nothing as well. This is DigiPet, your digital and quite friendly play-along pet. This pet does have the same needs as any other, of course: It gets hungry, gains weight, and does other assorted things (need I list them?). But this one travels with you wherever you go and requires no trips to the vet, no shots, and not even a bath every now and then. It's the digital pet lover's digital dream.

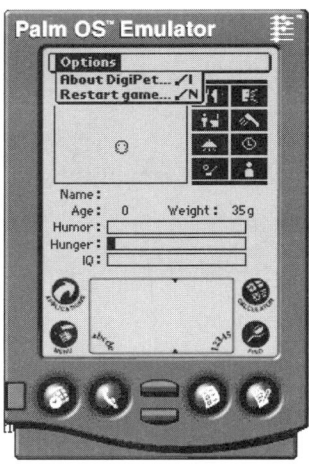

### Getting Started with DigiPet

Once you start DigiPet, you have to give your pet a name. As you play the game, various tasks arise (such as feeding and walking your pet). You win the game if your digital pet doesn't die.

### DigiPet: The Important Commands

The DigiPet commands are:

| Menu | Command | Shortcut | What It Does |
|------|---------|----------|--------------|
| Options | About DigiPet | /I | Tells you all about DigiPet |
| Options | Restart Game | /N | Introduces you to a new digital pet |

# 65 The Cleanest (and Most Ridiculous) Shave Possible: McRazor

Name of Program: McRazor
E-Mail Address: McRazor@MikeMcCollister.com
Web Address: http://www.MikeMcCollister.com/palm
Version: 2.03
Type of Software: Freeware
Cost: Free

You can turn it off and turn it on, and it even comes with sound. What else is there to say? As the very clever developer, Mike McCollister, says, "Just don't cut yourself."

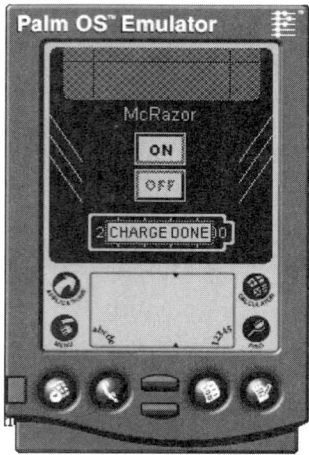

## Getting Started with McRazor

Bzz, bzz, bzz—how to get the shave of a lifetime.

**1.** Wash your face, legs, or whatever with a mild soap.

**2.** Launch McRazor.

**3.** Shave.

# 66 Work Wonders on Your Enemies: Voodoo Doll

Name of Program: Voodoo Doll
E-Mail Address: info@sickpuppy.com
Web Address: http://www.sickpuppysoftware.co.uk
Version: 0.9.6
Type of Software: Freeware
Cost: Free

This one *really* works. All you need to do is launch it, then enter the name of the person to whom you would like to inflict (theoretical) grievous injuries. Then just tap on the voodoo doll and—Shazam!—he or she is in trouble. I suspect there's some other magical Palm application that will reverse these effects, but I have yet to find it.

# Having Fun: Games and Entertainment

**A**dmit it, you've always thought of your Palm device as a toy—a business toy, perhaps, but a toy just the same. For even more entertainment, you can put a few games on it, too. The selection of available games is vast and offers various game types. This section offers up a collection of games that includes a word game, a puzzle, a card game, action games, and a maze game.

Some games will tax your brain. Most will eat your time. Occasionally, though, that may be just the thing you want. And with your Palm device keeping you on track the rest of the time, it only makes sense that it makes fun use of your downtime, too.

# 67 A New Twist on Word Games: AlphaTwist

Name of Program: AlphaTwist
E-Mail Address: miaowsoft@aol.com
Web Address: http://members.aol.com/miaowsoft/index.html
Version: 1.01
Type of Software: Shareware
Cost: $4

AlphaTwist is a little bit of word search, a little bit of Scrabble, a little bit of Tetris. Word-game lovers are sure to have a good time with it, because it provides plenty of options to make the game easier or more difficult, depending on your mood.

With this application, you try to form words from letters that appear on your screen, and you pay a penalty if you claim that a word is there but it isn't. You also pay a penalty if you opt to skip letters. The instructions below should get you going, but the best way to learn, as with most games, is to get in there and do it!

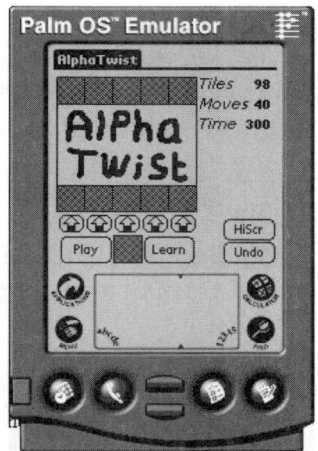

# Getting Started with AlphaTwist

Here's how to get started with AlphaTwist!

**1.** Install AlphaTwist and its dictionary.

**2.** Tap Learn to start off slow.

**3.** You will see a list of options available. Tap the Information icon (*i*) at the top right of the screen for explanations. Tap on your selection to change the settings according to your preferences. (You may want to turn off the Manual Claim option to start so that AlphaTwist will identify words for you.)

**4.** The object of the game is to score points by making words on the grid, either across or down. To begin, tap Play.

**5.** A letter appears at the bottom of the screen between the Skip and Claim options. Tap one of the squares on the bottom row, and the letter will appear in it.

**6.** Now another letter will appear at the bottom of the screen. Tap one of the squares on the bottom row, or tap the arrow beneath an existing letter, to place the new letter in the row and to move the existing letter up one square on the grid.

**7.** Continue placing letters until you see a word formed.

**8.** Tap Claim. AlphaTwist will give you a word and ask if you want to claim the word. If so, tap Yes. If it "sees" a word you don't want to claim because it would mess up the one you *do* want to claim, tap No and then tap Yes when your word appears.

**9.** The letters in that word disappear, and any extra letters will fall into the empty slots.

**10.** Continue to place letters and build more words with new letters until you run out of time or letters.

## AlphaTwist: The Important Commands

Here are the important AlphaTwist commands.

| Menu | Command | What It Does |
|------|---------|--------------|
| **Prefs** | **Word Preferences** | Lets you choose how AlphaTwist should search for words (e.g., minimum word length and word direction) |
| **Prefs** | **Game Preferences** | Lets you choose among several preferences in how the game is played |
| **Prefs** | **Super Challenge** | Lets you make the game more challenging in several ways |
| **HiScores** | **AlphaTwist Experts** | Shows high scorers in regular AlphaTwist play |
| **HiScores** | **AlphaTwist Trainees** | Shows high scorers among AlphaTwist beginners |
| **HiScores** | **FreeTwist Experts** | Shows high scorers in regular FreeTwist play |
| **HiScores** | **FreeTwist Trainees** | Shows high scorers among FreeTwist beginners |
| **HiScores** | **Clear HiScores** | Clears scores in HiScores lists |

# 68 No Tilt Allowed: Balls!

Name of Program: Balls!
E-Mail Address: info@deepnettech.com
Web Address: http://www.deepnettech.com
Version: 1.23
Type of Software: Shareware
Cost: $5

Balls! is one of those easy-to-play, hard-to-win games. In other words, if you want to kill time, this game will do it. It resembles those cheap little plastic games with tiny metal balls and a little maze inside. Instead of tilting the game to make the balls move, Balls! lets you reconfigure the maze in an effort to move each ball all the way from one side of the screen to the opposite side without falling into any of the holes.

Reconfiguring the maze is easy. You just tap on one of the diagonal walls, and it rotates 90 degrees. The hard part is figuring out which wall to rotate. Once you solve the puzzle a couple of times and you're ready for something more difficult, you can choose from eight levels of difficulty.

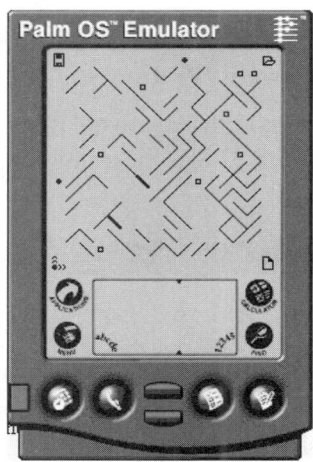

## Getting Started with Balls!

Follow these steps to get started with Balls!

1. When you launch, you will see a fresh game board. Tap the silk-screened Menus button and select Options.

2. Select Trivial (which means you'll have to deal with only one ball) from the pop-up Level menu, and select Very Slow from the pop-up Speed menu. (Trust me, you'll want to start slow to get a little positive reinforcement.) Tap OK.

3. Study the maze. The little squares are holes that the ball can fall into. The ball will start rolling straight into the maze from its starting point, and will deflect at a 90-degree angle when it hits a wall.

4. You'll want to rearrange the maze so that the ball makes it to the opposite side without falling into a hole. Tap on a wall to turn it 90 degrees. It will become darker and thicker, so you'll know which walls you've turned. If you tap a wall twice, it will return to its original position but remain dark.

5. Test your solution by tapping on the Ball icon in the lower-left corner; the ball starts rolling. If your solution doesn't work, Balls! will tell you.

6. Tap OK, and keep trying.

7. If you give up and want to know the solution, select Show Solution (or shortcut /W) from the Board menu.

8. You did it? Way to go! Record your name in the Best Times score-board. Check your battery stock. You've been playing for an hour!

## Balls!: The Important Commands

Here are the menu commands for Balls!

| Menu | Command | Shortcut | What It Does |
| --- | --- | --- | --- |
| Commands | New Game | /N | Starts a new game |
| Commands | Save Game | /S | Saves current game so that you may resume it later |
| Commands | Load Game | /L | Lets you start saved game |

| Menu | Command | Shortcut | What It Does |
|---|---|---|---|
| Commands | Options | /O | Lets you set speed and level of difficulty |
| Commands | Best Times | /B | Displays best recorded times |
| Commands | Pause Game | /P | Pauses current game and timer |
| Board | Test Board | /T | Lets you test a game solution without penalty |
| Board | Restore Board | /R | Returns board to its starting configuration |
| Board | Show Solution | /W | Highlights walls you needed to change for correct solution |
| Help | How to Play | /H | Gives details of Balls! operation |

# 69 Two Great Games in One: BlackJack Solitaire

Name of Program: BlackJack Solitaire
E-Mail Address: jlee@seahorsesoft.com.com
Web Address: http://www.seahorsesoft.com
Version: 3.1
Type of Software: Shareware
Cost: $5

BlackJack Solitaire, as its name suggests, uses principles of blackjack and applies them to a game of solitaire. The object of the game is to score the most points, and you score points by accumulating cards in five rows.

Sounds simple, and it is, but there's more. Except for the practice round, the games are timed, so you have to make quick decisions. You can set the game so that it doesn't show the row totals, meaning that you have to figure them in your head (yikes!).

It's fun. And it's a nice in-between kind of game—diverting, entertaining, but it doesn't leave you breathless (usually). Darn, that timer makes a difference!

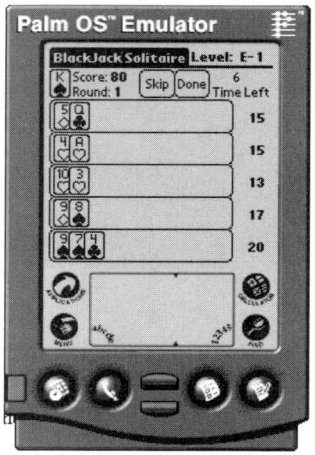

## Getting Started with BlackJack Solitaire

Get started with BlackJack Solitaire right here…

**1.** After launching BlackJack Solitaire, tap the silk-screened Menu button.

**2.** Select Settings from the Options menu.

**3.** Select P (for Practice) on the Level line. This level lets you play without a timer. Tap OK.

**4.** A card appears under the BlackJack Solitaire title bar. Tap the row where you want that card to go. Your goal is to get as many points as possible in each row without going over 21.

**5.** A new card will appear. Tap the row where you want that card to go. You may skip once per round (by tapping Skip).

**6.** Continue to place cards until you can't play any further without going bust (exceeding 21 points) in a line.

**7.** When you can play no more, tap Done to display your score.

**8.** Your score counts only if you get at least 95 points. You get bonus points for having time left when you finish (although not in a practice round) and for rows totaling 21. Tap OK.

**9.** To really play, return to the settings and set the level to 1.

**10.** Play as before, but note that the timer is running.

**11.** Cool! You made it to the Best Scores list? Tap Best Scores and record your glory.

## BlackJack Solitaire: The Important Commands

Here are the key BlackJack Solitaire commands.

| Menu | Command | Shortcut | What It Does |
|------|---------|----------|--------------|
| Options | New Game | /N | Starts a new game |
| Options | Settings | /S | Lets you select various play and display options |
| Options | Color Settings | /C | Lets color Palm users set colors |
| Stats | Best Scores | /B | Shows best scores recorded |
| Stats | Ultimate Score | /U | Shows best scores at easiest and hardest settings |
| Stats | Reset Best Scores | /R | Sets best scores to zero |
| Stats | Generate Code | /G | Shows you the level of difficulty for various codes. |
| Rules | How to Play | /H | Gives detailed play instruction |

# 70 Bursting Your Bubble: Bubblet

Name of Program: Bubblet
E-Mail Address: frank@oopdreams.com
Web Address: http://www.oopdreams.com
Version: 1.6
Type of Software: Shareware
Cost: $12

Bubblet is a Tetris-style game that comes with four different playing styles, from continuous to the standard drop-and-shift-when-empty mode that has a set number of bubbles.

Bubblet has other options, too. You can play alone or with up to four players. You can also set it up in Guest mode so that your friend doesn't mess up the game statistics you've worked so hard to accumulate. Once you're ready to start bursting bubbles, install Bubblet and give it a try.

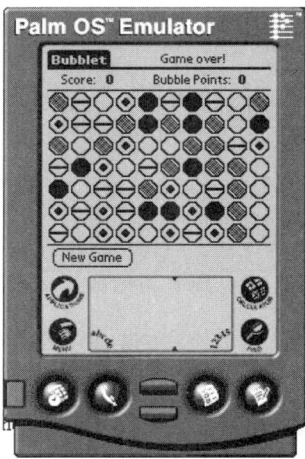

## Getting Started with Bubblet

Bubbles galore—here's how.

1. When you start Bubblet, it immediately starts moving. Go ahead and let it finish, accept the Welcome to Bubblet greeting, and psych yourself up.

2. Tap New Game. You will see a board filled with bubbles. Look for contiguous bubbles of identical patterns.

3. Tap on a bubble that abuts other bubbles of the same pattern to select all connected bubbles of that pattern.

4. Tap on your selection a second time. The selected bubbles disappear from the screen, and the bubbles above those shift down. (You can vary the shifting in the Preferences option under the Game menu.)

5. You score points each time you delete bubbles. The object is to score as many points as you can.

6. Continue selecting and deleting bubbles until you can remove no more, or until you have to stop. If you must stop before you're finished, tap End Game.

7. When your score appears on your screen, either tap Done to return to the screen you left or tap New Game to start a new game.

## Bubblet: The Important Commands

Here are the commands you need to know for Bubblet.

| Menu | Command | Shortcut | What It Does |
|------|---------|----------|--------------|
| Game | New Game | /N | Starts a new game |
| Game | End Game | /E | Ends current game |
| Game | Multi Game | /M | Lets you create a game for multiple players |
| Game | Replay Game | /R | Gives you a fresh crack at the game you just finished |

| Menu | Command | Shortcut | What It Does |
|------|---------|----------|--------------|
| Game | Undo Move | /U | Undoes last move |
| Game | Preferences | /P | Lets you choose game style, Guest mode, and other options |
| Info | Statistics | /S | Shows your highest score, average score, and number of game for each playing style |

# 71 Sea Battle Ahoy!: Derfflinger

Name of Program: Derfflinger
E-Mail Address: bermannj@gmx.de
Web Address: http://members.aol.com/bermannj
Version: 2.2
Type of Software: Shareware
Cost: $6

Derfflinger is a naval battle action game, full of strategy potential. It has different kinds of ships—carriers, cruisers, destroyers, tankers, and submarines—and each kind has different firing ranges and capabilities. In addition, each kind can survive a different number of hits.

Each ship also has a different viewing range. The trickiest part, therefore, may be that you can't always see all enemy ships; it depends on their distance from you. You can tap on an island (the circles on the screen) to get an overview of each side's ships, but that doesn't tell you where to find the ships.

The unregistered version lacks carriers (and, therefore, planes). Also, the unregistered version lacks certain game types. The $6 fee isn't much, though, and lovers of this kind of game will be eager to pay it.

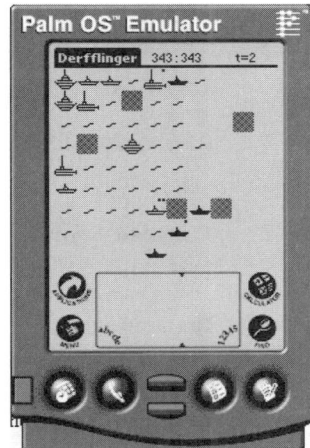

## Getting Started with Derfflinger

Here's how to "launch" Derfflinger.

**1.** Derfflinger starts with a cute little screen ordering you to "Sink all enemy cruisers!" You'll answer this command by tapping "Aye, Aye, Sir." (The orders won't always be the same, so read your commands!)

**2.** Your ships are gray; your opponent's ships are black. You'll want to move one of your ships to seek and destroy an enemy ship. Tap on your ship, wait for a selection box, and drag it where you want it to go. Different ship types can move different numbers of spaces at a time. The ships will shoot on their own.

**3.** If you want to know where you stand, tap on one of the islands (the circles) to see a lineup of your fleet.

## Derfflinger: The Important Commands

Here are the important Derfflinger commands.

| Menu | Command | What It Does |
| --- | --- | --- |
| Start | Normal Game | Starts a basic game |
| Start | Normal Game with Carrier | Starts a basic game that includes carriers |

| Menu | Command | What It Does |
|------|---------|--------------|
| Start | Easy Game | Starts an easy game |
| Start | Easy Game with Carrier | Starts an easy game that includes carriers |
| Start | Crowded Game | Starts a crowded game (registered version only) |
| Start | Dreadnought | Starts a game with a battleship |
| Start | Convoy | Starts a game with a convoy (registered version only) |
| Start | Random Game | Selects game type at random (registered version only) |
| Start | Restart Game | Restarts game |
| Options | Show All | Shows all ships |
| Options | Your Task | Shows you your task |
| Help | Rules | Explains ships' capabilities |

# 72  Coconut Catcher: Kanga.ru

Name of Program: Kanga.ru
E-Mail Address: comments@softava.com
Web Address: http://www.softava.com/kanga.ru
Version: 3.0
Type of Software: Shareware
Cost: $5

You've got to love Kanga.ru. It's just plain silly and fun. And it comes with striking graphics.

In the middle of your Palm screen, you'll see a happy kangaroo hanging onto its pouch. On either side of it are coconut palm trees. Coconuts fall out of the trees, and the kangaroo, with your help, tries to catch them in its pouch.

The animation in this game is smooth and quite funny. The kangaroo makes great faces, and if it gets hit in the head (and ends your game), it goes splat convincingly on the bottom of your screen. Forget those intellectually challenging games. Play Kanga.ru, and be a kid again!

## Getting Started with Kanga.ru

Getting started with Kanga.ru? Here's how.

1. The opening screen of Kanga.ru tells you what to do, so make sure to read that screen, and then tap New Game.

2. Select Help from the Kanga.ru menu to read how to use the hardware buttons or the stylus to play. Make your decision and tap Done.

3. Tap Novice to start the game.

4. Using either the hardware buttons or your stylus, help the kangaroo catch the coconuts in its pouch.

5. Keep playing until your kangaroo gets conked.

## Kanga.ru: The Important Commands

There isn't much in the way of Kanga.ru commands.

| Menu | Command | Shortcut | What It Does |
|------|---------|----------|--------------|
| Kanga.Ru | Help | /H | Shows you what each hardware button on your Palm device will do in this game and gives tips for stylus play |
| Kanga.Ru | Top Scores | /T | Shows top scores |

# 73 The Round Peg in the Round Hole: Pegged

Name of Program: Pegged
E-Mail Address: mobile@mobile.com.br
Web Address: http://www.mobile.com.br/palm/games/welcome.html
Version: 1.02
Type of Software: Shareware
Cost: $9

You may already know this game and know how maddening it can be. Pegged is another game that starts with a simple premise. You eliminate pegs from a board by jumping one peg over another, one at a time, into an empty space. The "jumped" peg is removed from the board. The idea is to end up with just one peg. Achieving that final result, naturally, is the hard part. Pegged has various configurations that you can use to find the solution of a puzzle. At $9, though, the price seems a little high for such a straightforward game that doesn't even provide solutions.

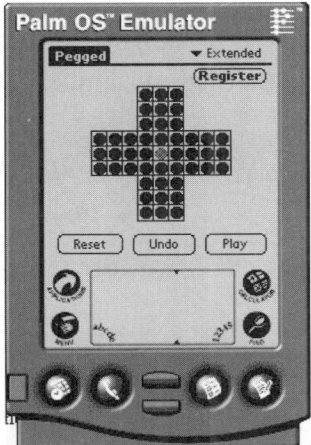

## Getting Started with Pegged

Here's how to play Pegged.

**1.** After the nifty animation at startup, you'll see what for many will be a familiar peg game layout: a giant plus sign with a blank square in the middle.

**2.** If you don't know the drill, information is available by tapping the silk-screened Menu button and selecting How to Play. Tap Done.

**3.** Once you're ready, touch the peg you want to move and drag the stylus to the empty spot where you want your peg to land. The peg you jumped over automatically disappears. Remember that you want to finish with just one peg left on your screen.

**4.** Continue moving until you can make no further moves. (Note that the Undo button doesn't work in the unregistered version.)

**5.** When Pegged tells you the game is over, tap OK.

**6.** Tap Reset to start over.

# Pegged: The Important Commands

Here are the Pegged commands.

| Menu | Command | What It Does |
|------|---------|--------------|
| Help | How to Play? | Gives you instructions |
| Options | Enable/Disable Intro Screen | Toggles introductory screen on or off |

# Seeing It All: Graphics Applications

**Y**ou know that pictures use a lot of memory, and you know that one thing the Palm lacks (at least compared with your Desktop computer) is a lot of memory. It follows, then, that Palm applications just can't do much with pictures, right?

Wrong! Developers have created some amazing and fun graphic applications for Palm devices. The selection here ranges from the simple to the complex, from still images to movies (really!). There's even one to share with a buddy.

So put on your beret and start creating drawings, animations, and movies—or download your favorites—for your Palm device.

## 74 Mirror, Mirror Images: Calei

Name of Program: Calei
E-Mail Address: ChipEra@mail.com
Web Address: http://www.geocities.com/janb_80687
Version: 1.0
Type of Software: Freeware
Cost: Free

You get a big bang for your buck with this free graphics application. Anyone who has ever been fascinated by a kaleidoscope will like this graphics program. It has two modes: automatic and manual. Choose automatic, and Calei will draw cool and complex kaleidoscopic images as you watch. Choose manual, and Calei translates your marks into kaleidoscopic patterns. Either way, you can choose whether it draws at 8 or 16 times the mirroring effect.

You can't save the drawings, but what do you expect for free? Besides, the ephemeral aspect of kaleidoscopic images is part of their charm. (I'm just sorry it isn't in color!)

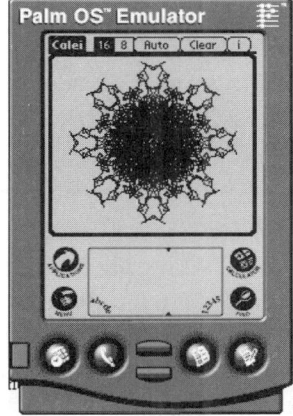

## Getting Started with Calei

Here's how to get great graphics with Calei.

**1.** Once you've loaded all three files and launched the application, you're ready.

**2.** Draw by moving your stylus (or finger) across your Palm device's screen. Watch as Calei translates your scratches into reflected images.

**3.** When you're done, tap Clear.

**4.** To try a different level of mirroring, tap the 8 at the top of the screen, or tap the 16 if the 8 is already highlighted.

**5.** Again, move your stylus across the screen and enjoy the effects.

**6.** Tap Clear.

**7.** Tap Auto, and see what Calei produces on its own.

**8.** Tap the screen to stop the automatic drawing.

# 75 Dynamic Doodler: Diddle

Name of Program: Diddle
E-Mail Address: mblevin@debian.org
Web Address: http://blevins.simplenet.com/diddle/diddle.htm
Version: 1.23
Type of Software: Freeware
Cost: Free

If you like doodling, you'll like Diddle, but Diddle gives you many more options than mere doodling. It offers all the basic black-and-white drawing tools, such as various pen widths, shape drawers, fill patterns, and text tools. And it's free, believe it or not.

Take a look at the Web site to see the amazing drawings that other users have created with this nice little application. This app lets you save your drawings when they go beyond doodles.

Here are the features:

◆ Freehand sketching with adjustable smoothing and filtering

◆ A variety of pen widths and shapes, including calligraphy

◆ Options for sketching lines, circles, rectangles, ovals, and other shapes

◆ Nine different fill patterns (from white to black) that can be applied to freehand sketching as well as to lines and shapes

◆ Option to insert text (three available fonts) into sketches

◆ Full-screen mode (or optional title bar)

◆ Copy-and-paste options

◆ A circular scratch buffer for quick doodles

◆ Ability to save your sketches with a title and keywords so that saved drawings can be found later using the Categories and Find functions

◆ Support for the Link Master protocol so that you can link directly to your sketches from any Link Container, such as Thoughtstream

◆ Ability to create new sketches using the hardware buttons

◆ Ability to lock your sketches to prevent accidental changing or erasing

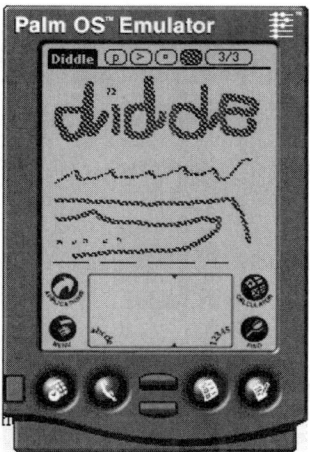

## Getting Started with Diddle

Here's how to get started with Diddle.

**1.** When you launch Diddle, all you need to do is start drawing. First, do a simple line by moving the stylus across the screen.

**2.** Change tools by tapping the P button at the top of the screen and selecting from the pop-up menu. Choose Smear and draw a shape with it.

**3.** You'd probably like the Smear more with a broader brush. Tap the Dot button and select Broad from the pop-up menu.

**4.** Tap the Equals Sign (=) button and select Smoother.

**5.** Got a full screen? Select Clear from the Edit menu, and start your next drawing.

**6.** Tap Diddle in the menu bar, and select a shape to draw.

**7.** Keep experimenting!

**8.** When you're done, just press a hardware button or return to the Applications/Home screen. Your drawing will automatically be saved, unless you clear it first.

# Diddle: The Important Commands

Here are the extensive Diddle commands.

| Menu | Command | Shortcut | What It Does |
|------|---------|----------|--------------|
| Page | New | /N | Creates new drawing page |
| Page | Duplicate | /D | Creates a duplicate of the current drawing |
| Page | Remove | /R | Removes drawing on display |
| Page | Previous | /- | Opens previous drawing in sketchbook |
| Page | Next | /+ | Opens next drawing in sketchbook |
| Page | Save | /S | Lets you name a drawing, attach a note to it, and categorize it |
| Page | Index | /I | Opens index of saved drawings |
| Page | Beam | /B | Lets you beam drawing to another Palm device |
| Page | Preferences | /H | Lets you select various display and function options |
| Edit | Clear | /X | Clears screen |
| Edit | Fill | /F | Fills screen with selected ink |
| Edit | Invert | /W | Reverses colors |
| Edit | Copy | /C | Copies selected text |
| Edit | Paste | /V | Pastes selected text |
| Edit | Insert Line | /K | Makes pen draw straight line |
| Edit | Insert Shape | /O | Lets you draw a selected shape with specific properties |
| Edit | Insert Text | /Z | Lets you specify text and text properties to insert into your drawing with a tap |
| Edit | Insert Last | /L | Inserts last object inserted |

| Menu | Command | Shortcut | What It Does |
|------|---------|----------|--------------|
| Edit | Toggle Title | /T | Toggles drawing title/button bar on and off |
| Mode | Paint | /P | Selects Paint mode |
| Mode | Smear | /M | Selects Smear mode |
| Mode | Erase | /E | Selects Eraser mode |
| Mode | Unsmooth | /< | Makes a less-clean line |
| Mode | Smooth | /= | Makes a smooth line |
| Mode | Smoother | /> | Makes a line even smoother |
| Pen | Fine | /. | Makes pen draw a fine line |
| Pen | Medium | /[square] | Makes pen draw a medium line |
| Pen | Bold | /i | Makes pen draw a bold line |
| Pen | Broad | /@ | Makes pen draw a broad line |
| Pen | F. Italic | /, | Makes pen draw a fine line of variable thickness, as with calligraphy |
| Pen | M. Italic | // | Makes pen draw a medium line of variable thickness, as with calligraphy |
| Pen | B. Italic | /; | Makes pen draw a bold line of variable thickness, as with calligraphy |
| Ink | White | /0 | Draws with white ink |
| Ink | 1/8 | /1 | Draws with 1/8 black ink |
| Ink | 2/8 | /2 | Draws with 2/8 black ink |
| Ink | 3/8 | /3 | Draws with 3/8 black ink |
| Ink | 4/8 | /4 | Draws with 4/8 black ink |
| Ink | 5/8 | /5 | Draws with 5/8 black ink |
| Ink | 6/8 | /6 | Draws with 6/8 black ink |
| Ink | 7/8 | /7 | Draws with 7/8 black ink |
| Ink | Black | /8 | Draws with black ink |

# 76 Video and More on View: FireViewer

Name of Program: FireViewer
E-Mail Address: support@firepad.com
Web Address: http://www.firepad.com
Version: 5.1
Type of Software: Freeware
Cost: Free

FireViewer is a jewel of a program that has become the standard in Palm image viewing. It lets you view HTML documents, images, and video files. It operates on black-and-white or color devices, and it's simple and easy to use. If you've got wireless capacity, FireViewer also supports hyperlinks for you. Additionally, you can convert your existing JPEG and GIF files to Fire-Viewer images. And for fun, lots of FireViewer movies are available online for downloading.

FireViewer features include the following:

◆ You can use FireConverter to convert JPEGs, GIFs, AVIs, and MOVs for viewing images and videos on your Palm.

◆ It offers the fastest, thinnest, and simplest document and media client for the Palm.

◆ You can view huge color images, text, hyperlinks, and video on Palm IIIC devices.

◆ You can view 16-level grayscale images, text, hyperlinks, and video.

◆ You can view 4-level grayscale images, text, hyperlinks, and video on all Palm devices.

◆ With 360-Degree Drag, you can easily move graphics larger than 8000 × 8000 pixels or 10 × 10 feet in any direction simply by dragging the stylus.

◆ You can preview large images on your Palm.

◆ You can zoom in on and out of large images.

◆ You can navigate through server-based documents by using images maps and hyperlinks.

◆ You can attach text notes to images.

◆ It offers support for Find and Beam functions.

In short, if you have images that you want to carry on your Palm, you'll want to get FireViewer.

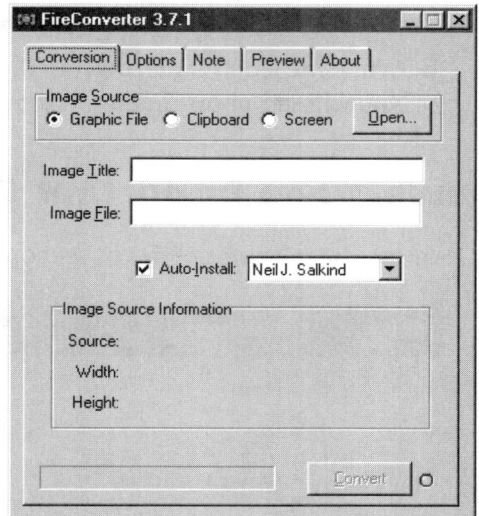

## Getting Started with FireViewer

Here's how to get started with FireViewer.

**1.** Install the application and at least one sample video or image file that has a PDB extension.

**2.** When you launch FireViewer, you will see a list of files you can view. The files may be images or hypertext. Images have a Flame icon, documents have a Document icon, and videos have a Film icon.

**3.** Tap and hold one of the items in your list. You will see a pop-up menu that shows the operations you can do with that item; the operations vary by type of item. Or, you can just tap the item, and it will default to View as the operation of choice.

**4.** Take a look at the item, and either tap the right-pointing arrow to see the next item in your FireViewer list or tap the Home icon to return home.

**5.** Open an image file to view it. Tap the silk-screened Menu button and select Preview to see a reduced but complete image.

**6.** Tap the % square to return the image to its full size. Tap the Home icon.

**7.** Tap a video item to play it.

**8.** While the video is playing, tap the screen. The video will pause, and you will see a pop-up menu from which to choose your next action.

## FireViewer: The Important Commands

Here are the important FireViewer commands.

| Menu | Command | Shortcut | What It Does |
| --- | --- | --- | --- |
| Info | Help | /H | Provides instructions on using FireViewer |
| Options | Open Location | /W | Opens to Web address |
| Options | Preferences | /R | Lets you choose among several display and operation options |
| Options | Assign Image Buttons | /I | Lets you assign FireViewer functions to Palm hardware buttons |
| Options | Advanced Configuration | None | Lets you preset a Fire-Publisher address |
| Options | Purge Cache | None | Deletes all FireViewer images and hypertext documents on your Palm device |

# 77 Drawing across the Room: IrSketch

Name of Program: IrSketch
E-Mail Address: handwatch@handwatch.com
Web Address: http://www.handwatch.com
Version: 1.1
Type of Software: Shareware
Cost: $19.99

Are you ready for this one? IrSketch lets you have real-time graphic information exchanges with another Palm device user. In other words, when you draw a sketch on your Palm, another person can see your drawing on his or her Palm device, thanks to infrared connections.

You can use it for fooling around—playing tic-tac-toe during a meeting, for instance—or for serious business, such as sharing design ideas. You and your Palm partner can even work on the same drawing.

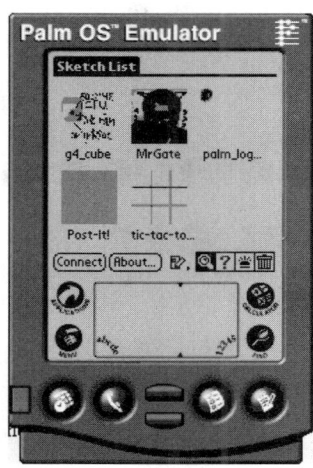

## Getting Started with IrSketch

Getting started with IrSketch is easy. Here's how…

**1.** Load IrSketch and the accompanying PDB files, then launch as usual.

**2.** Tap OK to leave the About screen.

**3.** Have the person with whom you will be sharing your file—we'll call that person your partner—launch his or her copy of IrSketch.

**4.** The opening Sketch List screen reveals five different files called sketch paper. Select one by tapping on it.

**5.** Make sure that your partner is within 15 feet of you, and then point the infrared ports of the two Palm devices toward each other.

**6.** Now, your partner must tap the Connect button on the opening Sketch List screen.

**7.** Wait a few seconds for the devices to exchange information.

**8.** Either one of you can now write or draw on the selected sketch paper, and the other person will be able to see it!

**9.** The default drawing tool is the pen, but you can select others from a pop-up menu that you open by tapping the Pen icon at the bottom of the screen.

**10.** The Dot icon at the bottom of the screen has a pop-up menu offering different line widths.

**11.** Press Done to return to the Sketch List screen.

# 78 Animation Just for Fun: Schmear

Name of Program: Schmear (was PalmSmear)
E-Mail Address: markyang@palmsense.com
Web Address: http://www.palmsense.com
Version: 1.0.2
Type of Software: Freeware
Cost: Free

OK, this one doesn't have much practical application, but it's kind of fun. You can think of Schmear as a revved-up doodler. It lets you take an image and manipulate it to create little animated movies. It comes with

11 celebrity images—from actors to Bill Gates to Bill Clinton—for you to fool around with. (Here's your chance to wipe that grin off of Clinton's face.)

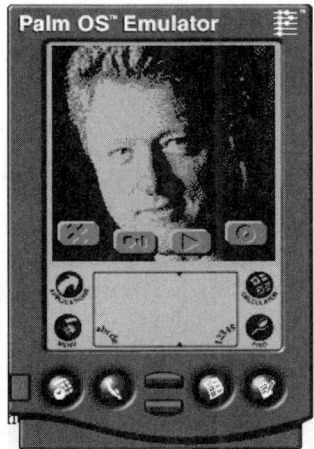

## Getting Started with Schmear

Here's the low-down on Schmear.

1. Install the application file and at least one image file.

2. Launch Schmear and tap OK to leave the Information screen.

3. Check to make sure that Edit is highlighted at the bottom of the screen.

4. Tap the name of the image you want to alter.

5. Tap the Menu button on your Palm device to open the Schmear Panel, a collection of tools and frames for your animation.

6. Tap on the leftmost empty frame to load the selected original image as the first one in your animation.

7. Tap on the Whirligig icon (the one on the top left); it's the Schmear button.

8. Tap on the top-right button, which is the Small Paintbrush selector.

9. Tap on the image, then wait a moment while the buttons disappear.

10. Tap your stylus on a part of the image you would like to change and drag the stylus in the direction you want the image to move. Stop

when you've moved partway to the location where you want the finished image to go.

**11.** Tap on the Menu button.

**12.** Tap on the second frame to store your keyframe.

**13.** Tap on the image again, and smear some more. (If you prefer, you can first choose a different tool: the Large Paintbrush tool, which is the middle button on the right, or the Unsmear tool, the middle one on the left.)

**14.** Tap the next frame to store your latest image. If you don't like your latest, tap the bottom-left button, which restores your image to its previous state.

**15.** Tap the right-pointing arrow to play your animation.

**16.** Tap the screen to stop the animation and return to the Smear Panel.

**17.** Tap the image to return to the Play screen. Tap the Bullseye image (far right) to return to the Schmear Files screen.

# 79 Painting in Miniature: TealPaint

Name of Program: TealPaint
E-Mail Address: contact@tealpoint.com
Web Address: http://www.tealpoint.com/softpnt.htm
Version: 4.76C
Type of Software: Shareware
Cost: $17.95

This application is unbelievable in its abilities. Unbelievable. Why? Because this Palm OS application lets you do just about anything you'd do with a Desktop paint program. You can make simple drawings or create complex animations. It works on color, grayscale, or black-and-white Palm devices. It lets you do darn near anything graphically, including share your work with your Desktop computer (PC only).

On top of it all, it's easy to use! You will begin to see how to use it in the steps listed on the next page. Then, you can spend as long as you want perfecting your artwork.

Look at this *huge* partial list of features:

- Multiple image databases
- Multiple annotated records
- Image templates
- Background locking
- Basic animation functions
- Dithered thumbnail images
- View-only Browsing mode
- Horizontal and vertical scrolling for oversized images
- Magnified Draw mode
- Freehand Draw tool
- Constrained 45- and 90-degree Line tool
- Erase tool
- User-defined image templates
- Coordinate-based lasso adjust
- 16 drawing patterns
- 12 brushes
- 90-degree copy-buffer image rotation
- Paste-to-fit image scaling
- Configurable hardware-button mapping
- Horizontal and vertical flipping
- Image compression
- Screen-grabbing Import function
- TealPaint Image Manager, a Windows import, export, and print utility
- PicUtil, a DOS command-line batch image converter

Now you can see why this application is unbelievable, too.

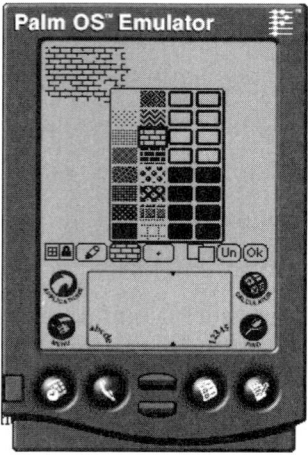

## Getting Started with TealPaint

Here's how to get started with the extremely powerful TealPaint.

**1.** Go ahead and tap OK when asked whether you want to name this database Pictures, then tap to pass the Information screen.

**2.** You might as well jump in and make a picture. Tap the empty square next to the words New Image. (The Edit button should already be highlighted.)

**3.** The next blank screen is your canvas. The default tools will appear at the bottom of your screen, showing a pencil, a black square, and a dot. Go ahead and draw a little with that setup to experiment.

**4.** Tap the silk-screened Menu button and select Clear Screen from the Edit menu. (We'll talk about saving in a minute.) Tap Yes to confirm.

**5.** Tap the Pencil icon and choose another drawing tool from those you see on the pop-up menu.

**6.** Tap the black square and choose another color or pattern from the palette. (Your options will depend on whether you have a black-and-white, grayscale, or color device.)

**7.** Tap on the third in that set of buttons, the Brush selector, and choose a different brush type.

8. If you have a color device, you can tap the pair of colored rectangles to make further color selections.

9. Create a new drawing. Oops! If you goof up, tap the Un button to undo your last step and then continue.

10. Tap the Lock button on the bottom of the screen to lock your current image so that you can draw over it.

11. When you're done, tap OK to save your masterpiece.

12. Now you'll probably want to give it a name. Just tap in the text line next to the image, delete the words New Image, and enter the new name.

## TealPaint: The Important Commands

TealPaint has plenty of commands to work with.

| Menu | Command | Shortcut | What It Does |
|------|---------|----------|--------------|
| Edit | Cut Selected | /X | Cuts selected area with the Rectangular Selection tool and copies it to the Clipboard |
| Edit | Copy Selected | /C | Copies the area selected with the Rectangular Selection tool to the Clipboard |
| Edit | Paste Selected | /P | Pastes contents of the Clipboard into current drawing |
| Edit | Paste Scaled to Fit | /W | Pastes contents of the Clipboard scaled to fit an area selected with the Rectangular Selection tool |
| Edit | Rotate Copy Buffer | /Z | Rotates, in 90-degree increments, image saved to the Clipboard (aka Copy Buffer); must use paste function to then place rotated image |

| Menu | Command | Shortcut | What It Does |
|------|---------|----------|--------------|
| Edit | View Full Image | /L | Lets you see entire drawing when it is larger than the screen |
| Edit | Previous Image | /A | Opens previously viewed picture |
| Edit | Next Image | /B | Opens next picture in database |
| Edit | Clear Screen | None | Clears contents of current screen upon confirmation |
| Edit | Close Without Saving | None | Closes current drawing without saving any changes |
| Select | Select All | /S | Selects entire screen contents |
| Select | Select None | None | De-selects your selection |
| Select | Nudge (Up, Down, Left, or Right) | None | Lets you fine-tune your selection in given direction |
| Select | Flip Horizontal | /H | Flips selection in horizontal plane (left to right) |
| Select | Flip Vertical | /V | Flips selection in vertical plane (up and down) |
| Select | Fill Area | /F | Fills selection with color or pattern in palette |
| Select | Erase Area | /E | Deletes all contents in selected area |
| Select | Invert Area | /I | Reverses background color and foreground color in selected area |
| Select | Coordinates | /? | Gives X and Y coordinates as well as height and width of selection |

| Menu | Command | Shortcut | What It Does |
|------|---------|----------|--------------|
| Anim | Previous Image | /A | Opens previously viewed picture |
| Anim | Next Image | /B | Opens next picture in database |
| Anim | Replicate Frame | /O | Creates an identical picture to the current one (especially for use in animation) |
| Anim | Junk Current Frame | /J | Deletes the current picture and opens the next one in the database |
| Anim | Set Animation Speed | None | Lets you set the speed at which images progress in your animation |
| Anim | Play Animation | /Y | Plays all the frames in current database in sequence for animation |
| Special | Text Font/Options | /T | Lets you select text properties |
| Special | Button Mappings | None | Lets you assign certain functions to hardware buttons |
| Special | Grid Snap Dist | None | Lets you set size of invisible grid (for when you use Grid option) |
| Special | Swap Fg/Bg Colors | /M | Changes background color to foreground color and vice versa |

# Taking Care
of Business:
Business' Best

**A** Palm device can be good for business. Literally hundreds of applications exist for business use. Information about some of these—such as calendars and document readers—are included in other chapters. This chapter will focus on Palm applications that let you handle everything from time management to project tracking to financial matters.

Specifically, these applications will help you do the following:

- ◆ Compute loan payments
- ◆ Figure the value of a business
- ◆ Track inventory
- ◆ Organize your ideas
- ◆ Make hierarchical To Do lists
- ◆ Figure price quotes
- ◆ Watch your investments
- ◆ Compute your retirement needs
- ◆ Reorganize your contact lists
- ◆ Make success a habit
- ◆ Help to keep your life in balance
- ◆ Do sophisticated statistical analyses
- ◆ Keep your checkbook and other accounts up-to-date
- ◆ And much more!

Those application developers have been busy, and their work can mean a productivity increase for you. (And that leaves you more time to try out those great Palm device games!)

# 80 You Can Count on It: powerOne Finance

Name of Program: powerOne Finance
E-Mail Address: info@infinitysw.com
Web Address: http://www.infinitysw.com/
Version: 2.0
Type of Software: Commercial
Cost: $49.99

Holy bean counter! powerOne Finance (a cousin of plain ole powerOne) has enough functions to keep you calculating in your sleep. It does everything but count your inventory for you. It'll even figure out how much interest you'll have to pay on a loan to buy this nifty, but expensive, application. The company says that this app has more than 430 functions. I didn't count 'em, but I believe it. powerOne Finance has all the financial functions found in the popular HP 12C, HP 17B, HP 19B, or TI BAII+ hardware calculators. It offers RPN (Reverse Polish Notation) and standard input modes, 14-digit number entry, and quick store and recall functions.

The functions cover business, statistics, and scientific calculations. Just for starters, you can figure loan payments and annuities, analyze the cash flows of investments, calculate depreciation four different ways, and convert units of measure from one standard to another (such as from metric to English).

Here are some of the (almost) endless features:

◆ Enter up to 14-digit numbers with 12 distinct decimal place settings

◆ Modify stack and history data using drop, duplicate, move, copy, and rotate functions

◆ Customize the calculator's buttons

◆ Recall and store up to 10 memory locations

◆ Review past calculations

◆ Input data using the pop-up Input screen

powerOne stores the product manual on your Desktop computer and loads the handheld application onto your Install tool for transfer during synchronization. You'll then need to install and save the application file to your Desktop computer, and then open it to start the installation process. When the installer is finished, synchronize your handheld computer to transfer the program.

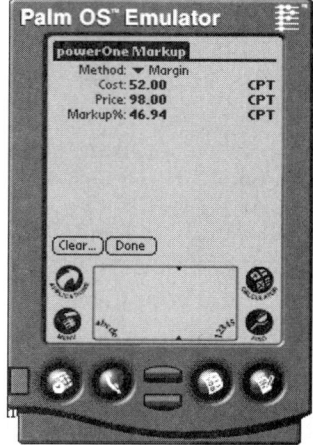

## Getting Started with powerOneFinance

Get a hold of your massive fortune beginning with these steps:

**1.** When you start up powerOne Finance the first time, it will ask whether you want its calculator to override the built-in calculator, and it will also ask whether you want to enter equations the standard way or RPN ("Don't know" *is* an option). Answer the questions, and you'll arrive at the basic powerOne Finance screen. Try it out as a simple calculator just for fun. Then we'll get serious.

**2.** Tap the selection bar at the top of the screen to choose the type of analysis you want to do. Select from the Finance, Business, Convert, Stats, Calendar, and Solver functions. Then enter your equation and make your calculation.

**3.** When you've finished with a calculation, tap Done.

**4.** Back at the main screen, choose another function and keep on calculating!

# powerOne Finance: The Important Commands

Here are the important commands for powerOne Finance.

| Menu | Command | Shortcut | What It Does |
|------|---------|----------|--------------|
| Edit | Copy | /C | Copies the selected text to the Clipboard |
| Edit | Paste | /P | Pastes the selected text from the Clipboard onto the entry field |
| Edit | Graffiti Help | /G | Provides help with graffiti keystrokes |
| Options | Clear All | /A | Clears the current math function, the history, and the memory list |
| Options | Clear History | /H | Clears only the history list |
| Options | Clear Memory | /Y | Clears only the memory list |
| Options | Error Help | /E | Displays information about an error when one occurs |
| Options | Keystroke Help | /O | Displays information about using graffiti keystrokes in powerOne Finance |
| Options | Back Up Options | /B | Lets you select from options for backing up your data |
| Options | Preferences | /R | Lets you select from various calculator preferences, such as the number of decimals shown, and lets you set programmable buttons on the calculator |

# 81 Keeping the Numbers Straight: Accounts & Loans

Name of Program: Accounts & Loans
E-Mail Address: jleung@direct.ca
Web Address: http://persweb.direct.ca/jleung/AL_Doc/AL.html
Version: 2.08c
Type of Software: Shareware
Cost: $15

With this straightforward handheld application, you can keep track of your checking accounts, savings accounts, and loans. You can also create a loan, complete with amortization schedule, and Accounts & Loans will automatically generate loan payment entries from the specified account. The registered version allows an unlimited number of accounts, categories, and loan entries. The unregistered version limits you to three accounts and two loans.

Accounts & Loans also interacts nicely with your built-in Date Book, To Do List, and Memo Pad. You can use Accounts & Loans and any of those applications to place payment reminders. The accompanying user's manual is detailed and useful, which is important for an app that gives as many options as this one does.

Here are the features:

◆ Unlimited number of expense categories

◆ Automatic loan payment entries

◆ Automatic recurring transaction entries

◆ Automatic reminder in Date Book, To Do List, or Memo Pad for recurring transactions or loan transactions

◆ Account summary and expense category summary reports

◆ Memorized transactions

◆ Data export to and import from Memo Pad in CSV format

◆ Support for Quik Budget, a PC-based personal finance application

◆ On-screen clock for checking the time as needed while you work in Accounts & Loans

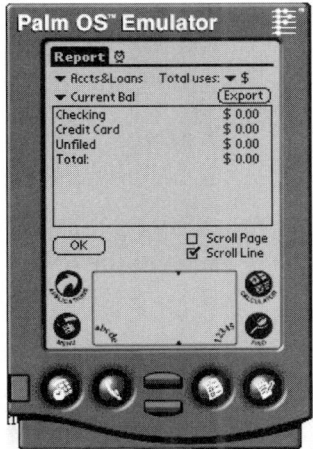

# Getting Started with Accounts & Loans

Follow these steps to find out just how much you owe:

**1.** Start Accounts & Loans to get to the main A&L screen. For this example, set your preferences to start. Tap the silk-screened Menu button. Note that the Home Currency field is already set to dollars; change it if you'd like.

**2.** Tap Account List. You can add any accounts you think you might need beyond the preset Checking and Credit Card accounts.

**3.** From the Account List, select Checking.

**4.** Tap Edit and provide any helpful information in the Edit screen. For example, the Last Cheq. # field will be particularly useful. (In this case, "Cheq." stands for the Canadian spelling for "check.") Use graffiti, or pop up the keyboard from the Graffit screen on your handheld.

**5.** Tap OK when you're done. Back at the Edit Accounts screen, either tap New to add another account or tap OK when you're done.

**6.** Tap Quick Entry to enter a transaction.

**7.** The Transaction screen automatically enters the current time and date. Enter a description in the Desc blank, or choose one from the pop-up menu. Tap DB for a debit and CR for a credit. Enter the amount in the next blank, and tap the equals sign. You can also choose a category from the pop-up menu and select the source of the money in the Transfer pop-up menu.

**8.** Tap OK.

**9.** To enter a loan, tap the Loan button on the main screen.

**10.** Tap New. Enter three of the four loan items (principal, annual interest rate, number of the payment, payment amount).

**11.** Tap Calc, and Accounts & Loans will figure the fourth item. Tap Amort, and you will see the amortization schedule for the loan you've entered.

## Accounts & Loans: The Important Commands

Here are the important commands for Accounts & Loans.

| Menu | Command | Shortcut | What It Does |
|------|---------|----------|--------------|
| Setup | Home Currency | /H | Lets you set the currency your accounts will generally use |
| Setup | Unfiled Account | /F | Lets you give an account name to any account you haven't categorized |
| Setup | Account List | /A | Brings up the Account List screen |
| Setup | Account Group List | /Z | Lets you add or change account groups (such as personal, business) |
| Setup | Currency List | /Y | Lets you add or change currencies in the currency list |
| Setup | Category List | /L | Lets you add or change transaction categories |
| Setup | Save to Memory | /M | Lets you add or change memorized transaction descriptions |
| Setup | Options | /O | Lets you select among various display options |

# 82 Take Action Quickly and Comprehensively: Action Names

Name of Program: Action Names
E-Mail Address: support@iambic.com
Web Address: http://www.iambic.com/pilot/actionnames/
Version: 4.56
Type of Software: Commercial
Cost: $19.95

Action Names is a nifty little application that integrates your built-in Date Book, To Do List, and Address Book. With a tap here and a tap there, you can go easily from contacts to To Do items to appointments.

You can look at your appointments and To Do's simultaneously, allowing you to schedule an appointment and call up your contact list from the same screen. Choose a contact from the pop-up list, and then look up his or her phone number or other contact information with a simple tap on another icon. From the same screen, you can set the time and the date of the appointment, make it a recurring event, write a note about it, and designate an icon for the type of meeting. (I like to use the fork and knife for lunch meetings!)

With Action Names, you can look at your schedule by day, week, month, or quarter, and still keep the contact links. Also, because it uses the Palm-native address, To Do, and contact applications, Action Names goes easy on memory and can synchronize with your Palm Desktop software. It will also synchronize with Microsoft Outlook and other such programs.

Action Names also offers these features:

◆ You can repeat To Do items.

◆ You can add alarms to your To Do's.

◆ It has powerful filtering capabilities.

◆ It offers easy-to-use Contact views with advanced sorting and grouping options.

◆ It offers snooze alarms.

◆ You can connect links to specific meetings.

◆ You can customize and edit existing icons.

◆ It is available in English, German, French, Italian, Danish, Spanish, and Japanese.

◆ You can make journal entries and call records.

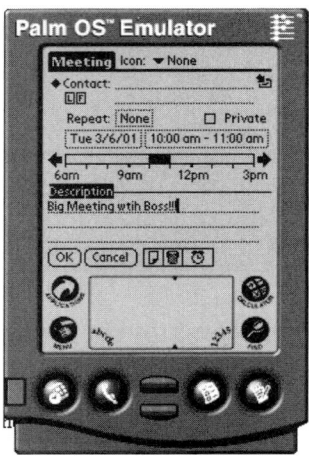

## Getting Started with Action Names

Follow these steps to get organized and get going with Action Names:

**1.** After starting up Action names, you will see the basic Journal page.

**2.** Tap the People icon. The Contact List screen opens. You will see the names and addresses you've previously entered in your Address Book. Tap on the first letter of a last name to browse by last name, or enter what you're looking for in the Go To blank.

**3.** Tap on the Document icon (the sheet of paper with a turned-down corner). Select Contact to go to the Edit Contact screen. Enter a contact name and any related information about that contact. Tap Done.

**4.** Tap the hardware Address Book button (the one with the telephone receiver), and there's your new contact. Cool! The same principle works for your appointments and To Do's.

**5.** Tap the numeral 1 at the bottom left of the screen to bring up your one-day appointments and To Do List. (The numeral 7 shows your week's schedule, 31 shows the month, and 1/4 shows a calendar quarter.)

**6.** Tap the triangle in the bottom-right corner to change the display type from Split to List. If you don't like it, you can change it back.

**7.** Tap on the Magnifying Glass icon to select which items you want displayed.

**8.** Tap on the Document icon to switch to another entry screen. (Try the Meetings screen to see the great features there.)

## Action Names: The Important Commands

Here are the important commands for Action Names.

| Menu | Command | Shortcut | What It Does |
|---|---|---|---|
| Record | New Meeting | /M | Opens new Meeting Scheduler entry screen |
| Record | New Call | /Z | Opens new Call entry screen |
| Record | New To Do | /T | Opens new To Do entry screen |
| Record | New Journal Entry | /W | Opens new Journal entry screen |
| Record | New Contact | /Y | Opens new Contact entry screen |
| Options | Preferences | /R | Lets you choose Alarms, Contacts, Views, and more options |
| Options | Performance | /N | Gives you options to increase application's performance |
| Options | Purge | /E | Lets you purge old items to increase memory; lets you save archive copy on your Desktop |
| Options | Edit Icons | /V | Lets you remove icons or add new icons |
| Options | Default Settings | /1 | Resets all settings to their defaults |

# 83 Make Contact Many Ways: AddressPro

Name of Program: AddressPro
E-Mail Address: info@zingware.com
Web Address: http://www.zingware.com
Version: 5.5
Type of Software: Shareware
Cost: $19.95

The built-in Palm OS Address Book certainly is handy. But, let's face it, it could be handier. AddressPro steps in and builds on your existing Address Book so that you can search it or sort it any number of ways. These search and sort features are the big deal. They allow you to display your Address Book contents by, say, company first, then contact name, and you can choose any field for the main sort and display. You also can choose any field for the secondary sort and any field for the phone display. Also, you can choose how any category gets sorted, such as reverse alphabetical order or numerical order.

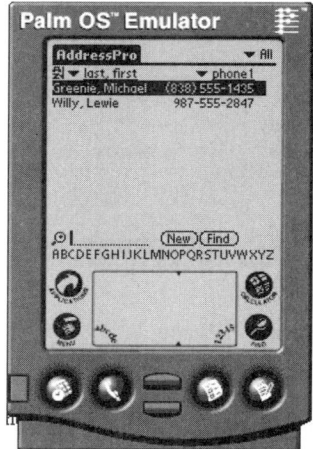

AddressPro makes data entry easy. Because it lets you duplicate records three different ways, you have less information to enter in similar records. It also has a contact-management feature for recording your last contact time, and AddressPro's search-and-replace function easily handles such annoying changes as new area codes. Meanwhile, you still get such built-in Address Book options as renaming custom fields and beaming, and your Address Book stays compatible with your Desktop application.

## Getting Started with AddressPro

You won't ever misplace an address or phone number again. Follow these steps to use AddressPro:

1. When you first open AddressPro, the introductory screen reminds you to register. Tap OK.

2. Then, you'll see the main AddressPro screen, which is the kind of screen you're used to seeing in your Palm Address Book. On the left side is a list of names (which AddressPro got from your built-in Address Book), and on the right is the first telephone number for each person. But you'll see some differences, too. Next to the Last, First column is an arrow (next to AZ). Tap it to re-sort the names in reverse alphabetical order.

3. Getting started with AddressPro is simply a matter of trying out the indicators you don't see on your regular Address Book. For example, tap the triangle next to the Last, First label. You'll get a pop-up display of all the other fields you can choose to display in that left column.

4. Select Company, First to display a list showing the company name and then the first name of all your contacts. Select Other at the end of the list to get a pop-up window that lets you choose any combination of sort fields.

5. If you know exactly whom you want to find, tap a letter at the bottom of the screen and the Palm cursor jumps to names that start with the specified letter. Or write a letter using graffiti in the blank next to the Magnifying Glass icon.

6. Want to try a search-and-replace action? Tap the Find button. Fill in all necessary information in the Search & Replace screen, and then tap Go.

# AddressPro: The Important Commands

Here are the important commands for AddressPro.

| Menu | Command | Shortcut | What It Does |
| --- | --- | --- | --- |
| Beam | Beam Category | None | Lets you beam an entire category to another Palm device |
| Beam | Beam Business Card | None | Lets you beam your Palm business card to another Palm device |
| Edit | Undo | /U | Undoes your last action |
| Edit | Cut | /X | Cuts selected text and saves it to the Clipboard |
| Edit | Copy | /C | Copies text and saves it to the Clipboard |
| Edit | Paste | /P | Pastes text from the Clipboard |
| Edit | Select All | /S | Selects all entries on the screen |
| Edit | Keyboard | /K | Allows you to use the keyboard to enter information |
| Edit | Graffiti Help | /G | Displays graffiti strokes |
| Options | Font | /F | Lets you choose a font for AddressPro |
| Options | Preferences | /R | Takes you to the Sorting & Preferences screen so you can choose your sort fields and other display options |
| Options | Rename Custom Fields | None | Lets you assign names to address entry blanks initially labeled Custom 1, Custom 2, etc. |

# 84 Keep Track of Your Track Record: CVKeeper

Name of Program: CVKeeper
E-Mail Address: handekeeper@infowest.com
Web Address: http://www.HandeKeeper.com
Version: 2.5
Type of Software: Commercial
Cost: $5

CVKeeper provides a simple and easy-to-understand way to keep track of your curriculum vitae, or resume. Although CVKeeper doesn't have an export function, you can copy and paste within this little application.

CVKeeper could be handy for transferring any data regarding your work and education history from bits of paper in your file cabinet to your Palm device. And when you remember something such as an award you received for a research project back in 1983, you can jot it down in CVKeeper. It's also helpful when you're filling out job applications, because the tab-style format will let you easily find needed information according to category.

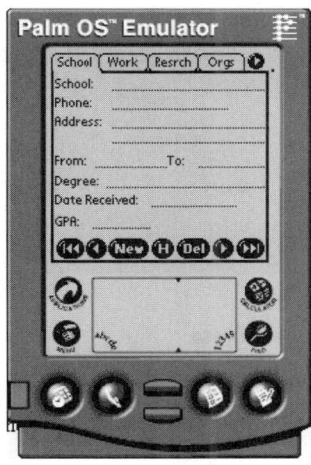

# Getting Started with CVKeeper

Follow these steps to make sure that your CV goes with you to every job interview:

1. Start entering data from the CVKeeper screen. The School tab is on top, so start with your school information. Just leave blank anything you don't know.

2. Tap New to add another school entry.

3. Tap Work to enter work experiences.

4. Tap Research to enter research experiences.

5. Tap Orgs to enter organizations of which you are (or were) a member.

6. Tap the right-facing arrow at the top-right corner of your screen to see four more entry tabs.

7. Tap Lead to enter leadership positions you've held.

8. Tap Serve to enter volunteer service information.

9. Tap Honors to enter honors and awards you have received.

10. Tap Refs to enter information about your references.

# CVKeeper: The Important Commands

Here are the important commands for CVKeeper.

| Menu | Command | Shortcut | What It Does |
|------|---------|----------|--------------|
| Edit | Undo | /U | Undoes your last action |
| Edit | Cut | /X | Cuts selected text and saves it to the Clipboard |
| Edit | Copy | /C | Copies text and saves it to the Clipboard |
| Edit | Paste | /P | Pastes text from the Clipboard |
| Edit | Select All | /S | Selects all entries on the screen |
| Edit | Keyboard | /K | Allows you to use the keyboard to enter information |
| Edit | Graffiti Help | /G | Displays graffiti strokes |

# 85 Project Tracking Made Easy: EZ Pro

Name of Program: EZ Pro
E-Mail Address: sauceydog_2000@yahoo.com
Web Address: http://hotfiles.zdnet.com/cgi-bin/texis/swlib/
hotfiles/info.html?fcode=001EBR&b=zdpalm
Version: 1.1n
Type of Software: Shareware
Cost: $5

This application provides a simple, straightforward solution for tracking projects (the "Pro" in EZ Pro comes from "projects"). It does what it's intended to do, and it won't confuse you with features you don't need. Instead, it lets you very simply create a project and note its deadline and the key project contacts. Also, for each contact person, you can record up to five contact numbers—such as pager, fax machine, and telephone—and notes about that person.

It also lets you keep track of any project meetings by time and date and record the key points of the meetings. It couldn't be simpler. The developers do note, though, that it isn't intended to replace your Palm device's Address Book; for a permanent record of phone numbers, EZ Pro recommends using the regular Palm address and phone application.

## Getting Started with EZ Pro

Keep projects on track by following these directions:

**1.** After starting EZ Pro, enter the information as indicated: project name, deadline, and people associated with the project.

**2.** Tap Info next to a person's name. In the Assoc screen, fill in such details as the company name for the contact and up to five contact numbers. Choose the contact type (such as work phone, mobile, e-mail, etc.) by tapping the down-pointing arrow to the left of the dotted lines.

**3.** Tap Notes to record added information or reminders about your associate.

**4.** Tap Back to return to the Assoc screen, or tap Done to return to the EZ Pro screen.

**5.** Tap the Meetings List button at the bottom of the EZ Pro screen. On the Meetings screen, record the time and date of your meeting, tap the right-facing arrow at the end of the line, and enter any meeting notes you might have.

**6.** Tap Done, and you're set! If you have other projects to keep track of, just tap New at the bottom of the EZ Pro main screen and follow these same steps for each project.

## EZ Pro: The Important Commands

Here are the important EZ Pro commands.

| Menu | Command | Shortcut | What It Does |
|------|---------|----------|--------------|
| Edit | Undo | /U | Undoes your last action |
| Edit | Cut | /X | Cuts selected text and saves it to the Clipboard |
| Edit | Copy | /C | Copies text and saves it to the Clipboard |
| Edit | Paste | /P | Pastes text from the Clipboard |
| Edit | Select All | /S | Selects all entries on the screen |
| Edit | Keyboard | /K | Allows you to use the keyboard to enter information |
| Edit | Graffiti Help | /G | Displays graffiti strokes |

# 86 Reach the Top of Your Game: FocusOnSuccess

Name of Program: FocusOnSuccess
E-Mail Address: success@ematthews.net
Web Address: http://palmgear.com
Version: 2.85
Type of Software: Shareware
Cost: $10

If you want to be the best you can be, you need to know what works and what doesn't. FocusOnSuccess's developer says, "Success is a habit, not an accident." This program gets you into the success habit by giving you a clear, easy-to-use and easy-to-maintain system for keeping track of your successes. FocusOnSuccess also lets you record quotes that inspire or challenge you.

By using FocusOnSuccess to record what works, you can, in a short time, generate enough success notes to take advantage of the program's browsing and categorizing features. You can look at all the great ideas that worked for meeting sales goals, for getting the hot date, for avoiding traffic jams, or for whatever topics you want to create. When you look at your successes together, you'll see patterns, which will lead you to even greater success.

# Getting Started with FocusOnSuccess

Follow these steps to insure that VP promotion:

1. When you start FocusOnSuccess, you'll first see the Success tab. Enter the information about who, where, and what.

2. Tap Edit next to the Topic drop-down arrow or the Who drop-down arrow to add items to the pop-up menus. Tap Return when you're finished entering your new information.

3. Tap Details. Record why your idea worked and/or what you learned from it.

4. Tap Return.

5. Tap the Thoughts tab. Record a meaningful quote that you heard or read. Tap the drop-down arrow next to Topic to categorize it. Tap Return when you've finished, and record the author.

6. Tap the arrows at the bottom of the screen to browse through previously recorded thoughts, or tap All to see a list of all of them.

7. Tap the Ideas tab. It gives you four idea options. The first, Idea Generation, is a resource to help you brainstorm. It provides cues to get the juices flowing. The Promote Idea, Design Idea, and Implement Idea options were still under development at the time of this writing and were promised as a free update to registered users.

# FocusOnSuccess: The Important Commands

Here are the important FocusOnSuccess commands.

| Menu | Command | Shortcut | What It Does |
| --- | --- | --- | --- |
| Edit | Undo | /U | Undoes action |
| Edit | Cut | /X | Cuts text |
| Edit | Copy | /C | Copies text |
| Edit | Paste | /P | Pastes text |
| Edit | Select All | /S | Selects all text |
| Edit | Keyboard | /K | Displays keyboard |
| Edit | Graffiti Help | /G | Displays graffiti strokes |

# 87 Name Me a Price: Handy Quote

Name of Program: Handy Quote
E-Mail Address: info@computassist.hypermart.net
Web Address: http://computassist.hypermart.net/hq/
Version: 2.0
Type of Software: Commercial
Cost: $16

This nice little program lets you offer price quotes wherever you are, whenever you need to. It lets you export your existing product database into the Desktop version of Handy Quote (for Windows only). The Desktop version then configures the data for downloading to your handheld device. It even has provisions for multilevel pricing, that is, for offering price breaks. Once your catalog is on your handheld, you can make fast, accurate quotes whenever you want.

Here are some features of this latest version:

◆ You can edit catalogs on your Palm and add, change, or delete items and prices without reimporting.

◆ There is no limit to catalog size (only limit is your Palm device's memory).

◆ Catalog items can be members of multiple departments.

◆ A Notes field lets you record additional information about a quote.

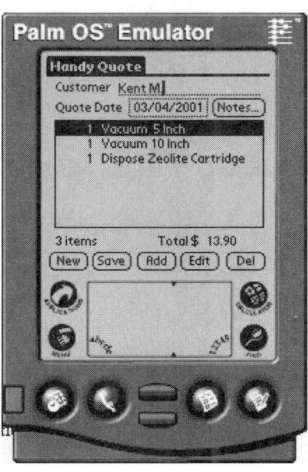

If you don't want to fiddle with making your database conform to the set-up required by Handy Quote, you can send your database to the developer, who will convert it to a Handy Quote database for $10. Not bad.

## Getting Started with Handy Quote

Quote me a price and I'll see what I can do.

1. Launch Handy Quote. Select the catalog your quote will come from.

2. You will make your quote from the New screen. First enter a customer name.

3. Tap Add. Select an item from the catalog by paging through it with the PgUp and PgDn buttons, or tap one of the departments at the top of the screen to narrow the list.

4. Tap the desired item; the base price appears on the right side of the screen.

5. Enter a quantity in the blank shown. Handy Quote automatically changes the price if the quantity carries a tax break, and it figures the total cost for that item.

6. Tap Add to add it to your customer's quote.

7. Repeat the selection and quantity steps until you've added all the items the customer requires.

8. Tap Quit. Handy Quote returns you to the main screen and totals all the items selected.

9. Tap Save to save the quote. Indicate whether to save the quote as Readable, which saves to the Memo Pad, or as CSV (comma-separated values) for later reading on a database or spreadsheet program.

## Handy Quote: The Important Commands

Here are the important Handy Quote commands (sorry, no shortcuts).

| Menu | Command | What It Does |
| --- | --- | --- |
| File | Edit Saved Quote | Lets you make changes to a quote you saved in CSV format |

| Menu | Command | What It Does |
| --- | --- | --- |
| File | Load Catalog | Lets you use a different catalog than the one currently loaded for your quote |
| File | Catalog Manager | Lets you delete, create, or rename catalogs you have on your Palm device |
| Edit | Cut | Cuts selected text and saves to the Clipboard |
| Edit | Copy | Copies selected text and saves to the Clipboard |
| Edit | Paste | Pastes text saved to the Clipboard |

# 88 Putting Your Priorities into Play: Life Balance

Name of Program: Life Balance
E-Mail Address: support@llamagraphics.com
Web Address: http://www.llamagraphics.com
Version: 2.6.1
Type of Software: Commercial
Cost: $39.95

You'll know right away that Life Balance is a different kind of personal management application; it doesn't have a user's manual, it has an Advice Book. Fair enough; when we're using an application, advice is what we really want.

The Advice Book opens with its philosophy, which is basically that Life Balance aims to help you take advantage of the limited amount of time in a day, a week, or a lifetime. To do so, you enter your long-term and short-term goals, and Life Balance records tasks in such a way as to replace your Palm device's built-in To Do List.

Life Balance does work with your Palm, though. It lets you import your current To Do entries and link Life Balance entries to events in your Date

Book. Then Life Balance uses this information to balance the time of day, upcoming deadlines, the relative importance of the task, and other details to help you figure out what you should be doing at any particular time.

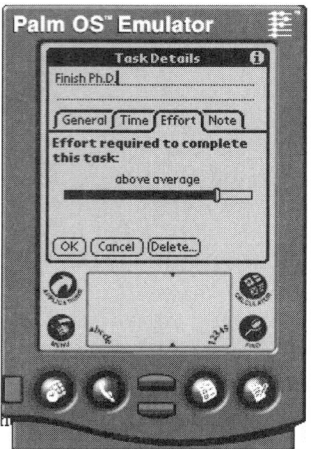

## Getting Started with Life Balance

Out of time? Try Life Balance by following these directions:

1. The opening Life Balance screen is the Outline screen. It already comes with a couple of work goals (pertaining to Life Balance software). The other goal categories are intended to be your big-picture life goals.

2. To enter a health task, tap on either the word Health or in the circle next to it.

3. To add a health subtask, tap the right-hand button next to New. Enter a task, such as **Walk 2 miles a day**. (If you accidentally tap another button, tap Details, then tap Delete, and then tap OK to get rid of the unwanted new task.)

4. Tap Details and enter the details requested under each tab: General, Time, Effort, and Note. (Under the General and Effort tabs, change the level by dragging the sliding marker on the scale with your stylus. The label above the scale will change as you move the marker.) Tap OK.

**5.** Tap the Bullet List icon (the second from the left) at the top of the screen to see or add to your To Do List.

**6.** Tap Update to include tasks recorded in the Outline screen.

**7.** Select your location from the pop-up list at the top left of the screen, and follow any further instructions from Life Balance.

## Life Balance: The Important Commands

Here are the important Life Balance commands.

| Menu | Command | Shortcut | What It Does |
|---|---|---|---|
| Task | New Task | /N | Creates a new task |
| Task | New Subtask | /I | Creates a new subtask |
| Task | Details | /T | Adds details to a task you've selected |
| Task | Duplicate | /O | Creates a duplicate of a selected task |
| Task | Move | /M | Moves a selected task from one point in your outline to another |
| Task | Delete | /D | Deletes a selected task |
| Task | Collapse All | /1 | Closes all Outline screen subtasks, showing only the top level |
| Task | Expand All | /2 | Opens all subtasks in Outline screen |
| Options | Preferences | /R | Opens Preferences screen |
| Options | Phone Lookup | /L | Looks up the related phone number for the item you've selected |

# 89 Put It All Together: LinkPak

Name of Program: LinkPak
E-Mail Address: sales@silverware.com
Web Address: http://www.silverware.com
Version: 1.7
Type of Software: Shareware
Cost: $24.95

With LinkPak, you can write yourself a memo and link it to an address, a To Do item, or the Date Book, all without leaving your Memo Pad. The reverse is true, too. LinkPak actually combines four applications: AddressLink, DateLink, MemoLink, and ToDoLink. These applications work with the built-in versions and look just like them, but they can link to each other with a tap.

Let's say, for example, that one of your To Do items is to call and wish your brother a happy birthday. With LinkPak, you can just tap the Link button to set up a link between the To Do item and your brother's phone number. It couldn't be much easier! Because these linking applications read and write to the built-in applications, they use little memory and they synchronize with your Desktop version. Also, if you decide you don't want to keep the apps after the 30-day trial period, you can switch back to the original applications without losing anything (but the links) you entered in the LinkPak apps.

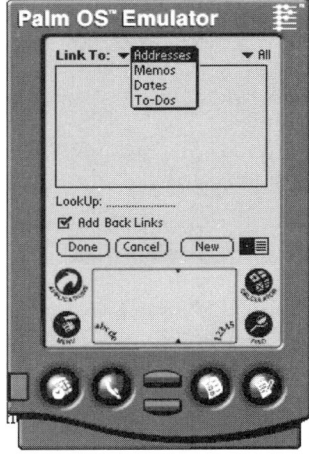

## Getting Started with LinkPak

Link and get going!

1. When you start up LinkPak, it will ask you whether you want the Palm buttons to launch the link applications. Tap Yes (unless you don't want them to, of course).

2. Now try the phone call example. Tap ToDoLink, or press the hardware To Do button.

3. Tap New. Enter the item using graffiti or the keyboard.

4. Tap Link. Select Addresses from the pop-up menu next to Link To.

5. Tap on the box next to the person you need to call to select it.

6. Tap Done.

7. Back in the To Do List, tap somewhere in the To Do text line to select it. Notice that the Link button at the bottom of the screen is now bold to indicate that item has a link.

8. Tap Link. A pop-up box shows the link to the person you selected in step 5 (or to your brother, as in the earlier example), and a little telephone next to his or her name shows the kind of link. The box also has a Link To indicator, which you can tap should you wish to make another link.

9. Continue to use your Date Book, To Do List, Memo Pad, and Address Book as before, but add links whenever you want!

## LinkPak: The Important Commands

Here are the important LinkPak commands.

| Menu | Command | Shortcut | What It Does |
|--------|-------------|----------|-------------------------------|
| Record | New Event | /N | Creates a new event |
| Record | Delete Item | /D | Deletes selected item |
| Record | Attach Note | /A | Attaches note to selected item |
| Record | Delete Note | /O | Deletes note from selected item |

| Menu | Command | Shortcut | What It Does |
|------|---------|----------|--------------|
| Record | Purge | /E | Deletes completed items and archives them on the Desktop |
| Record | Beam Item | /B | Beams selected item to other Palm device |
| Record | Beam Category | None | Beams selected category to other Palm device |
| Edit | Undo | /U | Undoes your last action |
| Edit | Cut | /X | Cuts selected text and saves it to the Clipboard |
| Edit | Copy | /C | Copies text and saves it to the Clipboard |
| Edit | Paste | /P | Pastes text from the Clipboard |
| Edit | Select All | /S | Selects all entries on the screen |
| Edit | Keyboard | /K | Allows you to use the keyboard to enter information |
| Edit | Graffiti Help | /G | Displays graffiti strokes |
| Options | Font | /F | Lets you change display font |

# 90 Know What You've Got: On Hand

Name of Program: On Hand
E-Mail Address: support@stevenscreek.com
Web Address: http://www.stevenscreek.com/palm/support.html
Version: 3.0
Type of Software: Commercial
Cost: $79.95

On Hand does more than provide a convenient list of the products your company carries. It also keeps you up-to-date on inventory, and it's as simple as synchronizing.

To use On Hand, you will first either create a text file of your product list or download a text file (such as an export file from your database). Then you can actually add the inventory counts into your Palm device at your warehouse or other location. You can do this either of two easy ways: Enter them with your stylus on a regular Palm device, or use the built-in bar code scanner of the Symbol SPT 1500. Its software is entirely button driven, so you can take a complete inventory simply by holding the device in one hand and placing the items to be inventoried in front of the scanner.

On Hand is additionally useful because it will sort your inventory by name, bar code number, or however else you tell it to. It also supports printing the results of your inventory collection and printing any bar codes inputted during your inventory if you have the appropriate added software.

On Hand is also a dream-come-true for taking orders off-site, because you know right away whether or not a product's in stock. As you might imagine, an application that does all this is a little more complicated than, say, a To Do List. Fortunately, On Hand comes with thorough and clearly written documentation.

## Getting Started with On Hand

What have you got on hand? Follow these directions to keep track:

1. Install On Hand and your product catalog according to the directions in the User Guide.

2. Open On Hand on your Palm device. The opening screen shows the inventory as downloaded from your Catalog file.

3. If your downloaded file includes quantities, immediately identify out-of-stock items by tapping =0 in the upper-right portion of the screen.

4. Select Sort from the Inventory menu. Specify sort order. Tap OK.

5. To change an inventory quantity, tap on the product name. A side-pointing arrow beside the item indicates that it is selected. Tap –1 to indicate that you've reduced (sold!) one unit from that inventory item.

6. Tap the up-pointing or down-pointing arrows in the middle of the screen to scroll through items, or tap a letter to jump to the first item starting with that letter.

7. Tap the C to clear the inventory quantity. Enter the new quantity with the on-screen numbers, with graffiti, or by using the +10 and +1 buttons.

8. To add an inventory item, choose Add New Item from the Inventory menu and supply the requested information.

## On Hand: The Important Commands

Here are the important On Hand commands.

| Menu | Command | Shortcut | What It Does |
|------|---------|----------|--------------|
| Inventory | Sort | /S | Lets you choose among print and sort options |
| Inventory | Reset Quantities | /R | Resets all inventory quantities to zero (after confirming your command) |

| Menu | Command | Shortcut | What It Does |
|------|---------|----------|--------------|
| Inventory | Purge New Items | /X | Deletes (after confirmation) all newly entered items |
| Inventory | Add New Item | /A | Opens Add Item screen to enter a new inventory item's information |
| Configure | Header | /H | Lets you enter information that will appear at the top of your Inventory report |
| Configure | Note/Location | /N | Lets you enter information into an item's Note area |
| Configure | Export | /E | Lets you set options for exporting data |

# 91 A Close Look at the Numbers: ProStats

Name of Program: ProStats
E-Mail Address: seisupport@home.com
Web Address: http://members.home.net/seisupport/index.html
Version: 2.3.4
Type of Software: Shareware
Cost: $13.95

ProStats offers business solutions for Palm users who need to make scientific and technical calculations. It's a program for serious statistical analysis written specifically for the Palm platform. It's definitely one for total stat nerds.

ProStats is fast and easy to use, and calculates more than 40 statistical values on two user-supplied data sets of up to 100 points each. You can look at the results by the numbers, or ProStats can create a graph, which is a very

nice option. Once you complete your analyses, you can then export your data in a CSV file for use on your Desktop computer. You also can import data this way.

Look at these features:

◆ Statistical calculations that include mean, standard deviation, standard error of the mean, variance, minimum, maximum, range, sum, and skewness

◆ Histogram and scatter plots

◆ Hypothesis testing (1 and 2 tailed t-testing), which can be done at 1%, 2.5%, 5%, and 10% significance levels

◆ Confidence intervals that can be calculated for the means of the data sets

◆ Probability calculations that can be done on all data or by parameters that can be entered individually

◆ Regression analysis that includes linear and exponential curve fitting, plotting, and interpolation

◆ Data entry from the screen or imported from a comma-delimited memo file

◆ Data export as comma-delimited memo files for transfer to a PC; written in Quartus Forth

◆ Box-and-whisker plots to calculate and display quartiles

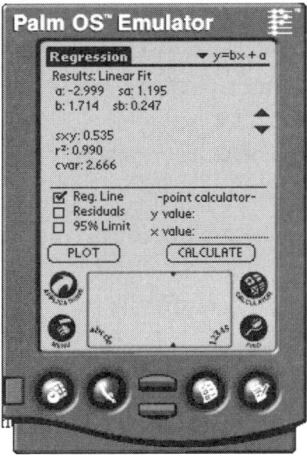

# Getting Started with ProStats

Follow these steps to calculate the regression coefficient for predicting sales this year from the days that your employees played hooky last year:

**1.** From the opening ProStats screen, enter your X and Y data using the graffiti number pad, and use a return stroke at the end of each entry. After you've entered your data, tap Enter. Palm Stats immediately registers your *n* value.

**2.** Tap in the boxes next to the list on the right side of the screen to select the standard descriptive statistics you want ProStats to do. Also, tap X, Y, or X,Y to indicate which data you want the statistics calculated for, and tap Calculate. Tap the Home button on the silk-screened portion of your Palm device to go back to the data entry screen, and notice that your data are still there. Whew!

**3.** Choose other analyses from the Analysis menu. Just be sure to tap Calculate whenever you change any aspect of the analysis.

# ProStats: The Important Commands

Here are the important ProStats commands.

| Menu | Command | Shortcut | What It Does |
|------|---------|----------|--------------|
| Analysis | Confidence Interval | /L | Calculates confidence intervals for the means of the X and Y data sets at 80, 90, 95, 98, or 99% confidence levels |
| Analysis | Hypothesis Test | /T | Tests for both X and Y as individual data sets against a given mean, X and Y against each other, or tests on user-supplied means |
| Analysis | Probability | /B | Calculates for both X and Y with respect to one or two values, or calculates user-specified data input |

| Menu | Command | Shortcut | What It Does |
|------|---------|----------|--------------|
| Analysis | Sample Size Calculator | /Z | Calculates the minimum sample size required for a given confidence level, mean, standard deviation, and total error of the estimate |
| Analysis | Regression Analysis | /R | Conducts analysis using any of three regression models |
| Analysis | Histogram Plot | /H | Quickly determines the distribution of a data set |
| Analysis | Scatter Plot | /S | Graphically shows the relationship between the X and Y data sets |
| Analysis | Box & Whisker Plot | /W | Calculates and displays quartiles |
| Edit | Undo | /U | Undoes action |
| Edit | Cut | /X | Cuts selection and saves to the Clipboard |
| Edit | Copy | /C | Copies selection and saves to the Clipboard |
| Edit | Paste | /P | Pastes information from the Clipboard |
| Edit | Select All | /S | Selects all data |
| Edit | Clear Data | /. | Erases all the data contained in the field selected with the Data Selector (X, Y, or both) |
| Edit | Swap X-Y | // | Exchanges the X and Y datasets |
| Edit | Keyboard | /K | Displays keyboard |

| Menu | Command | Shortcut | What It Does |
| --- | --- | --- | --- |
| Options | Filer | /F | Opens Filer screen, which lets you export or import comma-separated data |
| Options | Preferences | /N | Lets you choose display items such as number of digits shown, decimal versus scientific notation, and more |

# 92 Accounting for Your Money: PMT-Personal Money Tracker

Name of Program: PMT-Personal Money Tracker
E-Mail Address: pmthelp@attglobal.com
Web Address: http://www2.viaweb.com/pilotgearsw/charlesmorris.html
Version: 6.2
Type of Software: Shareware
Cost: $19.95

First you moved your checkbook to your Desktop computer. Now you can shift it to your handheld with Personal Money Tracker, a virtual accounting program for your Palm device. With PMT, you can keep track of multiple checking accounts, credit card accounts, your business expense account, and more. It's a great way to keep track of your spending—as you're spending!

PMT will show you a quick balance sheet of your assets and liabilities, so you can know your financial status at the tap of a stylus. PMT organizes your accounts into asset, liability, income, and expense account categories, and it lets you set budgets for the last two. Therefore, besides accumulating expenses, PMT will also tell you, for example, whether what you're spending on car repairs is in line with your budget.

PMT requires that you enter new accounts in a certain order. It's simple and straightforward, and the application will stop you if you get off track,

but your understanding will be clearer if you read the documentation before you create your accounts. Fortunately, PMT includes a useful tutorial to get you over the startup bumps. What's also nice: When you become a registered user of PMT, updates will be e-mailed to you as they become available at no additional cost for one full year following registration.

Here's an official list of its many features:

◆ Recurring transactions and split transactions

◆ Easy entry and editing of income and expenses

◆ Easy selection of date ranges to view your entries

◆ Entry of future transactions and a display of your running balance to show you if you can meet your obligations

◆ Reminders for paying your bills

◆ Summary balance sheet and income/expense statements to show you where you stand and to make comparisons with your budget

◆ Overdraft warnings

◆ Easy reconciliation with your bank statements

◆ Easy synchronization, which allows you to view your financial data on your PC as well as to transfer your financial data to your PC, edit it, and transfer it back

◆ Export of balance sheet and income/expense reports to Memo Pad database

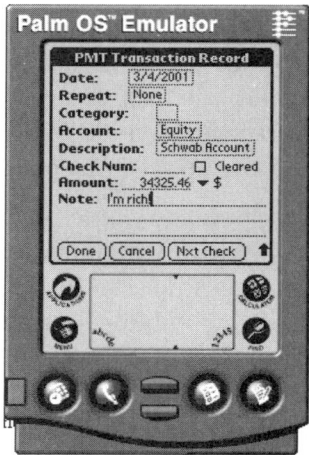

# Getting Started with PMT-Personal Money Tracker

Manage your money by following these directions:

**1.** The opening screen, the PMT Accounts List, will be empty when you first launch PMT. Tap New, which will present you with the PMT Transaction Record screen. Tap the Cash box next to Category. Choose Cash or Equity, or choose Edit to set up your own category. For this example, tap Edit to start.

**2.** On the Edit Accounts screen, tap New to add a new account. Enter a name for the account. Tap the Type pop-up menu and select the appropriate type. You'll need to start with your asset accounts, which include checking accounts. If you're not sure whether the account is an asset, liability, income, or expense account, tap the Information icon (*i*) for help.

**3.** Tap OK after entering an account. You should be back in the Edit Accounts screen.

**4.** To enter starting balances, select an asset account from your list, such as a checkbook account. Tap OK. This takes you back to the PMT Accounts List screen, with the selected account showing in the upper-right corner of your screen.

**5.** Tap New. In the PMT Transaction Record screen, tap on the box next to Account and change it to read Equity. Enter your starting balance in the Amount blank. Tap on the box next to Category, and select the name you've given your checking account. You will notice the labels change to read Transfer To [*your checking account's name*] and From Account (Equity). You might want to enter Starting Balance in the description space.

**6.** Tap Done.

**7.** Repeat the process with your other account balances.

**8.** Select the account and tap New from the starting screen to enter new transactions, such as purchases or expenses.

# PMT-Personal Money Tracker: The Important Commands

Here are the important PMT commands.

| Menu | Command | Shortcut | What It Does |
| --- | --- | --- | --- |
| Commands | Journal List | /J | Displays all transactions associated with a specific description |
| Commands | Reconciliation | /R | Allows you to reconcile the selected account |
| Commands | Balances Date | /B | Sets the "as of" date for the Balances screen |
| Commands | Purge Transactions | None | Starts dialog wherein you purge old transactions |
| Commands | Export | /T | Exports the currently displayed report (such as Balances) via the Memo Pad |
| Edit | Copy Transaction | None | Duplicates the displayed transaction |
| Edit | Delete Transaction | /D | Deletes currently displayed transaction |
| Edit | Edit Transaction | /E | Edits the currently displayed transaction |
| Edit | Copy Amount | /C | Copies the amount of the highlighted or displayed transaction to the Clipboard |
| Edit | Edit Accounts | /A | Brings you directly to the Account Edit dialog |
| Options | Lock | /L | Locks PMT, except when you enter a password |

| Menu | Command | Shortcut | What It Does |
| --- | --- | --- | --- |
| **Options** | **NoLock** | **None** | **Erases your PMT password and makes PMT accessible without one** |
| **Options** | **Preferences** | **/P** | **Lets you set various person- alized preferences such as display options** |
| **Options** | **Free Mem** | **None** | **Displays the total unused memory in your Palm organizer** |

# 93 No Longer Lost without Quicken: Pocket Quicken

Name of Program: Pocket Quicken
E-Mail Address: sales@landware.com
Web Address: http://www.landware.com
Version: 1.01r1
Type of Software: Commercial
Cost: $39.95

Intuit has licensed its famous Desktop checking manager and other account manager to LandWare for this slick mobile adjunct. Pocket Quicken isn't intended to stand on its own; its specific purpose is to let you record deposits, expenses, and other activities while you're away from your Desktop computer. It lets you record your credit card charges as you make them without worrying about keeping track of the receipt until you get home.

The same thing is true with bank deposits or ATM withdrawals. Just log them all into Pocket Quicken, then HotSync when you get the chance. In a few seconds, your activities will be recorded in your Desktop Quicken, and your Palm device will show your updated balances. (Pocket Quicken doesn't allow Desktop transactions to be downloaded to your handheld, which is probably a good thing if you think about the memory it would require.)

Its handy features include QuickFill, which will fill in the rest of a memorized transaction automatically once you enter a graffiti letter. You can also look up payee names from your built-in Address Book. Nice. You can also void transactions and look at previous transactions.

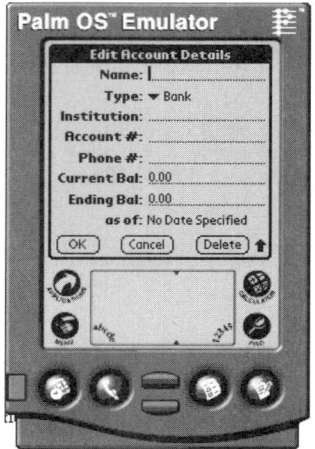

## Getting Started with Pocket Quicken

Follow these steps to use the best-selling finance program for the PC on your Palm:

**1.** The first thing you'll want to do after installing Pocket Quicken is to download your existing accounts, categories, and classes from your Desktop Quicken. Follow the directions in the User Guide.

**2.** The opening screen of Pocket Quicken will be the Accounts view. (If it isn't, just tap the Accounts button at the bottom of the screen.) Tap the account to which you want to record a transaction. For this example, choose your checking account. Pocket Quicken immediately opens the Register screen for that account.

**3.** Tap the New button and select Payment, Deposit, or Transfer from the pop-up menu.

**4.** The Edit Transaction screen lets you enter the appropriate information. The current date automatically shows, although you can change it by tapping on the date box. Enter a check number, or use the Ref pop-up screen to select Next Check#, ATM, or other reference options.

**5.** Enter the payee next to Pay, or use the Pay pop-up menu to select a memorized transaction.

**6.** Enter the check amount next to Payment and any notes on the Memo line.

**7.** Choose a category from the Category list and a class from the Class list. If you need to split the payment among categories, tap Split.

## Pocket Quicken: The Important Commands

Here are the important Pocket Quicken commands.

| Menu | Command | Shortcut | What It Does |
|---|---|---|---|
| Lists | Accounts | /A | Displays the Accounts List view |
| Lists | Register | /R | Displays the Register List view |
| Lists | Categories | /L | Opens the Categories list for viewing or editing |
| Lists | Classes | /S | Opens the Class list for viewing or editing |
| Lists | Memorized | /Z | Opens the Memorized Transactions list for viewing or editing |
| Actions | Pay Money | /M | Creates a withdrawal transaction |
| Actions | Deposit Money | /D | Creates a deposit transaction |
| Actions | Transfer Money | /T | Creates an account transfer transaction |
| Actions | Trim History | None | Removes transactions from the transaction history |
| Options | Security | None | Lets you create a PIN for Pocket Quicken |
| Options | Preferences | None | Lets you select various display and activity options |

# 94 Work, Overtime, and Vacation: PTimLog

Name of Program: PTimLog
E-Mail Address: PTimLog@mboenig.de
Web Address: http://www.mboenig.de, http://www.palmgear.com
Version: 4.00b3
Type of Software: Shareware
Cost: $5

PTimLog offers a handy way to help you keep track of your work time (if you're a wage earner) or your billable time (if you're self-employed). With PTimLog, you can record your regular hours as well as keep track of your overtime, holidays, and vacations. You can set up multiple projects and assign your work hours and costs to each project. You can preset lunch breaks and work shifts, and you can see a graphical representation of your sick time, vacation time, and other information. (And if you're a billionaire, you can keep track of all those people who made you rich.)

PTimLog has its quirks, however. Its original documentation is in German, and the English translations aren't always as smooth as you might hope. Also, it went by a different name (Job Time) in an earlier version, so you'll see that name crop up now and then. Still, it's a useful application, and the $5 price is hard to beat.

## Getting Started with PTimLog

You're underpaid, and your boss isn't. Compute what he or she owes you by following these directions:

1. The first time you start with PTimLog, you'll need to set your global preferences. To do so, tap OK on the introductory screen, and it will take you directly to the Global Preferences screen. Tap on the box next to any item you want PTimLog to apply.

2. For explanations of the different options, tap on the Information icon in the upper-right corner of your screen. When you're finished, tap OK.

3. Now you have the PTimLog main screen. Tap New to enter a new record, which is typically for your work day or part of a work day. The current date will automatically be entered, but you can change it if you'd like.

4. Enter the start time and finish time for your work. If appropriate, check the Billable box. Choose the type of work from the Description pop-up menu, and indicate whether the time specified includes a lunch break. If you'd like, enter a project name.

5. PTimLog returns you to the main screen and calculates how many work hours are remaining in your work week, in the current month, and in the year.

## PTimLog: The Important Commands

Here are the important PTimLog commands.

| Menu | Command | Shortcut | What It Does |
|---|---|---|---|
| Commands | Global Preferences 1 | /1 | Lets you set up displays and other preferences |
| Commands | Global Preferences 2 (DS) | /2 | Lets you change the preset date and times for daylight saving time |
| Commands | Global Preferences 3 | /3 | Lets you exclude over-time from the main screen |
| Commands | Select Client | /T | Selects the client for a record (not available to unregistered users) |
| Commands | Graphical Overview | /G | Shows a year's worth of monthly work and vaca-tion calendars |
| Commands | Create Memo | /C | Creates a memo in Memo Pad of PTimLog items you select |

| Menu | Command | Shortcut | What It Does |
| --- | --- | --- | --- |
| Commands | Create Date Book | /D | Creates Date Book entries from PTimLog data |
| Commands | Define Projects | /B | Creates a project and defines various details about it |
| Commands | Show Project Statistics | /S | Shows data about projects |
| Commands | Force Recalculation | /F | Recalculates figures in main screen |
| Records | New Record | /N | Opens New Record screen |
| Records | New Preferences | /P | Opens preferences from your first startup |
| Records | View All Records | /R | Displays a list of time records |
| Records | View This Week | /W | Displays list of this week's records |
| Records | View This Month | /M | Displays list of this month's records |
| Records | View This Year | /Y | Displays list of this year's records |
| Records | View User-Range | /U | Lets you choose date range for records display |
| Records | View Holidays | /H | Displays Holiday List screen |
| Records | View All Preferences | /L | Summarizes set preferences |

| Menu | Command | Shortcut | What It Does |
|------|---------|----------|--------------|
| Records | Delete Records | /X | Deletes records of your choice |
| Records | Delete All Preferences | /Y | Deletes all preferences (upon confirmation) |
| Utils | Day Calculator | /O | Counts the days within a given range and displays the number of work days, vacation days, and holidays in the range |

# 95 What's the Password: SAM

Name of Program: SAM
E-Mail Address: support@intellicodepro.com
Web Address: http://www.intellicodepro.com/
Version: 2.0
Type of Software: Shareware
Cost: $14.95

SAM (Security Account Management) can keep track of all the account names, account numbers, PINs, and passwords that seem to be required in today's electronic society. You can use SAM for personal accounts and business accounts of all kinds, including bank accounts, credit cards, online shopping accounts, network security accounts, frequent flier accounts, and more.

Besides keeping track of all those accounts, SAM also keeps them as secret as you could hope. You can choose to assign a password to SAM (you'll have to remember that one on your own, but SAM will give you a hint if you want it to) to prevent unauthorized access to your sensitive data. SAM also encrypts your data for additional security.

SAM includes these additional features:

◆ Navigating through SAM is easy, because its navigation is based on standard Palm navigation.

◆ You can tag records as "private" for added protection.

◆ You can customize each account's descriptions so that the descriptions in the pop-up lists fit your idea of the account's type.

◆ You can alphabetically sort accounts for easy access.

◆ You can organize your accounts with categories that you create.

◆ You can share your data with other applications and speed up data entry by using the cut, copy, and paste features.

◆ You can back up your data on every HotSync.

◆ You can find your accounts quickly and seamlessly using SAM's Category Cycler (which lets you browse by category), its Look Up feature, or Palm's Find feature.

◆ You can assign account entries to categories so that you can organize and view them in logical groups.

◆ You can use your PDA-assigned password or assign a new password to SAM for additional security.

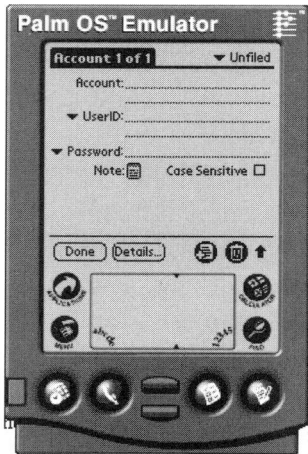

# Getting Started with SAM

Keep *everything* secret by following these directions:

**1.** From the opening SAM screen, tap the Add Account icon (it's the one with the plus sign).

**2.** Enter the account information. Besides giving the account name, choose from the pop-up menu whether your account identifier is a code, an ID, a number, password, PIN, or user ID.

**3.** Enter your account's identifier.

**4.** If you'd like, tap the Note icon and enter any notes you want to remember.

**5.** Tap the Category drop-down arrow in the upper-right portion of the screen, and choose a category for the account.

**6.** Tap Details and choose Private to make that account additionally secure. Tap Done.

**7.** Assign a password to SAM by tapping the silk-screened Menu icon. Select Password. Enter a Password and, if you'd like, enter a question (such as **When is my dog's birthday?**) and answer to remind you what your password is.

# SAM: The Important Commands

Here are the important SAM commands.

| Menu | Command | Shortcut | What It Does |
| --- | --- | --- | --- |
| Account | New Account | /N | Enters a new account |
| Account | Delete Account | /D | Deletes an account |
| Edit | Cut | /X | Cuts text |
| Edit | Copy | /C | Copies text |
| Edit | Paste | /P | Pastes text |
| Edit | Undo | /U | Undoes last action |
| Edit | Select All | /S | Selects all text |
| Edit | Keyboard | /K | Displays keyboard |
| Edit | Graffiti | /G | Displays graffiti strokes |

# 96 Start Your Savings: SavRetUtil

Name of Program: SavRetUtil
E-Mail Address: ed@witkowski-design.com
Web Address: http://www.Witkowski-Design.com
Version: 4.6
Type of Software: Shareware
Cost: $10

SavRetUtil provides an easy way to look into your financial future. Looking at your savings and retirement money is all it does, so you don't have to be some financial whiz to figure out what it's telling you. Because the application includes good documentation, the $10 cost is a sound investment in your retirement planning.

The savings portion of the application will quickly and easily figure out how much money you need to save to reach a specific goal, or how much money you'll accumulate at your current rate of savings. It also lets you try out various scenarios for 401K and other salary-based savings plans by making estimates based on expected annual salary increases and employer matches.

The retirement portion starts by telling you how much your current living expenses will cost you when you retire, based on your current age and expected age at retirement. Then, it tells you how much money you'll need to retire comfortably, depending on whether you want to live off the monthly interest or you intend to spend your entire savings.

With SavRetUtil, you can calculate the following:

- ◆ Long-term savings with or without taxing the interest
- ◆ The unknown interest rate
- ◆ The amount of money you need to start with to reach a goal

- The amount of money you will need at retirement to live off the interest

- The amount of money you will need at retirement to live off the entire amount

- Future value of a present amount of money

- Present value of a future amount

- The amount of money you should deposit to reach a goal

- The amount of time it will take to reach a goal

- Your final savings after a given number of years

- Your savings as you make withdrawals

- Savings based on your salary

And if that's not enough, SavRetUtil also offers these features:

- It allows for annual raises with a realistic salary cap.

- Employer contributions are based on matching each dollar you deposit.

- Employer maximum annual contribution is calculated as a percentage of your salary.

- Pop-up screen calculator helps you calculate annual deposits.

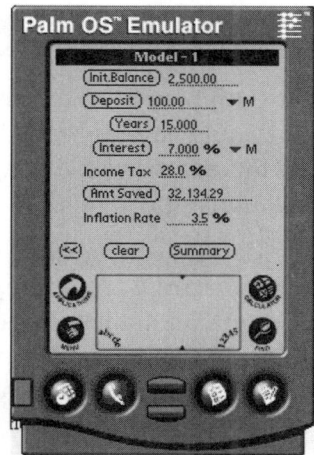

# Getting Started with SavRetUtil

Follow these steps to plan for the next 30 years:

1. The main SavRetUtil screen asks you to choose between the Savings Calculator and the Retirement Calculators. For this example, tap the Model-1 button to get started with the Savings Calculator Model.

2. The opening Model-1 screen gives you an example. Enter the amount you have currently in savings.

3. Enter the amount you think you will deposit to savings. Select the interval from the pop-up list (W for weekly, M for monthly, Q for quarterly, S for semiannually, A for annually).

4. Enter the number of years you expect to make these deposits.

5. Enter the annual interest rate you expect to earn, and designate on the pop-up list how often you expect the savings interest to be compounded.

6. Enter your tax rate. Or, if you want to know what your money will be worth (for example, with an IRA) without paying taxes on the interest, enter 0% for Income Tax.

7. Tap Amt Saved, and SavRetUtil automatically computes the amount of money you will have saved at the end of the time period you entered.

8. If you'd like, enter an estimate of the average inflation rate over the savings time period. This will affect your summary.

9. Tap Summary. The Summary screen shows the amounts of money you would have deposited, earned, and paid in taxes, as well as what the future total would be worth in today's dollars if you specified an inflation rate.

10. Tap Continue to return to the Model-1 screen, where you can try out other scenarios. For example, you can fill in the total amount you want to save in the Amt Saved blank, and leave one of the other variables—such as deposit—blank. SavRetUtil will tell you the value that variable needs to be to reach your savings goals.

11. Tap the button with two left-facing arrows to return to the main screen.

**12.** Tap Model-2 to figure 401K or other salary-based savings accounts, or tap Scenario under Retirement Calculators and follow the same fill-in-the-blank procedures for retirement calculations. It will walk you, step-by-step, through the scenarios. (Be careful; these can be scary!) You could also tap Inflation to determine values under various inflation rates.

# 97 Track Projects as Your Shadow Tracks You: ShadowPlan

Name of Program: ShadowPlan
E-Mail Address: support@skeleton.org
Web Addresses: http://www.icomm.ca/~skeezix/palm,
http://www.codejedi.com
Version: 1.5.4
Type of Software: Shareware
Cost: $12.99

If you like to make lists to get the job done, you'll love ShadowPlan. With ShadowPlan, you can create intuitive project outlines and manage projects. You will first create a main item that needs to be done, then you list all the tasks (and subtasks) that you need to complete to finish the job. Shadow-Plan will also allow you to sort, filter, and number your items in a variety of ways, as well as add notes, set priorities, and more. You can also rearrange your lists, label subcategories differently than the main category, and choose from display options that make ShadowPlan work the way you like to work.

An especially useful feature is that ShadowPlan lets you link your project lists to your Palm device's built-in To Do List and Date Book. Excellent documentation guides you through this powerful, yet easy-to-use, application.

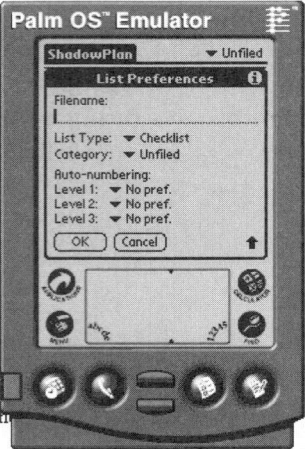

# Getting Started with ShadowPlan

Use ShadowPlan by following these directions:

**1.** The first time you start ShadowPlan, you'll get a blank screen, so tap New to get started.

**2.** The List Preferences screen you see next lets you set up how a new project or list will be arranged. These choices are specific to the new item you're creating. First, enter a name for your new list.

**3.** Select your list type from the pop-up list. (Checklist is a basic list with check boxes. Tasklist is a fancy one with priorities, dates, and so on.) You can change the preference at any time.

**4.** Assign the project to a category. If you don't see one that applies on the pop-up list, select Edit Categories and create your own.

**5.** Select the kind of automatic sequencing (A, B, C or 1, 2, 3, for example) you want ShadowPlan to use for each level of your project outline, or leave it at No Pref. Tap OK.

**6.** Now you're ready to enter your list. Tap New to create a list item. Assign target, start, and finish dates. Tap Note if you want to attach a note. (If you chose the Tasklist format, you'll also need to assign a priority and other information.)

**7.** Tap Options to create links to the To Do List and Date Book. Tap OK.

**8.** If you have subtasks to add to your project, tap Child. Enter the pertinent information, then tap OK.

**9.** Proceed until your project outline is done.

## ShadowPlan: The Important Commands

Here are the important Shadow Plan commands.

| Menu | Command | Shortcut | What It Does |
|------|---------|----------|--------------|
| Item | New Item | /N | Creates a new item in your project list |
| Item | New Child | /H | Creates a new subitem in your project list |
| Item | Delete Item | /D | Deletes selected item |
| Item | Delete Children | None | Deletes subitems from selected item |
| Item | Promote Item | /Q | Moves item up a notch in your project list |
| Item | Move Item | /W | Moves item down a notch in your project list |
| Item | Item Options | /O | Opens Item Options screen for selected item |
| Item | Glance | /G | Pops up details for selected item |
| List | Preferences | None | Opens List Preference screen |
| List | Revert to Last | /R | Reverts list to last saved version |
| List | Save Now | /U | Saves work without exiting screen using Done |
| List | Sort | /S | Opens Sort screen for reordering a list |
| List | Filter | /F | Opens Filter screen that lets you filter out particular items for viewing |
| List | Hilight | None | Lets you select type of items to highlight on list |

# 98 Who Needs a Stock Broker?: Stock Manager

Name of Program: Stock Manager
E-Mail Address: StockManager@TinyStocks.com
Web Address: http://www.tinystocks.com/
Version: 3.05
Type of Software: Shareware
Cost: $24.95

Can't stand not knowing how your portfolio is doing? Stock Manager does what its name suggests. It will keep the values of your portfolio up-to-date every time you HotSync, which you can do in a number of ways: through your Windows or Mac computer, by connecting your Palm handheld to a modem or mobile phone, or by using a Palm VII. It also tells you the day's high, low, change, and volume in a special window that you can scroll through easily.

You aren't just limited to the New York Stock Exchange, either. Stock Manager supports the stock exchanges in the United States, Canada, most of Europe, Australia, New Zealand, Singapore, Kuala Lumpur, Hong Kong, Taiwan, Korea, Indonesia, and India. And you can see your stock statistics in a range of currencies.

The people at TinyStocks.com have thought of just about everything for you and your stocks. You can organize your stocks into different portfolios, and you can look at your stock statistics—profit, profit change, profit per annum, current value, and cost—on a per stock basis, per portfolio basis, or for all your stocks.

You can even export your portfolio to a CSV file, which you'll appreciate come tax time since you'll be able to read that information in Excel and other spreadsheet applications. Windows users can take advantage of Stock Manager's Desktop tool that lets you check on your stocks without HotSynching or launching your browser. You can even get the program in four languages—English, French, German, and Italian.

Look at what you can do with Stock Manager:

◆ You can easily see your portfolio cost, value, profit, and other statistics.

◆ With the portfolio charts, you can quickly see how your money is distributed across all your investments.

◆ Support for multiple portfolios allows you to keep your different investments well classified.

◆ After every update, quickly see which stock has gone up or down since the last update with handy visual indicators. Also see the profit change of your portfolio since the last update.

◆ Stock Manager downloads the current stock price, the day's high, the day's low, the day's change, the previous close, and the volume values.

◆ Stock alerts will warn you after an Internet update of important changes in your portfolio. Alerts can be set on a stock's price, profit, profit percentage, or daily change.

◆ You can manage different portfolios in different currencies and see the portfolio statistics in either the portfolio's native currency or in your base currency.

◆ Individual stock charts allow you to see a stock's price history for 1.5, 3, or 6 months at a time.

◆ It also keeps track of the cash available in each portfolio.

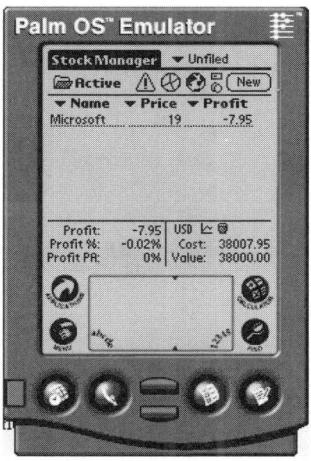

## Getting Started with Stock Manager

Follow these steps to use Stock Manager:

1. Start by entering your stocks into Stock Manager. Choose New Stock under the Record menu, or tap New at the top of the screen. Enter the stock name, its ticker symbol, and any other pertinent information. Tap OK.

2. Repeat step 1 for as many stocks as you'd like. You can also sort them into portfolio categories.

3. Under the Network menu, go to Network Panel. Provide the required information on your wireless service provider, the type of connection you'll be making, your username, and telephone number. Tap on Details to make sure the default settings for your connection are correct. Tap OK. Tap Done.

4. HotSync to update your stock information.

## Stock Manager: The Important Commands

Here are the important Stock Manager commands.

| Menu | Command | Shortcut | What It Does |
|------|---------|----------|--------------|
| Record | New Stock | /N | Adds another stock to your Stock Manager portfolio |
| Record | Stock Details | /I | Shows information about a stock you select |
| Record | Delete Stock | /d | Deletes a stock from your Stock Manager list |
| Record | Delete All Stocks | None | Removes all stocks from Stock Manager |
| Record | Split Stock | None | Handles a split of a stock you select |
| Record | Sort Stocks | /D | Lets you choose a range of sort options for your stocks |
| Record | Preferences | None | Lets you choose from a range of options, such as password protection |

| Menu | Command | Shortcut | What It Does |
| --- | --- | --- | --- |
| Record | Portfolio Charts | /H | Presents a graphical display, in a bar graph or pie chart, of your portfolio |
| Record | Currencies | None | Lets you change the currency type of a given portfolio |
| Network | Update Stocks | /U | Updates stocks upon making Internet connection |
| Network | View Log | /V | Shows when you connect to the Internet |
| Network | Disconnect | None | Disconnects your handheld from the Internet |
| Network | Network Panel | /T | Lets you set preferences for your Internet service, password, etc. |
| Network | Modem Panel | /M | Lets you choose your modem type |
| Network | Network Settings | None | Lets you work around a firewall or stay connected after updating stocks |

# 99  $50 per Hour and Climbing: TrackFast

Name of Program: TrackFast
E-Mail Address: TrackFast@vision7.com
Web Address: http://www.vision7.com
Version: 1.4b3
Type of Software: Commercial
Cost: $30

Where does the time go? If you can't remember, TrackFast will help you. In fact, it will not only remember all those details for you—who you saw, what

you talked about, what follow-up actions you need to take—but it will organize them, too.

TrackFast will also help you keep track of your progress toward goals, the completion of assigned tasks, and preparation for events. Also, TrackFast links to the existing items on your Palm Address Book, Date Book, To Do List, and Memo Pad. What you will really love is its keyword and name-completion features. They let you enter data quickly and painlessly with just a few strokes of the stylus.

TrackFast first organizes your activities into tracks and entries. You will create a track for anything you want to monitor over time, such as an important customer contact, a project, your exercise habits, an event, or your diet. For each track, then, you'll eventually create a list of entries. Entries keep a record of specific activities within a track. They contain a date and optional start and stop times to help you view them chronologically and to show you how much time you're spending (or not spending) on an activity. For example, if you're a runner, you might create an entry for each time you run and note the distance, time, and how you felt.

Additional features add to TrackFast's usefulness:

◆ Both tracks and entries can be assigned to categories to assist in finding information or quickly checking on the number of a particular type of project or activity (business, personal, phone calls, meetings, memos, etc.). You can customize your category list to reflect the types of activities you want to track.

◆ Both tracks and entries can contain links to items in your Palm Address Book, Date Book, To Do List, and Memo Pad applications so you can reference important contacts, appointments, etc., from within the TrackFast software. What's really cool is that when you, say, change a phone number in your Palm Address Book, the number will automatically change when you use the link in TrackFast.

◆ You can jump to view or edit a linked item directly from the TrackFast application, and then return to the Tracks view, Entries view, or Edit Entry view you left. Deleting a linked item automatically deletes the link, so you don't have to worry about removing them manually.

◆ The name-completion feature uses the Palm Address Book to look for matching first names and enters the full name upon selection. Just enter one or two letters using the graffiti writing area and tap the Keyword box to insert the word or name shown. Keywords are completed from a keyword database, which you can customize to include words that you frequently use and then organize so that the most common word will appear in the keyword selector. An expanded pop-up menu lets you pick a keyword or name from a list of matches.

◆ Multiple links can be added to any track or entry so you can reference more than one contact or a mix of contacts, appointments, and so forth. For example, you can track all the attendees to a meeting entry by adding multiple links to Palm Address Book items and one link to a Date Book item.

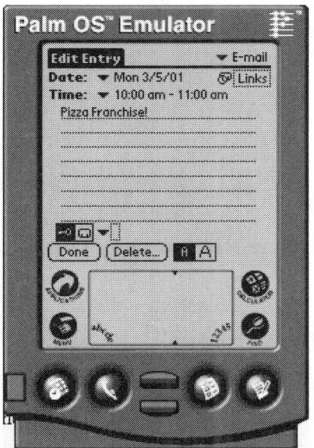

## Getting Started with TrackFast

Track time and details by following these directions:

**1.** When you first start TrackFast, the main screen is essentially blank. Tap New to create a new track. Enter a title for a track.

**2.** Tap the Category pop-up menu (it currently reads Unfiled), and assign a category to your track by tapping on your selection. To create a new category, tap Edit Categories from the menu, tap New, and enter your new category. Tap OK, then tap OK again on the Edit Categories screen.

**3.** Tap Save to save your new track.

**4.** Tap the arrow next to a track to display the Entries screen for that track. Tap New. The Edit Entry screen automatically enters the current date (although you can select another date if you'd like). Select a time from the Time pop-up menu, or leave it at None.

**5.** Enter the pertinent information about the activity. The Keyword icon (a key) at the bottom of the screen will be preselected. Notice as you enter the information that words will appear in the box to the right of the icon. They're based on the first letter or two of a word as you enter it. When a word appears that you want to use, just tap it, and Track-Fast will complete the word for you. Tap the arrow next to Unfiled if you wish to categorize your entry.

**6.** Tap the Links selector in the upper-right corner of the dialog box to go to the Links view. Tap the Add button. Tap the icons on the right side of the lower screen to go to the regular Palm Address Book, Date Book, To Do List, or Memo Pad. Select a link item and tap Add. Tap Done. Tap Done again to return to the entry.

## TrackFast: The Important Commands

Here are the important TrackFast commands.

| Menu | Command | Shortcut | What It Does |
| --- | --- | --- | --- |
| Options | Go to Top | None | Moves you to the top of your track list |
| Options | Go to Bottom | None | Moves you to the bottom of your track list |
| Options | Keywords | /Y | Takes you to the Edit Keywords screen, where you can add or delete words in your keywords list |
| Options | Help | /H | Provides help and tips for working with TrackFast |
| Track | Move Up | /U | Moves selected track up one spot on the list |
| Track | Move Down | /D | Moves selected track down one spot on the list |
| Track | Move to Top | /T | Moves selected track to top of list |
| Track | Move to Bottom | /B | Moves selected track to bottom of list |
| Track | Sort | /S | Sorts tracks alphabetically |

# 100 What's It Worth to You?: Valuer

Name of Program: Valuer
E-Mail Address: `info@performancetools.com`
Web Address: `http://www.performancetools.com`
Version: 1.01
Type of Software: Shareware
Cost: $29.95

If you want to know how much your business is worth, Valuer will walk you through the steps to make your estimate. It lets you use different assumptions, from irrational exuberance to patent pessimism. It can't get much simpler—at least in operation—than Valuer.

Valuer takes you from the general (questions about the economy, the industry, and so on) to the very specific (the business' sales figures, for instance). The accuracy of it as a valuation tool, of course, depends largely on the accuracy of the assumptions you make, such as your estimate of expected sales growth. Still, it can be handy to make a quick estimate of a business' worth, as well as to try out different assumptions and see what would happen to the business, for instance, if the economy bombs.

Valuer isn't likely to replace detailed pro forma analyses of businesses, but it's a pretty painless way to find out whether to go to the trouble of doing such an analysis.

## Getting Started with Valuer

Find out the value of your business by following these directions:

1. The opening screen gives you a list of economic items—inflation, interest rates, unemployment, currency, and import/export operations—for the company in question. Tap in the appropriate box to indicate your best estimate. (Tap on the Information icon if you aren't sure what the abbreviations stand for.)

2. Note the bar on the bottom of the screen that indicates whether the economic situation is favorable or unfavorable. Tap Next.

3. Now check the appropriate answers for the industry. Tap Next.

4. Continue making your choices in the Local Market window.

5. Now is the hard part. Enter the numbers for the business in the left column and the expected annual change in those numbers in the Percent column. Enter the dollar figures as thousands; for example, enter **47** in the Cost of Goods Sold field if the actual figure is $46,785.

6. Tap Next. The Net Income 1 screen extrapolates your figures for the current year plus two more years.

7. Tap Next to see an additional two years of projections (the Net Income 2 screen).

8. Continue tapping Next through the remaining screens to get the projected book value.

9. Tap Next. Enter the values of equity, short-term loans, and long-term loans and of the expected return to shareholders.

10. Tap Calculate. Valuer now shows your weighted average cost of capital.

11. Tap Next. The Valuation screen gives the estimated value of the business.

12. Tap Next. Read and, if you'd like, consider the recommendations that Valuer makes about your business.

## Valuer: The Important Commands

The only command you need to know for Valuer is the Reset command on the File menu, which clears existing answers so you can make a fresh analysis.

# 101 Keeping Currency Current: BCalcPalm

Name of Program: BCalcPalm
E-Mail Address: info@belcaf.com
Web Address: http://www.belcaf.com/english/bcalc.htm
Version: 2.01
Type of Software: Shareware
Cost: $13.99

You might think a currency calculator belongs in the travel section of this book, but this isn't just any currency calculator. It's the kind you need if you're involved in international trade, because it can calculate for 165 different currencies (several more than even your most intrepid traveler might need). In addition, it allows you to configure buttons for specific currencies, and its Web site, from which you download currency values, is updated every 30 minutes. What's more, you can update those values through your cellular phone, as well as when you synchronize with your PC. It all adds up to an amazing currency tool for doing international business.

Look at the features:

◆ All functions of a conventional calculator, including usage of memory

◆ Calculation histories (up to 10)

◆ Use of copy-and-paste feature for values

◆ Configurable buttons for quick specifying of currencies

◆ List of 165 national currencies

◆ Option of currency rates updates by direct request from your Palm

◆ Direct PDB file downloading via your Internet browser

◆ IR-port support

◆ Support for cellular phone updates

◆ Support for color customization

◆ Manual currency rate changes

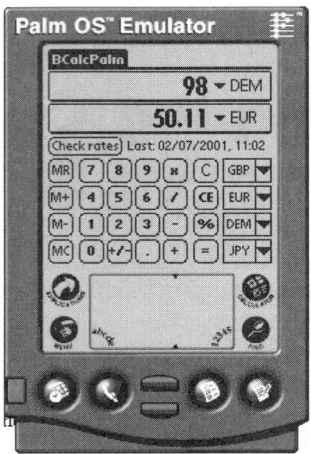

## Getting Started with BCalcPalm

How much for that bratwurst? That crème brulee? Figure it out with BCalcPalm:

**1.** The first step is to choose the currencies you're interested in. To do so, tap the triangle in the display strip across the top of the screen to get a pop-up menu of currencies. Tap in the box next to the desired currency to select it. You can uncheck any that you don't want to see in your pop-up list. You also can refer to the list to see the definitions of any abbreviations you don't understand.

If you don't see the one you'd like, tap the silk-screened Menus button and then choose Options from the currency menu.

**2.** Conversions don't get much faster. Use the on-screen keypad to enter a value, which appears in the top of the two display strips across the top of the screen. As you enter the value, BCalcPalm converts it to the selected currency and displays it in the bottom display strip.

**3.** Tap one of the currency buttons on the right to convert the same initial amount to other currencies.

**4.** To update rates, tap Check Rates.

**5.** Select the connection you will be using.

**6.** Tap Connect.

## BCalcPalm: The Important Commands

Here are the important BCalcPalm commands.

| Menu | Command | Shortcut | What It Does |
|------|---------|----------|--------------|
| Edit | Copy | /C | Copies text and saves it to the Clipboard |
| Edit | Paste | /P | Pastes text from the Clipboard |
| Edit | Interface Color Setup | None | Sets preferences for color (not available in demo version) |
| Currency | Options | /O | Lets you choose among scores of currencies for pop-up menus |
| Currency | History | /S | Displays the last 10 calculations |
| Help | Help | /H | Provides on-screen guidance for using BCalcPalm |

# 102 Slide Shows in Miniature: Flip Chart

Name of Program: Flip Chart
E-Mail Address: stephen@middlecross.com
Web Address: http://www.middlecross.com
Version: 3.2
Type of Software: Shareware
Cost: $14

 With Flip Chart, you don't need a screen, a digital projector, and a laptop to be able to give an electronic slide show. Sure, the handheld slide shows don't do all the flip-flops that some PC-based shows (like PowerPoint) allow, but Flip Chart gives you flexibility in type and color selections, and it allows you to use FireViewer images.

Besides showing a sequence of slides, Flip Chart also allows you to create an interactive presentation with a set of linked slides, which is called Jump Charts. Your path through your Jump Charts show will depend on screen selections you make as the show progresses.

Flip Charts are super-easy to create, and you can beam your results to others. Wouldn't you rather get a show than a memo?

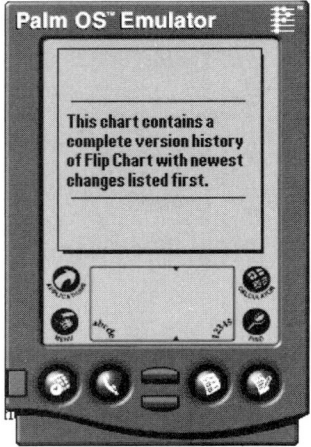

## Getting Started with Flip Chart

Who needs Bill Gates and PowerPoint when you have Flip Chart? Create charts by following these directions:

1. When you install Flip Chart, also install a couple of the PDB files as sample slide shows.

2. The first screen you'll see with Flip Chart gives a listing of slide shows that are saved on your Palm device. For now, they are the samples. To see the slide show, tap on the name of one of the samples.

**3.** The first slide will appear. After you read it, press the lower hardware scroll button to see the next slide.

**4.** When you finish looking at the slide show, tap anywhere on the Flip Chart Slide screen to return to the Flip Chart Home screen.

**5.** To create your own sample slide show, tap New. Then tap Flip.

**6.** Next to Title, enter the title that you want to appear on your first slide and on the home list of slide shows. For this example, enter **My Resume**.

**7.** Next to File Name, enter a name for the PDB file you're creating. Unlike the title, the PDB file can't have any spaces or punctuation.

**8.** Next to Author, enter the name of the Flip Chart show creator; it will appear on the opening slide.

**9.** Enter a password next to Pswd if you want your file to be unchangeable by anyone but you. If so, you'll also want to check the Locked box.

**10.** Check Private if you want your show to be private, and check Intro if you want an introduction slide before yours appears (more on that in step 20). Tap Done.

**11.** You're back home. Now you can create your slides. Tap the name of your new slide show. Tap New to create a new slide.

**12.** Tap the appropriate number under one of the first five available slide styles that appear on your screen. (The sixth style is for Jump Charts, the interactive kind of slide show, which won't be detailed here.) Each set of lines represents a text block that you can individually format in terms of text style and color (if you have a color Palm).

**13.** Enter some text in the first text block on your new slide.

**14.** Tap the double angle brackets button next to the text block.

**15.** In the Text Block screen that appears, select the font and color for the text from the pop-up menus under the triangles. Then turn on the Sep Bar with its pop-up menu. (The Sep Bar is a horizontal line that you can choose to appear in your slide between text blocks.)

**16.** Repeat steps 13–15 for any other text blocks on your slide. When you finish, tap the Checkmark icon.

**17.** Now you're back at the My Resume home screen. It shows the first line in your first slide, and it displays the style number of the slide on the right.

**18.** Tap New to create another slide. Repeat the slide-making process.

**19.** When you finish with your last slide, select Start Slide Show from the Chart menu.

**20.** If you checked Intro back on the Slide Show Properties screen, you'll first see an intro slide that lists the show's title, author, and date, and provides two sentences on how to operate the show.

## Flip Chart: The Important Commands

Here are the important Flip Chart commands.

| Menu | Command | Shortcut | What It Does |
|------|---------|----------|--------------|
| Chart | Start Slide Show | /S | Starts the active slide show |
| Chart | Set Chart Properties | None | Lets you select among options, such as whether to have an intro slide, for the active slide show |
| Chart | Quick Paint | None | Lets you quickly change the colors (if you have a color handheld) of all slide text or separator bars |
| Chart | Delete Chart | None | Deletes selected slide show |
| Beam | Beam Flip Chart App | /A | Beams Flip Chart application to another Palm device user |
| Beam | Beam Chart | /B | Beams a slide show to another Palm user who has Flip Chart |

# 103 Get It Down Quickly: My Ideas!

Name of Program: My Ideas!
E-Mail Address: MyIdeas@SandsUSA.com
Web Address: http://www.SandsUSA.com
Version: 2.1
Type of Software: Shareware
Cost: $10

If you like simplicity, My Ideas! fills the bill. All it does is provide a simple way for you to record, classify, and organize your ideas. That's it. It doesn't let you beam them. It doesn't synchronize the ideas with Outlook or Palm Desktop. It just keeps your ideas percolating on your Palm device until you're ready to share them with others.

When that time comes, you can copy the idea from My Ideas! and paste it in the Memo Pad, the To Do List, the Calendar, or an outlining or project application, and pass it on when you synchronize.

Entering your ideas is easy, and you can create your own status and categories to suit your needs. A simple, useful, and private application is just what you need for those incubating ideas.

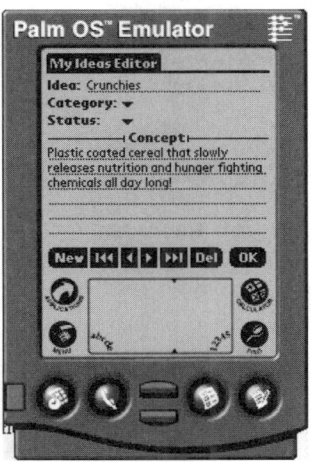

## Getting Started with My Ideas!

Whose ideas? Your ideas!

**1.** Tap New in the opening My Ideas! screen.

**2.** Enter a title in the blank next to Idea.

**3.** Enter additional information about the idea in the lines under Concept. Tap OK.

**4.** Tap Config now that you're back at the main screen if you'd like to assign a category or status to the idea.

**5.** Tap Edit Categories. Enter a category name in the blank. Tap OK.

**6.** Tap Edit Status List.

**7.** To create additional categories or statuses, enter them the same way.

## My Ideas!: The Important Commands

Here are the important My Ideas! commands.

| Menu | Command | Shortcut | What It Does |
|------|---------|----------|--------------|
| Edit | Undo | /U | Undoes your last action |
| Edit | Cut | /X | Cuts selected text and saves it to the Clipboard |
| Edit | Copy | /C | Copies text and saves it to the Clipboard |
| Edit | Paste | /P | Pastes text from the Clipboard |
| Edit | Select All | /S | Selects all entries on the screen |
| Edit | Keyboard | /K | Allows you to use the keyboard to enter information |
| Edit | Graffiti Help | /G | Displays graffiti strokes |

# 104 Where Does Time Go?: Time Journal

Name of Program: Time Journal
E-Mail Address: fullerrw@bellsouth.net
Web Address: http://hotfiles.zdnet.com/cgi-bin/texis/swlib/
hotfiles/info.html?fcode=001CIJ&b=zdpalm
Version: 1.3
Type of Software: Shareware
Cost: $14

If you need to keep track of your time by date, by project, or by client, Time Journal could be for you. It doesn't provide some of the features that other time applications do—such as running a timer—but it does give you lots of options for recording your information the way you want to and need to record it.

For such a simple, intuitive application, it has remarkably thorough documentation by the developer, who created it to fit his own time-tracking needs.

## Getting Started with Time Journal

Use Time Journal by following these directions:

1. Time Journal's opening screen will remain empty until you fill it up. Tap New to get started.

2. Enter a filename. Make it something that corresponds with the way you need to keep track of your time, such as a name for a week. Tap Done.

3. Next you'll see another blank screen for you to fill! Tap New to add your first Time Journal entry.

4. At the New Entry screen, tap the diamond next to the Project field.

5. Enter a project name using graffiti or the keyboard. The name will appear on the blank at the bottom of the screen. When you finish with an entry, tap Add and enter your project codes. When you finish entering project codes (and there's no need to enter them all now), tap OK.

6. Tap the diamond next to the Act (for Activity) blank. Enter an activity (or activities) just as you did your project name(s).

7. If desired, add any notes about the current activity that you're recording.

8. The current date, as you can see, automatically appears in the upper-left corner of the screen.

9. Record the amount of time used. Select hours from the pop-up menu indicated by the H, and select minutes from the pop-up menu indicated by the M.

## Time Journal: The Important Commands

Here are the important Time Journal commands.

| Menu | Command | Shortcut | What It Does |
|------|---------|----------|--------------|
| Record | First Record | /F | Takes you to the first record in the active file |
| Record | Last Record | /L | Takes you to the last record in the active file |
| Record | Delete Record | /D | Deletes the selected record |

| Menu | Command | Shortcut | What It Does |
| --- | --- | --- | --- |
| Options | Maintain Action Codes | /M | Opens the Action Codes screen to add, edit, or delete codes |
| Options | Maintain Project Codes | /P | Opens the Project Codes screen to add, edit, or delete codes |
| Options | Copy/Export Settings | /Y | Lets you choose among various copying and exporting options |
| Options | Preferences | /E | Lets you choose viewing and entry options |
| Help | Graffiti | /G | Shows graffiti strokes |

# 105 The Big Itty-Bitty Spreadsheet: TinySheet

Name of Program: TinySheet
E-Mail Address: sales@iambic.com
Web Address: http://www.iambic.com
Version: 3.12
Type of Software: Commercial
Cost: $19.95

Don't you just love Excel? Don't you wish your Palm did, too? With TinySheet, it does.

If you're an Excel user, you will feel right at home with TinySheet. It operates very much like Excel. You can do everything from entering numbers and formulas to applying a range of formats to cells. You can export to and from the Memo Pad in tab- or comma-separated formats, which means

you can create a spreadsheet with Excel and use it with TinySheet. The reverse is also true. You can do simple or complex operations, make big (multiple sheets) or small (single sheet) workbooks, and make huge worksheets with thousands of cells.

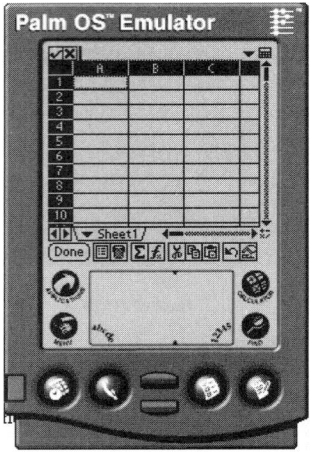

The price is definitely modest for such a versatile and functional application. Here are the features:

◆ Familiar and intuitive Excel-like spreadsheet interface

◆ Supports color and can be installed on devices that are color-enabled (e.g., Palm IIIc)

◆ Supports separate sheets within one workbook

◆ Size of spreadsheets limited only by Palm device memory

◆ Adjustable columns *and* rows

◆ Advanced built-in functions including financial, date and time, math and trig, statistical, and logical

◆ Ability to cut and paste cell values and formulas

◆ Handles sophisticated formulas, including absolute and relative cell references and references between sheets

◆ Advanced formatting options (cell data alignment, word wrap, fonts, decimals, borders, protections, etc.)

◆ Calculator-style keyboard for entering formulas quickly and without handwriting

◆ Fast cell navigation, scrolling, and paging, including graffiti support

◆ Currency, Percent, Date, and Time cell styles

◆ Negative numbers can be shown in brackets, e.g., [$100]

◆ Locked sheets with optional password

◆ Beaming support so you can share your spreadsheet data with coworkers or friends

## Getting Started with TinySheet

Here's another tip of the hat to the original spreadsheet program's developer, Dan Bricklin. Follow these steps to do more than imagine a spreadsheet on your Palm:

**1.** Tap on New to create a new spreadsheet. This view will look familiar, with its numbered rows and lettered columns.

**2.** Enter a few numbers to try it out. In column A, enter a series of numbers for rows 1 through 5. Tap the first cell in the upper-left portion of the screen, which we'll call A1. The number you enter appears on the entry line at the top of the screen.

**3.** Tap another cell, such as A2. The number you entered for A1 should now appear in the cell. Enter another number in A2.

**4.** Repeat until you have numbers in the first five cells of column A.

**5.** Now enter a formula. Tap A6 and tap the sigma at the bottom of the screen. (The sigma is the third icon from the left. It's the Greek letter that resembles a funny-looking E.)

**6.** TinySheet automatically highlights the cells you previously entered, and it shows in the data entry line **SUM(A1:A5)**. How did it know? Don't ask me, but you'll notice that the **A1:A5** portion of the formula is highlighted. Thus, if you want to total different cells, you just enter those by tapping. But for this example, you want to total A1 through A5, so tap the checkmark next to the formula. Voilà! The sum of those five lines appears in A6.

**7.** Tap the Sheet 1 tab at the bottom of the screen.

**8.** Select Rename from the pop-up menu.

**9.** Enter a name for our first workbook, as TinySheet calls these worksheets.

**10.** Tap the Workbook Details icon, which is the first one on the left at the bottom of the screen.

**11.** Name the workbook to which this sheet will belong, and select from various display options.

**12.** Tap the pop-up triangle next to Category, and select a category for it.

**13.** Tap OK and then tap Done.

**14.** Notice that your new workbook appears now that you're back in the TinySheet home screen.

## TinySheet: The Important Commands

Here are the important TinySheet commands.

| Menu | Command | Shortcut | What It Does |
|------|---------|----------|--------------|
| Book | New Workbook | /N | Creates a new workbook |
| Book | Delete Workbook | /D | Deletes current workbook |
| Book | Duplicate Workbook | /1 | Creates a duplicate of current workbook and lets you name it |
| Book | Beam Workbook | /B | Beams current workbook to another Palm user |
| Book | Default Format | /V | Lets you change the application's default cell-formatting settings |
| Book | Details | /4 | Opens the Workbook Details screen for setting display preferences |
| Edit | Undo Cell | /U | Undoes entry in last cell |
| Edit | Clear | /L | Clears contents of selected cell |
| Edit | Cut | /X | Cuts selected text and saves it to the Clipboard |

| Menu | Command | Shortcut | What It Does |
|------|---------|----------|--------------|
| Edit | Copy | /C | Copies text and saves it to the Clipboard |
| Edit | Paste | /P | Pastes text from the Clipboard |
| Edit | Select All | /S | Selects all entries on the screen |
| Edit | Insert Column | /A | Inserts a column to the left of selected column |
| Edit | Delete Column | /Q | Deletes selected column |
| Edit | Insert Row | /J | Inserts a row above the selected column |
| Edit | Delete Row | /M | Deletes selected row |
| Edit | Keyboard | /K | Allows you to use the keyboard to enter information |
| Edit | Graffiti Help | /G | Displays graffiti strokes |
| Cell | Format | /F | Lets you edit formatting in selected cell |
| Cell | Freeze | /Z | Lets you freeze a column or row to keep it from scrolling and to act instead as headers |
| Cell | Unfreeze | /3 | Unfreezes frozen column or row |
| Cell | Home | /H | Selects cell A1 |
| Cell | Top | /T | Scrolls to top of current worksheet |
| Cell | Bottom | /W | Scrolls to bottom of current worksheet |
| Cell | Go To | /2 | Lets you specify a specific cell to go to |

| Menu | Command | Shortcut | What It Does |
|------|---------|----------|--------------|
| Tools | Fill Series | /Y | Lets you set up automatically entered data series, such as consecutive numbers |
| Tools | Calculate Now | /O | Calculates values |
| Tools | Import Sheet | /I | Lets you import tab- or comma-separated data from Memo Pad |
| Tools | Export Sheet | /E | Lets you export data as tab- or comma-separated data to Memo Pad |
| Tools | Preferences | /R | Lets you select functional options |
| Tools | Sort | /4 | Lets you sort data |
| Tools | Repair Workbook | None | Checks and repairs any work-book errors |

# Connectivity Applications

**H**otSyncing your Palm device to your Desktop computer is only the beginning when it comes to PDA connectivity. Nowadays, connectivity applications let you view your actual Desktop computer applications, read Internet content, send and receive faxes, or send and receive e-mail—all from the convenience of your handheld computer. With these applications, all you need is a wristband for your Palm device, and you'll be way ahead of Dick Tracy's two-way wrist radio.

# 106 Take the News with You: AvantGo

Name of Program: AvantGo
E-Mail Address: `info@avantgo.com`
Web Address: `http://avantgo.com/frontdoor/index.html`
Version: 3.3
Type of Software: Freeware
Cost: Free

With AvantGo, you can take advantage of tons of Web content without suffering the extremely slow interaction common with some Web applications for handhelds. On the AvantGo Web site, you can choose the channels that you want to view and then HotSync with your Web browser running to download their content. Its channels range from business to wireless and feature such content providers as Bloomberg Personal, *Business Week*, TV Guide Online, Yahoo!, the *New York Times*, *USA Today*, ZDNet to Go, and much more. You can get such information as stock quotes, flight schedules, movie listings, restaurant reviews, and weather.

AvantGo features include the following:

- ◆ Web-based user interface for end users
- ◆ Dial-up, wireless, synchronization, or kiosk support
- ◆ HTML 3.2–compliant forms and documents
- ◆ Symbol Technologies scanner integration
- ◆ Online or batch connectivity

◆ Remote handheld management via AvantGo Server

◆ Data compression

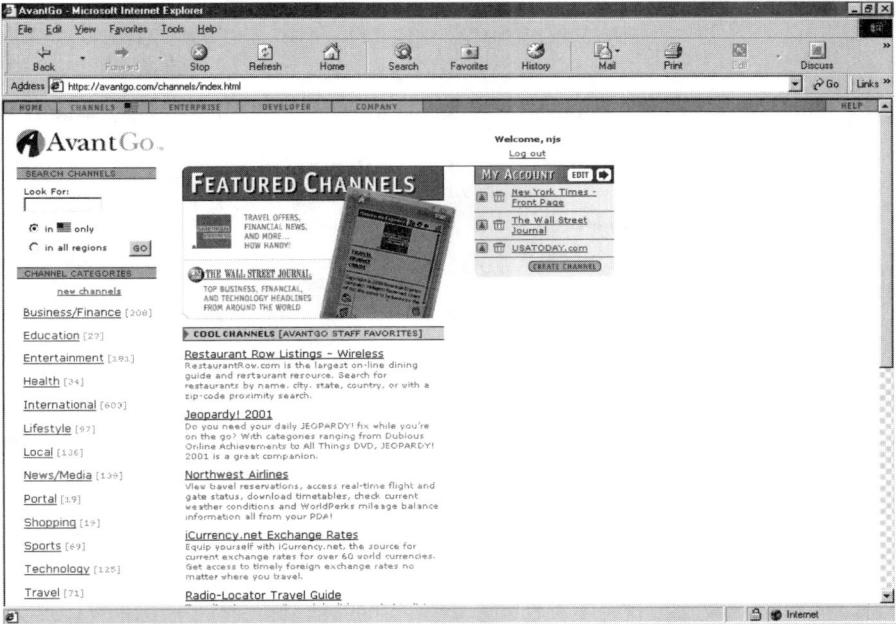

## Getting Started with AvantGo

Here's how to get started with AvantGo.

**1.** Go to the AvantGo Web site, `www.avantgo.com/setup`, and create your account. Follow the steps through configuring and synchronization. Choose the Channels (content providers) you want to have. HotSync with your handheld.

**2.** Start up AvantGo on your Palm device.

**3.** Tap the channel you want to view.

**4.** Tap the particular selection you want. Enjoy your reading!

**5.** Tap the left-pointing arrow at the top of the screen to go back to the previous screen.

**6.** Tap the Home icon to go back to the Channels listing, then tap your next selection.

# AvantGo: The Important Commands

Here are the important AvantGo commands.

| Menu | Command | Shortcut | What It Does |
|---|---|---|---|
| Channels | Open Page | /O | Opens Web page |
| Channels | Reload Page | /L | Reloads (refreshes) Web page |
| Channels | Forms Manager | /M | Manages AvantGo forms that are submitted to channels |
| Channels | Channel Manager | /E | Manages your selection of channels |
| Channels | Online Cache Manager | None | Manages the channels that you have saved |
| Channels | Modem Sync | None | Adjusts your modem settings for synching with AvantGo |
| Channels | Connect | None | Connects with Internet service |
| Channels | Disconnect | None | Disconnects from Internet service |
| Go | Home | /H | Returns browser to your pre-set Home site |
| Go | Back | /B | Goes to last Web page viewed |
| Go | Forward | /W | Goes to next Web page |
| Options | Preferences | /R | Lets you choose among options, including whether or not graphics and tables are displayed |

# 107 On the Road, on the Web: DPWeb

Name of Program: DPWeb Basic and DPWeb DX
E-Mail Address: info@digitalpaths.com
Web Address: http://digitalpaths.com
Version: 2.2
Type of Software: Shareware
Cost: $20

If you have the wireless PDA, DPWeb has the power to link you to World Wide Web text. When you request a Web page, DPWeb retrieves, transforms, and reformats it into text-only content. DPWeb Basic is free and gives you access to standard Web sites. DPWeb DX requires a registration fee, and it enables Secure Sockets Layer (SSL), cookie (yum!) support, bookmarking, and advanced search capability. If you have a Palm VII, you probably already know that Web access is handy, but it certainly isn't like surfing the Web via your DSL or cable modem. It's significantly slower, but hey, in the middle of another boring meeting, who cares?

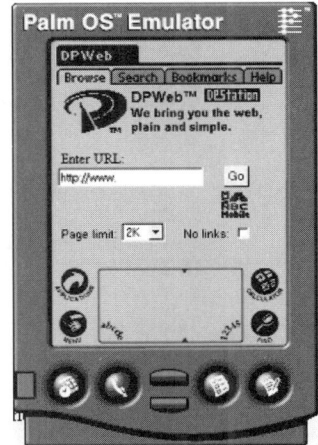

## Getting Started with DPWeb

Here's how you get started with DPWeb.

**1.** From the main DPWeb screen, tap the Browse tab (if it isn't already active).

**2.** Enter the URL you wish to see and tap Go.

**3.** Tap Next.

**4.** Tap any link you wish to follow.

**5.** Tap DPWeb when you want to return to the main screen.

**6.** To search, tap the Search tab and enter your search criteria. Select your favorite search engine from the pop-up menu. Tap Search.

**7.** Questions? Tap the Help tab.

## DPWeb: The Important Commands

Here's a summary of the important DPWeb commands.

| Menu | Command | Shortcut | What It Does |
|------|---------|----------|--------------|
| Options | Get ID | /L | Gets your registration ID |
| Options | Quit Program | /Q | Quits program |
| Edit | Cut | /X | Cuts text |
| Edit | Copy | /C | Copies text |
| Edit | Paste | /P | Pastes text |
| Edit | Undo | /U | Undoes action |
| Edit | Select All | /S | Selects all text |
| Edit | Keyboard | /K | Displays keyboard |
| Edit | Graffiti | /G | Displays graffiti strokes |

# 108 Just the Fax, Ma'am: Fax

Name of Program: Fax
E-Mail Address: info@markspace.com
Web Address: http://www.markspace.com
Version: 1.0 (a public beta)
Type of Software: Shareware
Cost: $29.95

With Fax, all you need to do is connect a compatible modem or cellular phone to your Palm, and you're ready to send a fax. You can even send and receive faxes in some foreign languages. The Fax application lets you preview a fax and add graphics before you send your fax.

Take a look at more of its features:

- ◆ Generation of the fax page before or during the transmission
- ◆ Management of created faxes in a dedicated database
- ◆ Insertion of bitmap drawings
- ◆ Editable header and footer
- ◆ Easy modem configuration through dialog boxes
- ◆ Support for dialing prefixes and calling cards
- ◆ Online help and tips

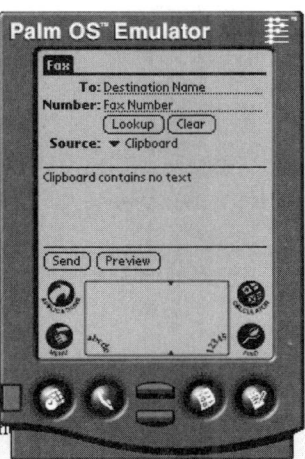

## Getting Started with Fax

Here's how to use Fax.

1. From the Fax screen, enter the receiving name and fax number in the blanks, or get them from the list you've created by tapping Lookup.

2. Locate the material you want to fax. Tap the pop-up menu to choose from the Clipboard, the Memo Pad, or another fax document.

3. Tap Preview to see what the fax will look like.

4. Tap Send.

5. To receive a fax, tap Receive.

## Fax: The Important Commands

Here are the commands you'll need in Fax.

| Menu | Command | Shortcut | What It Does |
| --- | --- | --- | --- |
| Options | User Settings | /U | Sets up or changes your fax ID, fax phone number, and any dialing prefixes |
| Options | Page Setup | /S | Sets margins, headers, and more |
| Options | Modem Config | /M | Configures modem, port, and more |
| Options | Phone Lookup | /L | Displays fax phone list |
| Options | Delete Fax | None | Deletes existing fax |
| Options | Display Log | /D | Displays log of fax activity |
| Options | Register | None | Register Fax |
| Options | About | None | All about Fax |
| Edit | Undo | /U | Undoes most recent operation |
| Edit | Cut | /X | Cuts text |
| Edit | Copy | /C | Copies text |

| Menu | Command | Shortcut | What It Does |
|------|---------|----------|--------------|
| Edit | Paste | /P | Pastes text |
| Edit | Select All | /S | Selects all text |
| Edit | Keyboard | /K | Displays keyboard |
| Edit | Graffiti | /G | Displays graffiti strokes |

# 109 E-Mail Control Like Poetry: iambic Mail

Name of Program: iambic Mail
E-Mail Address: support@iambic.com/pilot/mail
Web Address: http://www.iambic.com
Version: 1.01
Type of Software: Commercial
Cost: $14.95

iambic Mail lets you keep up with your e-mail even when you're out of the office. Its screens are clear and easy to understand and view. With iambic Mail, a Palm device, and a Palm modem you can send and receive e-mails anywhere in the world, using either a cell phone or a telephone outlet.

Besides ease of use, iambic Mail also offers lots of features that you can set to your personal preferences:

◆ Choose to download your e-mail messages or just the subject lines.

◆ Include signature text.

◆ Save copies of sent e-mails.

◆ Handle multiple e-mail accounts.

◆ Choose whether you want to include the original e-mail in your replies.

It works a lot like your Desktop e-mail program. For example, you can identify in an instant, thanks to helpful icons, which e-mails you've already opened and read, and you can designate recipients, copy recipients, and specify subjects just as you would on a Desktop e-mail program. Tap the Details button to add a priority, a BCC (blind carbon copy), and a signature. Also, the Reply, Reply to All, CC, Forward, and Redirect buttons ease your e-mail tasks.

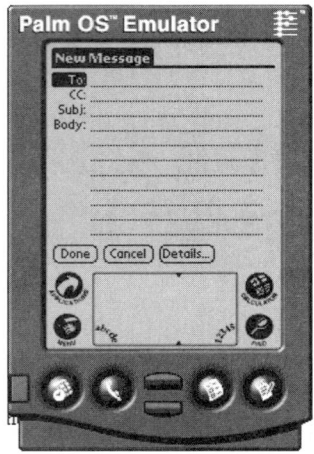

## Getting Started with iambic Mail

Follow these steps to get running with iambic Mail.

1. Start up iambic Mail from your Palm. Tap the Menu icon on the bottom of the Palm device, choose Accounts from the Tools menu, and then tap New.

2. Fill in the blanks for an account label (such as work or home), the name that appears on the account, and the actual e-mail address.

3. Tap the Settings tab. Fill in the POP3 (incoming) and SMTP (outgoing) e-mail servers, plus the username and password for the servers.

4. Tap the Options tab. Choose how the account will be handled and tap OK. The program will let you know if you've left anything blank.

5. Tap Done when you finish setting up accounts.

**6.** Now you're ready to send and receive mail. Tap New to create a message. Fill in the To: line, CC: line (optional), and Subject line, and then add your message. You can also tap Details to change priority settings, to designate BCCs, or to add a signature.

**7.** Tap OK in the Details box, then tap Done. Your message will now be in your iambic Mail outbox.

**8.** After connecting to your outgoing server, tap the Send/Recv button. From the pop-up menu, indicate whether you want to send and receive all selected e-mails, to receive only, or to send only, and choose from specific accounts that you created. Tap the Service Connection button (between the Show and Send/Recv buttons).

## iambic Mail: The Important Commands

You'll need these commands to manage iambic Mail.

| Menu | Command | Shortcut | What It Does |
|---|---|---|---|
| Message | New | /N | Sets up New Message screen |
| Message | Purge Deleted | /E | Purges deleted messages from your Palm device |
| Message | Purge Sent | /Y | Purges sent messages |
| Tools | Accounts | /H | Lets you set up e-mail accounts |
| Tools | Preferences | /R | Lets you choose the font that your e-mails will display |
| Edit | Undo | /U | Undoes last action |
| Edit | Cut | /X | Cuts selection |
| Edit | Copy | /C | Copies selection |
| Edit | Paste | /P | Pastes what you've cut or copied |
| Edit | Select All | /S | Selects all text available |

| Menu | Command | Shortcut | What It Does |
|---|---|---|---|
| Edit | Keyboard | /K | Allows you to use the keyboard to enter information |
| Edit | Graffiti Help | /G | Allows you to access Graffiti Help |
| Options | Font | /F | Lets you choose your e-mail font |
| Options | Preferences | /R | Designates how messages are handled, what your signature says, and more |

# 110 Keep That Internet Info Coming: Mobile Internet Kit

Name of Program: Mobile Internet Kit
E-Mail Address:
http://www.palm.com/support/contact/chat_or_mail.html
Web Address: http://www.palm.com/software/mik
Version: 1.0
Type of Software: Commercial
Cost: $39.95

Palm, Inc. offers its own Internet connectivity software, the Mobile Internet Kit (MIK). This software allows you to get Internet access, e-mail, and short messaging through your mobile phone or modem. MIK uses the built-in data capability of your mobile phone to establish a connection to the Internet from your Palm via the dial-up number from your Internet Service Provider. Once you've made the connection, MIK lets you use Web clipping applications to get whatever Internet information you want.

If you are using a GSM phone (Global System for Mobile Communications, a digital mobile telephone system), MIK allows you to compose short text messages (SMS) on your Palm handheld and the MIK. You can also send and receive corporate and personal e-mail from Yahoo!, EarthLink, Hotmail, or other POP3/IMAP4 accounts.

Another nice thing about MIK is that it comes with dozens of Web clipping applications for travel (so you can access other airline schedules when you're delayed), news (such as WSJ.com), reference (dictionary and encyclopedia), and Web portals (such as Yahoo!). But don't get too excited; it doesn't let you access AOL or MSN e-mail, nor does it download attachments.

### Getting Started with Mobile Internet Kit

Here's how to get started with Mobile Internet Kit.

1. Install the Mobile Internet Kit software on a compatible Palm handheld.

2. Connect your handheld to a data-enabled mobile phone or modem using a cable or infrared connection.

3. Log on to your ISP using the mobile phone or modem.

4. Send or receive short messages or e-mail using your Palm handheld, or tap on a Web clipping icon or the WAP (Wireless Application Protocol) browser to access information on the Web.

# 111 Visit Your Desktop from Mars!: PalmVNC

Name of Program: PalmVNC
E-Mail Address: harakan@btinternet.com
Web Address: http://www.harakan.btinternet.co.uk/PalmVNC
Version: 1.40
Type of Software: Freeware
Cost: Free

VNC, which stands for Virtual Network Computing, is a remote display system that allows you to view a computing desktop environment not only on the machine where it is running, but from anywhere on the Internet.

With PalmVNC and a VNC server, you can view your desktop computer—be it PC, Mac, or Unix—on your Palm handheld over a normal TCP/IP connection. Therefore, you can view it from just about anywhere that your Palm can connect.

Key features abound:

◆ Less than 40KB of Palm memory used

◆ Servers available for a wide variety of operating systems

◆ Color displays on Palm IIIc devices

◆ Server-side scaling support

◆ Data stored in Flash memory

## Getting Started with PalmVNC

Here's how you can "go remote" with PalmVNC.

**1.** After starting up PalmVNC, tap the Menu icon on the bottom of the screen and select Open from the Server menu.

**2.** Enter the name or IP address of your VNC server. You must also specify a display number, which is normally 0 for Windows servers or 1 for Unix servers. (You only have to enter this information the first time you connect.)

**3.** Once you have connected to the server, your Palm device will display a portion of the Desktop. To see other parts of the Desktop, use the stylus to drag the black bar along the horizontal or vertical scroll bar. The Up, Down, To Do, and Memo buttons on your handheld will also scroll the Desktop up, down, left, and right, respectively.

**4.** If your server supports the scaling extensions, you can scale down your Desktop view using the scale commands under the View menu.

**5.** Tap the stylus on the screen to single-click as you would with the left mouse button (for you Windows folks). Double-click by tapping twice in rapid succession, or drag the stylus across the screen.

**6.** Use the graffiti pad to enter text.

**7.** Tap Close under the Server menu to end your session.

## PalmVNC: The Important Commands

Here are the important PalmVNC commands.

| Menu | Command | Shortcut | What It Does |
|------|---------|----------|--------------|
| Server | Open | /O | Lets you connect to your server |
| Server | Close | None | Ends your VNC session |
| Server | Hang Up | None | Ends VNC session and disconnects your modem |
| Server | Network | None | Lets you change your connection information |
| Send | Palm Clipboard | /B | Transfers the contents of the Palm Clipboard to the server's Clipboard buffer |
| Send | Ctrl+Alt+Del | /X | Sends this 3-key Windows command |
| Send | Alt+F4 | /A | Closes Windows applications |
| Send | NT Login | /I | Assists with NT login |
| Send | NT Logout | /T | Assists with NT logout |
| Send | NT Lock | /L | Locks NT |
| Send | NT Reboot | None | Reboots NT |
| Help | Help | /H | Gets help |
| Help | About | None | About PalmVNC |

# 112 On the Road Again: MyPalm

Name of Program: MyPalm
Web Address: http://www.palm.net
Cost: Free

Question: What's not on your Palm or on your Desktop PC but lets you track all the info on your Palm and on your Desktop PC?

Answer: MyPalm, an Internet-based application, allows you to HotSync the data on your Palm to your own Internet site. It's terrific when you are on the road without your Palm and you have to look up a contact, and it's even terrific as a backup. And because it's on the Internet and available to all who can sign in, you can easily notify your team members, employees, roomies, family members, or whomever about a change in plans.

You can do these tasks with MyPalm:

◆ Manage meetings with more than one Palm user

◆ Send e-mail reminders

◆ Share group calendars

◆ Find out about and track events through the Event Club (including your state's holidays, local and national sporting events, and more)

◆ Send out personalized party invitations (wuh-hoo!)

◆ Track all your accounts (banking, Internet, airline, etc.)

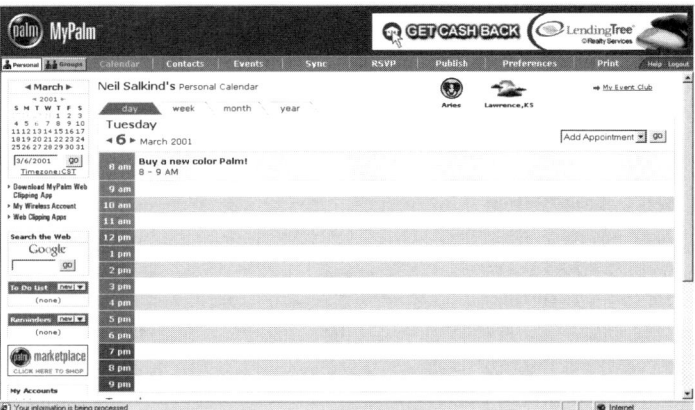

## Getting Started with MyPalm

To get started with MyPalm, follow these steps:

**1.** Go to www.palm.net and register.

**2.** Personalize any information that you might want added.

**3.** Download and install the Synch Software (click the Synch tab).

**4.** Select the information you want to synchronize.

**5.** Synchronize with MyPalm, and then everything you selected that is on your Palm Desktop software is also on your MyPalm account.

# Travel Applications

It's always nice to get away, but it's just as nice to know where you're going and what you can do once you get there! The outstanding Palm applications in this section can do everything from alerting you when it finds a cheaper flight to finding out the weather at your destination. When you travel, these tools can help you at every stop along the way.

## 113 Find Shopping, a Broadway Show, or a Hot Pastrami: CitySync

Name of Program: CitySync
E-Mail Address: info@lonelyplanet.com
Web Address: http://www.lonelyplanet.com
Version: 1.04
Type of Software: Commercial
Cost: $49.95 (plus $19.99 for additional cities)

Next time you go to New York, Chicago, Los Angeles, San Francisco, or any number of other cities, ditch the oversized travel guide. Instead, try City-Sync, your Palm's guide to shopping, eating, sleeping, and generally touring about town.

CitySync includes scrollable street maps, restaurant hours, transportation options, night spot listings, and just about any other information you might need while travelling. In addition, you can keep your own travel notes and even beam them to others, and bookmark your favorite sites. What fun!

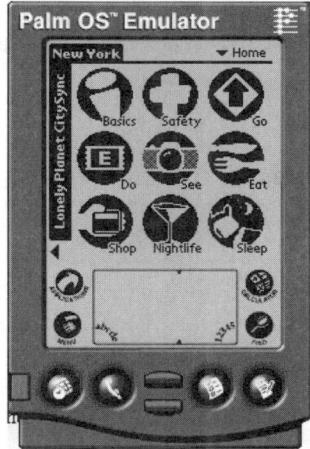

## Getting Started with CitySync

Find out what to do and where to go in Mexico City, Paris, Los Angeles, etc.

**1.** Install CitySync and select four cities. (Note that you may install only four cities if you purchase the program. One city may be downloaded and unlocked, but that demo city is good for only 24 hours.)

**2.** Tap the CitySync icon.

**3.** Tap the city you want to use.

**4.** Tap Basics, Safety, Go, Do, See, Eat, Shop, Nightlife, or Sleep, depending on what you want to do.

**5.** To enter comments and such, tap the Notes icon.

## CitySync: The Important Commands

These are the important CitySync commands.

| Menu | Command | Shortcut | What It Does |
|------|---------|----------|--------------|
| **CitySync** | **Bookmarks** | **/B** | **Bookmarks a site or City-Sync page** |
| **CitySync** | **Load City** | **/L** | **Loads a new city** |

| Menu | Command | Shortcut | What It Does |
|------|---------|----------|--------------|
| CitySync | Global Search | /E | Searches for a CitySync feature |
| CitySync | About CitySync | None | Tells all about CitySync |
| Edit | Undo | /U | Undoes your last action |
| Edit | Cut | /X | Cuts selected text and saves it to the Clipboard |
| Edit | Copy | /C | Copies text and saves it to the Clipboard |
| Edit | Paste | /P | Pastes text from the Clipboard |
| Edit | Select All | /S | Selects all entries on the screen |
| Edit | Export All Notes | /W | Exports notes to the Memo Pad |
| Edit | Delete All Notes | /Z | Deletes all notes |
| Edit | Keyboard | /K | Allows you to use the keyboard to enter information |
| Edit | Graffiti Help | /G | Displays graffiti strokes |
| Options | Help | /H | Provides help |
| Options | Font | /F | Changes font |
| Options | Register | None | Registers CitySync |
| Vehicle | Totals | /T | Shows total spending by vehicle for fuel, oil, service, tire rotation, miscellaneous costs, and trip costs |

# 114 Baby, You Can Drive My Car Records: AutoBase

Name of Program: AutoBase
E-Mail Address: herbo@earthlink.net
Web Address: http://home.earthlink.net/~herbo/palmos_sw.html
Version: 1.3.4
Type of Software: Freeware
Cost: Free

It isn't quite as good as having a chauffeur, but AutoBase keeps track of all those tiresome auto details a hired driver would handle for you—such as mileage, fuel costs, miles per gallon, and maintenance schedules—and it reminds you when it's time for general periodic maintenance. It even produces nifty reports that you can parse any way you'd like: mileage for all your cars, for instance, or oil changes for only your Chevy.

AutoBase has many features, such as the following:

◆ Supports up to 15 vehicles

◆ Tracks fuel entries

◆ Calculates distance and reimbursement costs

◆ Reminds you of service visits

◆ Tracks miscellaneous expenses

◆ Generates an overall report for each vehicle, showing total costs for fuel, oil, service, and tires

◆ Calculates miles per gallon since last fueling and for the life of the vehicle

◆ Provides detailed on-screen help for many screens

A downside of AutoBase is that it can be a bit of a nag. It will keep reminding you of that oil change you need until you enter the new information (this is where the chauffeur could be really, really handy).

## Getting Started with AutoBase

Track your mileage (and more) with AutoBase:

**1.** After starting AutoBase, tap All in the top right of the screen.

**2.** Choose Edit Categories and then tap Rename to change Car1 and Car2 to more memorable designations and to add any other vehicles you want to track.

**3.** Select a vehicle (note that its name appears in the top right of the screen). Tap the Menu spot on the bottom of the Palm screen. If you'd like, you can go to the Vehicle option and change the settings for the frequency of oil changes, tire rotations, and other regular services. You also can set the mileage reimbursement rate for tax purposes or for reporting expenses to your employer. Tap OK.

**4.** Tap Add. On the Entry screen, choose the vehicle. The time and date will default to your Palm's time and date. Add the location of service or fuel, or add your trip destination. Enter your current mileage.

**5.** Tap the drop-down arrow next to the Mileage field and choose the type of activity you're recording, such as Trip. The screen now provides a space to record the mileage at the destination.

**6.** Once you arrive at your destination, record your ending mileage and tap Calc. AutoBase computes your mileage and mileage reimbursement amount.

## AutoBase: The Important Commands

Here are the important AutoBase commands.

| Menu | Command | Shortcut | What It Does |
|------|---------|----------|--------------|
| Options | Preferences | /P | Designates units of measure including miles per gallon and dollars |
| Vehicle | Settings | /S | Specifies mileage reimbursement rate and intervals for maintenance procedures |
| Vehicle | Export to Memo | None | Automatically exports displayed data to Palm's Memo Pad |
| Vehicle | Fuel Usage | /F | Calculates miles per gallon for any vehicle |
| Vehicle | Totals | /T | Shows total spending by vehicle for fuel, oil, service, tire rotation, miscellaneous costs, and trip costs |

# 115 Umbrella or Shades?: AWS WeatherNet

Name of Program: AWS WeatherNet
E-Mail Address: info@aws.com
Web Address: http://aws.com/palm/
Version: 1.0
Type of Software: Freeware
Cost: Free

Finally! You can get weather reports when you need them—now. AWS WeatherNet is a Web clipping application that provides live, real-time reports on weather conditions for more than 4,000 sites in the U.S. through your wireless Palm connection. It works in conjunction with 103 local television stations, whose neighborhood weather stations can tell you if it's raining on the north side of town even though the sun is shining on the south side.

Want to be really cool? WeatherNet also works with your Internet-ready cell phone. You just point your mobile phone browser at aws.com, and you can access the weather from the available locations around the U.S.

## Getting Started with WeatherNet

Follow these steps to find out what the weather is where with AWS:

1. Go to aws.com/palm/.

2. Download and install the application.

3. Tap the AWS WeatherNet icon.

4. Enter the zip code of the location whose weather you want to know.

5. Tap Search. WeatherNet connects to its own weather service (on the Net) and provides you with a report.

# 116 Travel Info Update: Biztravel

Name of Program: Biztravel Unwired
E-Mail Address: customerservice@biztravel.com
Web Address: http://www.biztravel.com
Version: 2.0
Type of Software: Freeware
Cost: Free

Holy cow! You may never need a computer or travel agent again. With Biztravel Unwired, you can book air, rental car, and hotel reservations through your Palm-powered PDA. Just tell it where and when you want to go, and it can set up the reservations. To make reservations, you must become a Biztravel member, but even if you don't want to join, you can still get up-to-the-minute flight departure and arrival times plus gate and terminal assignments from Biztravel. It also provides flight schedules, fares, and seat availability information and hotel and car rental information. Best of all, it only tells you what is *really* available, so the hotels or cars or flights it offers are those that have rooms or vehicles available or seats that aren't booked.

Once you sign up, you can expect the following help from Biztravel in arranging everything from your Lincoln Town Car limo to tickets for next year's World Series.

- ◆ You can automatically request automated airline upgrades, whether you are flying on a qualifying coach fare, you have frequent-flyer status, or you use an upgrade coupon. Also, you will receive notification of your upgrade via e-mail.

- ◆ You can use FareGuard to search for the lowest fare up until the time of departure and to alert you if it finds a better price.

- ◆ You can use CalendarDirect to automatically import your Biztravel.com itinerary into your calendar software on your Palm.

## Getting Started with Biztravel

Follow these steps to stay in touch and on time with Biztravel:

1. From the Biztravel main screen, tap your choice of these options: Flight Status, Flight Availability, Hotel Reservations, or Rental Car Reservations.

2. Fill in the information requested.

3. Follow the directions to complete your travel planning.

# 117 Travel with Fodor's

Name of Program: Fodors.com
E-Mail Address: http://www.fodors.com/about/write/
Web Address: http://fodors.com/mobile/
Type of Software: Freeware
Cost: Free

Fodor's, longtime publisher of travel guides, offers a Web clipping application that provides information on thousands of hotels and restaurants in numerous cities across the U.S. The Palm.Net service accesses Fodors.com's Web content for free in real time to provide this information, so you won't need to synchronize your handheld with a Desktop computer. Fodors.com is also available for free through AvantGo using a sync through the computer and a couple of other programs.

# 118 Maps and More Maps: HandMap

Name of Programs: HandMap, HandMap Deluxe, HandMap Pro
E-Mail Address: support@evolutionary.net
Web Address: http://www.handmap.net
Version: 3.1
Type of Software: Freeware, Shareware
Cost: Free (HandMap), $16 (HandMap Deluxe), $35 (HandMap Pro)

With HandMap and its variations, you can know a city like the Palm in your hand. And, HandMap Deluxe and Pro are doubly handy because they can read maps created with MapIt, a popular map-making program. The three variations of HandMap are priced according to varying needs. The basic HandMap has a nice selection of features for free. HandMap Deluxe adds Address Book links, clearer maps, and a third-party map-reading capability.

The top-of-the-line HandMap Pro offers these features:

◆ Full GPS (Global Positioning System) tracking capabilities

◆ U.S. county map viewing

◆ Viewing of third-party maps created with MapIt (`www.handmap.net/mapit.htm`)

◆ Address Book links

◆ Map rendering using diagonal street labels

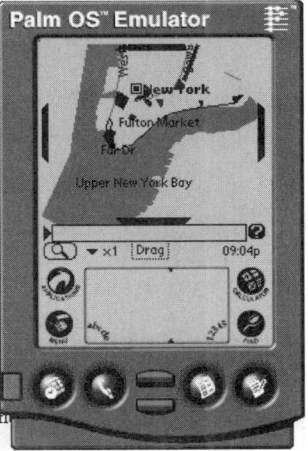

## Getting Started with HandMap

Make a right on Broadway and follow these instructions to find out where to go next:

**1.** After you install HandMap and at least one map module, tap on the HandMap icon. The program opens with the first map that it finds at the initial zoom level, called x1.

**2.** Press the Up hardware button to zoom in, doubling the magnification at each zoom level. Press the Down hardware button to zoom out, which cuts the magnification by half at each level.

**3.** Tap on a map feature. Notice that it flashes, and HandMap identifies it in a little window at the bottom of the screen.

**4.** Tap on the scroll tabs that line each side of the screen to scroll the map one-half the screen in the direction you specify.

**5.** Tap the Magnifying Glass icon at the bottom of the screen. Choose the For Name option from the pop-up list. Start entering the name of the street or landmark you're looking for, and a list will appear. Tap on your choice, then tap Go To.

**6.** The location you specified now appears flashing on the screen.

**7.** Tap the Magnifying Glass icon and choose For Intersection. Enter the street names and tap Go To. You'll now see the intersection, also flashing.

**8.** Tap the square at the bottom of the screen that reads Drag. Select Calc Dist from the pop-up menu. Tap and drag your stylus across the map; the distance (in miles) covered on the map appears in the text bar at the bottom of the screen.

**9.** Tap the same square and select Show Coord. Tap a spot on the map, and the latitude and longitude coordinates appear in the text bar.

## HandMap: The Important Commands

Here are the important HandMap commands.

| Menu | Command | Shortcut | What It Does |
|---|---|---|---|
| View | Options | /O | Lets you personalize map views |
| Search | For Name | None | Searches for street or landmark name |
| Mode | Normal | None | Pops up street and landmark names when you tap the stylus on the screen |
| Mode | Drag | None | Scrolls map when you drag the stylus on the screen |
| Mode | Calc Dist | None | Reveals distance when you drag the stylus over the screen |

| Menu | Command | Shortcut | What It Does |
|------|---------|----------|--------------|
| Mode | Show Coord | None | Reveals geographic coordinates when you tap on the screen |

# 119 Staying in the Zone: Location Manager

Name of Program: Location Manager
E-Mail Address: locmgr@star-pilot.com
Web Address: http://www.star-pilot.com/locmgr/
Version: 1.50
Type of Software: Freeware
Cost: Free

Don't you just hate it when you have to reset your time zone in several applications when you travel? Location Manager lets you set your location once and change it easily as you change time zones. It will even adjust for daylight saving time automatically (unless you tell it not to). You can add custom locations, too, for the places you go that aren't on Location Manager's database, or choose to use a different location database. Location Manager utillizes a single interface that works with more than one program.

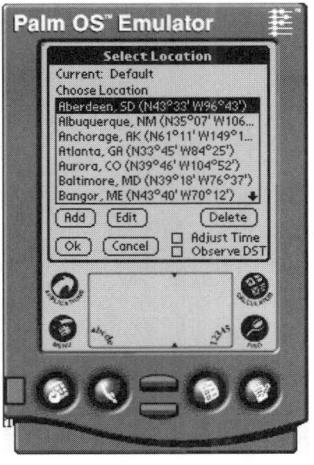

## Getting Started with Location Manager

Follow these steps and stay in the right zone:

1. The opening screen, Select Location, displays the cities in Location Manager's standard database. It goes from Aberdeen, South Dakota, to Worcester, Massachusetts. Find and highlight your location.

2. If you want Location Manager to calculate daylight saving time, check the box next to Observer DST.

3. Tap OK.

4. When you change locations, select a new location. If your new location is in a different time zone, Location Manager automatically checks the Adjust Time box. Tap OK, and all of your Palm clocks will set to your new time zone.

5. To add a location not included on the database, tap Add, and fill in the blanks for the location's latitude, longitude, and time zone.

# 120 Take the A Train: Metro

Name of Program: Metro
E-Mail Address: patriceb@worldnet.fr (program) or
frank.vancaenegem@worldonline.fr (subway data)
Web Address: http://home.worldnet.fr/~patriceb/Technique/
Main.html?main=Metro/Metro-en.html
Version: 2.2.6
Type of Software: Freeware
Cost: Free

Forget complicated subway maps; Metro can tell you the shortest route and (if different) the route with the fewest connections on more than 140 subway networks around the world. The handiest databases are those—such as for Chicago, Paris, and Hiroshima—that provide a list for places of interest as well as for train lines, to make your route planning easier. The lines are updated weekly, and the program comes in 10 languages, including Chinese, Russian, and Portuguese.

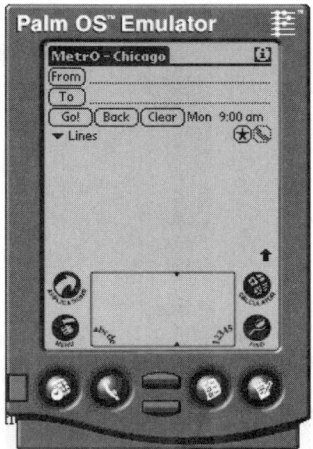

## Getting Started with Metro

Remember that most subways don't allow eating, but you will get there by following these instructions:

**1.** Delete any version older than 2.2.0, then download the latest version (in your desired language) and install the software. Once the app is installed on your PC, read the User Guide and select the cities desired.

**2.** Go to the Options menu; select Network.

**3.** Choose the city whose subway system you want to use. Tap OK.

**4.** Enter the name of station you're leaving from, or select it from the Lines list.

**5.** Enter the station you're going to.

**6.** Tap Go.

**7.** Tap Back to determine your return trip.

**8.** You can also copy and paste the results into another application.

## Metro: The Important Commands

Here are the important Metro commands.

| Menu | Command | Shortcut | What It Does |
| --- | --- | --- | --- |
| Edit | Cut | /X | Cuts selected text and saves it to the Clipboard |
| Edit | Copy | /X | Copies text and saves it to the Clipboard |
| Edit | Paste | /P | Pastes text from the Clipboard |
| Edit | Keyboard | /K | Uses the keyboard to enter information |
| Edit | Graffiti | /G | Uses graffiti to enter information |
| Options | Network | /N | Lets you choose a different city's subway system |
| Options | Preferences | /P | Lets you select user preferences |
| Options | About Metro | None | Tells all about the Metro application |

# 121 Did You Remember to Pack It?: My Luggage

Name of Program: My Luggage
E-Mail Address: sales@palmsoftnet.com
Web Address: http://www.palmsoftnet.com/myluggage/index.htm
Version: 1.0
Type of Software: Shareware
Cost: $5.50

If you're forever losing that list of things to take on your next trip, or if you just haven't gotten the hang of packing well, you need My Luggage. With this reasonably priced shareware, you can use My Luggage's list or make your own packing list on your never-to-be-lost PDA. Then you can check off things as you pack them. You'll know not only what to pack, but whether or not you packed it.

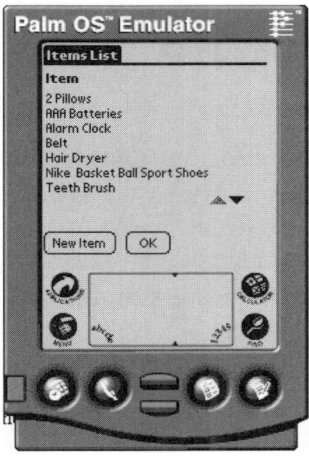

## Getting Started with My Luggage

You won't forget your belt, your red socks, or your list with My Luggage:

1. On that blank first screen (the first time you open My Luggage), tap New to create a packing list.

2. Fill in as many of the blanks as you'd like: Luggage/Bag, Who, Trip, Date (has a pop-up calendar), and Size.

3. Tap CheckList. Each drop-down arrow lists possible packing items from which you can select. Highlight an item you want listed, and My Luggage adds it to your list. When you finish, tap OK. Tap OK again on the Details screen.

4. Tap Items on the main screen. Tap New Item to add to the decidedly limited list that comes with the demo version. You have to register, however, to add to the list.

# 122 Flight Information on the Fly: OAG Mobile

Name of Program: OAG Mobile (with or without wireless Internet access)
E-Mail Address: helpdesk@oag.com
Web Address: http://www.oag.com
Version: 1.1
Type of Software: Commercial
Cost: $59.00

OAG Mobile puts airline information at your fingertips. For those PDAs with wireless Internet access, OAG Mobile provides up-to-the-minute information on flights worldwide. Plus, you can get such other useful travel information as airline telephone numbers, airport ATM information, and hotel reservation phone numbers.

On the regular version, you can download schedules for pairs of cities (say, for Memphis and Detroit) for later reference, and update them every week or so. It will store your PDA schedules for 5 different round trips or 10 unique city pairs. The Internet version even lets you set yourself up for e-mail notification of flight information.

## Getting Started with OAG Mobile

Be where you need to be when you need to be there.

1. From the main window, your choices are Flight Schedules, Reservation Numbers, or the Airport Services Guide. For Internet versions, the choices are Flight Schedules, Flight Status, and E-Notification. For this example, tap Flight Schedules.

2. Enter your departure city, your destination, and the date and approximate time you want to travel. Tap Find Flights.

**3.** The Flight Results screen reports information on available flights, including flight numbers, arrival and departure times, and the types of planes on the route. On the version without Internet access, tap Reservation #s to get the airline's toll-free reservation telephone number.

On the Internet version, tap Availability to find out whether the flight has room for you.

# 123 Get There from Here: Quo Vadis

Name of Program: Quo Vadis
E-Mail Address: info@marcosoft.com
Web Address: http://www.marcosoft.com
Version: 2.0, 2.0c
Type of Software: Commercial
Cost: $44.95; $49.95 for color

You'll never have to fold a map again with Quo Vadis. But what good is a 2-inch map, you say? Besides being compact, of course, these 2-inch maps are great because you can zoom in or out to many levels and you can scroll your maps in any direction with a mere drag of the stylus. Street names appear in the larger scale maps. The scrolling goes fast, but a little practice using the zooming and scrolling features will help you get the most out of the maps.

Even better, Quo Vadis includes full GPS support and tracking, which means your actual position will appear on the map and move as you move. The maps cover the 50 U.S. states, U.S. territories, and even many small towns; a total of 23,000 are available. The maps also include cute little symbols for such travel necessities as golf courses and shopping centers. Oh, yes, and airports, too. Of course, having all these features means that you won't have any excuse for getting lost again.

# Getting Started with Quo Vadis

Follow these steps so you'll know exactly where you are in the Grand Canyon:

**1.** Tap Mode, then tap Directory.

**2.** Select the map you wish to use.

**3.** Tap View.

**4.** Under the Options menu, tap Find.

**5.** Select your current location or starting point from the list provided. The location will then appear on your map with a bull's-eye.

**6.** Under the Navigate menu, tap Select Destination. Choose your destination from the same list. Your destination will appear as an X on the map.

**7.** The tracker, a circle with a short line extending from it in the center of your screen, will point the direction from your current location to your destination.

**8.** Tap and hold your stylus to the screen to choose Zoom In or Zoom Out, or write the letter **i** or **o** on your graffiti pad.

**9.** Scroll a map by dragging your stylus toward the area you wish to see, or tap the screen in the direction you want to see more of.

# Quo Vadis: The Important Commands

Here are the important Quo Vadis commands.

| Menu | Command | Shortcut | What It Does |
|---|---|---|---|
| Mode | Directory | /D | Lists maps you've downloaded |
| Mode | GPS | /J | Shows GPS settings |
| Mode | Map | /M | Switches to Map view |
| Options | Help | /H | Provides context-sensitive help |
| Options | Find | /F | Lets you find and mark current location |
| Options | Preferences | /R | Selects details for map display |

| Menu | Command | Shortcut | What It Does |
|------|---------|----------|--------------|
| **Navigate** | **Select Destination** | **None** | **Lets you find and mark destination** |
| **Navigate** | **GPS Position On/Off** | **None** | **Turns on GPS positioning** |

# 124 Never Ask for Directions Again: StreetFinder Deluxe

Name of Program: StreetFinder Deluxe
E-Mail Address: webmaster@randmcnally.com
Web Address: http://www.randmcnally.com
Type of Software: Commercial
Cost: $49.95

Noted mapmaker Rand McNally applies its expertise to the really small screen with StreetFinder Deluxe. After you get directions from one address to another from the Internet, you can download the directions—along with the map (like the one you see here)—to your Palm. It also has full GPS support to help you find your way.

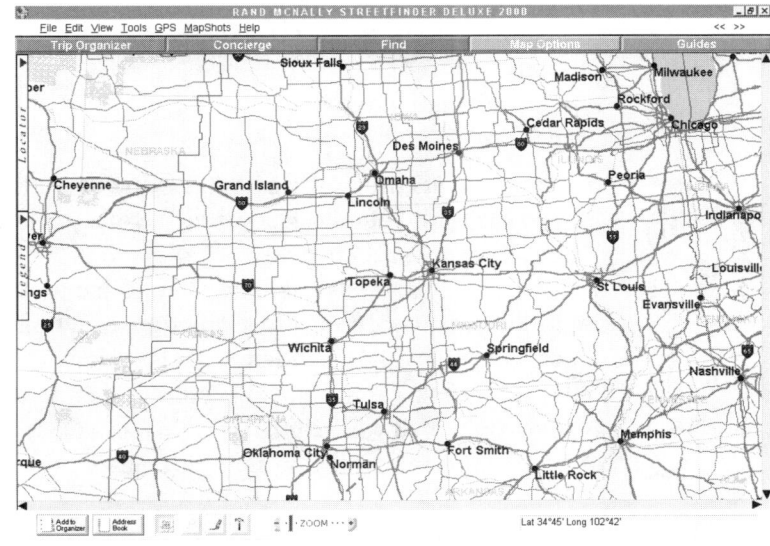

StreetFinder has a ton of features including finding restaurants and museums close to your location, specifying the longitude and latitude of your location (just in case!), measuring distances, and even providing important addresses from your Address Book. It also features Mobil Travel Guide listings and ratings for restaurants and hotels, and it includes recommendations for the best in food, lodging, and nightlife for 100 cities.

### Getting Started with StreetFinder

Make a left, or make a right? How about using StreetFinder instead?

1. Using the Windows-based version of the software, create the map you want to use by clicking MapShots ➤ Export to Palm Organizers.

2. HotSync, and your map will show up on your Palm. It's easy and very cool.

# 125 Trips Are More Fun with One: Travel Pal

Name of Program: Travel Pal
E-Mail Address: info@zingware.com
Web Address: http://www.zingware.com
Version: 1.5
Type of Software: Shareware
Cost: $24.95

Travel Pal covers the bases, from time and currency conversions to itinerary and car rental details. Its currency converter is the easiest and clearest of any I've seen, and Zingware promises to provide weekly online updates to the currency database. It allows you to see the details for any trip from the Itinerary screen, and Travel Pal's time function synchronizes your Palm's system clock to your trip itinerary. It also has an alarm you can set. If you like bells and whistles, it has pretty pictures—of a rotating Earth, for example—in color, no less (if you've got the right Palm OS unit). I can't promise they'll keep you entertained if your flight is delayed, however.

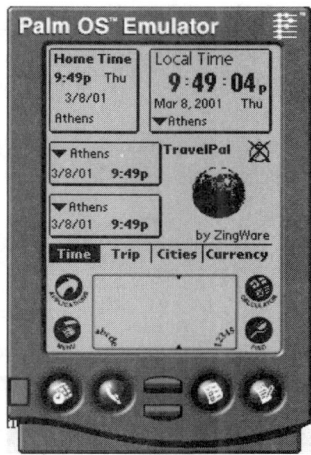

# Getting Started with Travel Pal

Three shekels equals how many dollars?

**1.** At startup, select your home location from the list.

**2.** Select up to three more locations.

**3.** Tap Trip to record your itinerary.

**4.** Tap Add to add a trip. Select Auto Rent, Transport, or Lodging, and fill in the blanks.

**5.** Tap Done.

**6.** For a quick look at your itinerary, go to the Trip screen and tap the appropriate icon at the top of the screen: the Jet icon for transportation info, Jet C for connections information, the House icon for accommodation, and the Car for car rental information. Then touch and hold on the trip you're interested in from your list of trips. The transportation details, for example, will appear on your screen as long as you hold the stylus down.

**7.** Tap Currency. Enter the value you want to convert, identify its currency type, and the currency type you wish to convert it to.

**8.** Tap Cities. Tap and hold on the city you want more information about, and Travel Pal will reveal its time zone and local currency.

## Travel Pal: The Important Commands

Here are the important Travel Pal commands.

| Menu | Command | Shortcut | What It Does |
| --- | --- | --- | --- |
| Edit | Copy | /C | Copies entry |
| Edit | Cut | /X | Cuts entry |
| Edit | Paste | /C | Pastes cut or copied text |
| TimeZone | Set Home Time Zone | None | Lets you reset your home time zone |
| Time Zone | Set Itinerary | None | Goes to Trip screen |
| Time Zone | Set Device Date & Time | None | Allows you to set the time and date of your Palm |
| Prefs | AM/PM Format | None | Sets A.M. and P.M. time display |
| Prefs | Military Format | None | Displays time in military format |

# 126 What a Long, Great Trip It's Been: Trip and Trip Deluxe

Name of Programs: Trip, Trip Deluxe
E-Mail Address: info@handshigh.com
Web Address: http://www.handshigh.com/html/trip.html
Version: Trip 3.01, Trip Deluxe 3.0
Type of Software: Commercial
Cost: $19.95 for Trip, $29.95 for Trip Deluxe

Trip and Trip Deluxe give you an easy way to keep track of your mileage for business, charitable, and any other reasons. You just need to enter your odometer reading, and the program figures the miles for you. Then you pick a category (such as Business or Charitable), and it will show your miles for that category only.

When you HotSync, Trip Deluxe automatically transfers your mileage reports to an Excel spreadsheet (you'll need to have Excel already, of course). With regular Trip, you can export to your Palm Expense program or to the Memo Pad.

Maybe you have a veritable fleet of cars. No problem. Trip and Trip Deluxe let you keep track of the mileage for up to 16 vehicles. Also, this pair of programs will make reporting your miles for tax purposes super-easy.

## Getting Started with Trip and Trip Deluxe

Follow these directions to get started with Trip:

1. After starting up Trip, choose Edit Cars from the drop-down menu.

2. Write in the name of the car whose expenses you want to track. Tap Done.

3. Tap New to record a trip.

4. Select the car for the trip; enter the starting and ending dates, time, and mileage. (The defaults are the current time and date and last recorded miles.)

5. Record the who, where, and why of the trip.

6. Tap on the Unfiled box in the top right of the screen, and select a category for the mileage type.

7. Look at all your mileage from the All selection in the main window, or tap the triangle and select a category, such as Business, to see the miles for that category only.

8. If you have Trip Deluxe, your Trip data will automatically export to your desktop computer every time you HotSync. Trip Deluxe includes a preprogrammed, customizable Excel spreadsheet that will automatically import your Trip data and format it into a mileage report.

## Trip and Trip Deluxe: The Important Commands

Here are the important Trip Deluxe commands.

| Menu | Command | Shortcut | What It Does |
|---|---|---|---|
| Options | Edit Cars | /E | Lets you add or delete cars to track |
| Options | Export | /X | Lets you export data to other applications |
| Options | Purge | /G | Purges records before a date you designate |

# 127 Get the Scoop on Going Out: Vindigo

Name of Program: Vindigo
E-Mail Address: http://www.vindigo.com/help/email.html
Web Address: http://www.vindigo.com/
Version: 1.0
Type of Software: Freeware
Cost: Free

Vindigo packs a lot of information in your Palm. Just tell Vindigo what you want in the way of shopping, restaurants, or nightlife, and it will tell you the latest on what is available in your city. You can browse through listings of restaurants and cafes in a variety of categories, or check out the shopping nearby. You can even have more than one city on your Palm.

To get the most up-to-date information, you'll need to sync your Palm OS device to your Desktop computer while connected to the Internet. And every time you synchronize your handheld to your Desktop while it's online, Vindigo is automatically updated. The movie listings alone are worth the trouble of updating.

One downside—or advantage, depending on your point of view—is that Vindigo uses ads. Say, for example, you're looking at information about an Indian restaurant in your Washington, D.C., neighborhood. An ad might appear at the bottom of your screen advising you that another restaurant, which it names, is nearby. The ads can be easily ignored, but you can choose to view the information about the advertised item if you tap the spot specified.

## Getting Started with Vindigo

Shop until you drop and know where you're going with Vindigo:

1. From the opening What screen, you can choose from the Eat, Shop, Play, or Give options. For this example, tap Eat.

2. The next screen, which tells who (it varies by city) provided the content, lets you select from different restaurant types. Tap the type you're interested in.

3. Tap the name of a specific restaurant you want to know more about.

4. A window with four tabs appears. The Detail tab, which is at the top, lists the telephone number and address of the establishment. Tap the Features drop-down arrow to get more information about the food.

5. Tap the Review tab to see what reviewers say about the place.

6. Tap Go to get walking directions from your home locale (which you set on the Vindigo home page).

7. Tap the Notes tab to record your own impressions and to add the restaurant to your personal list on Vindigo.

8. If you don't like the current selection, tap the left arrow at the top of the screen to go back to the previous screen and look at other restaurants.

9. Make another selection, or change your criteria for selecting. If you've been looking at the options by distance, for example, try finding a location by street intersection or by neighborhood. Tap OK.

10. To go back to the opening screen, tap the little Home icon at the top of the Vindigo screen.

11. The Shop feature works just like the Eat feature, except that there's no Review tab.

12. When you tap the Play feature, your next option will be Movies or Nightlife.

13. With the Movies option, the categories are Venue, which is a list of movie houses, and Movie Type, such as Action or Thriller. Thanks to regular updating, you will be able to see what movies are currently playing and at what times. Cool!

14. Once a week or so, update the listings by HotSynching while you're online.

## Vindigo: The Important Commands

Here are the important Vindigo commands.

| Menu | Command | Shortcut | What It Does |
|------|---------|----------|--------------|
| Edit | Undo | /U | Undoes last action |
| Edit | Cut | /X | Cuts selection |
| Edit | Copy | /C | Copies selection |
| Edit | Paste | /P | Pastes what you've cut or copied |
| Edit | Select All | /S | Selects all text available |
| Edit | Keyboard | /K | Allows you to use the keyboard to enter information |
| Edit | Graffiti Help | /G | Accesses graffiti help |
| Options | My City Preferences | /R | Lets you select the City database to be searched |
| Options | Submit New Listing | None | Lets you suggest additions to Vindigo |

# 128 Globe-Hopper's Companion: WorldMate

Name of Program: WorldMate
E-Mail Address: WorldMate@MobiMate.com
Web Address: http://www.MobiMate.com/worldmate/index.html
Version: 5.0
Type of Software: Shareware
Cost: $15

WorldMate provides four handy functions for international travelers: currency conversion, time conversion, clothing size conversion chart, and measurement conversion. If you can figure out where you are, it can tell you what your dollar or guilder is worth and what time it is locally and back home. If you are a registered user, you can add time zones, currency types, and other options as fits your personal needs. WorldMate works fairly intuitively, which is nice, even if it leaves a few things to puzzle over. For example, what does the abbreviation "kn" stand for? (It's found under the speed conversions, so "knots" is my best guess, but still....)

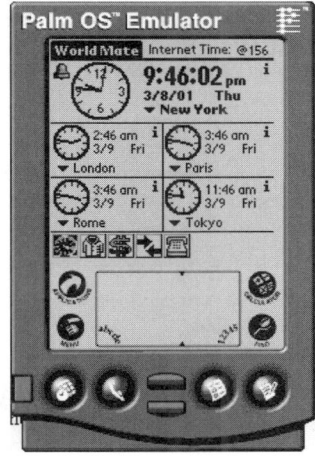

## Getting Started with WorldMate

Use WorldMate by following these steps:

1. Enter your home time and time zone as directed. (If you're anywhere in North America except in the eastern time zone, you'll have to add your city or zone to the list provided.)

2. The Clocks screen appears, showing the time in four other world cities. You can change the cities selected.

3. Tap Clothes (or the Shirt icon) to see the clothing size charts (displayed in U.S., U.K., and European sizes).

4. Tap Currencies (or the Money icon) to make money conversions between any of two dozen currencies.

5. Tap Converts to figure weights and measures, including speeds, in up to three different units at a time.

## WorldMate: The Important Commands

Here are the important WorldMate commands.

| Menu | Command | Shortcut | What It Does |
|------|---------|----------|--------------|
| Tabs | Clocks | /1 | Goes to the Clocks screen |
| Tabs | Clothes | /2 | Goes to clothing size charts |
| Tabs | Currencies | /3 | Goes to currency conversion |
| Tabs | Converts | /4 | Goes to measurement conversions |
| Tabs | International | /5 | Goes to Telephones screen |
| Edit | Undo | /U | Undoes typing |
| Edit | Copy | /C | Copies entry |
| Edit | Cut | /X | Cuts entry |
| Edit | Paste | /P | Pastes cut or copied text |
| Edit | Select All | /A | Selects all entries |
| Edit | Graffiti | /G | Shows graffiti writing strokes |
| Options | Preferences | /R | Customizes clocks |

# Appendix:
# The Best Palm
# Application List
# in the Universe

**TABLE A.1:** Business' Best

| Application | On CD? | Description |
| --- | --- | --- |
| **Abacus**<br>www.pmdc.pt/abacus<br>dvit@ceeeta.pt | | Advanced spreadsheet with 60 functions and a very friendly user interface. |
| **All Money**<br>www.iambic.com/pilot/allmoney/default.htm<br>support@iambic.com | X | Capture your personal expense and income data with three easy-to-use screens. |
| **BankBook**<br>www.bahsoftware.com<br>customerservice@bahsoftware.com | | Track your checking, savings, and other accounts. |
| **BizExpense**<br>south.dynip.com/~wilper/software.html<br>cwilper@yahoo.com | | For the business traveler. Track your business expense information and keep your manager happy with a timely expense report. |
| **Date Chart**<br>www.aloha.net/~malan<br>malan@aloha.net | | Displays a Gantt chart of selected events (or appointments) from the built-in Date Book application. View your selected Date Book entries as project tasks. |
| **Date Wheel**<br>www.members.tripod.com/~DeftSoft/DateWheel/<br>  index.html<br>DeftSoft@mailcity.com | | Electronic version of the plastic wheel-shaped calendar used by businesses to calculate lead times. |
| **Equipment Log**<br>www.palmgear.com/software/showsoftware.cfm<br>  ?sid=18607720001011234641&prodID=9434<br>jrbetts@hotmail.com | X | Track your possessions for insurance purposes or to recover stolen property. Keeps date, item, make, model, color, serial number, cost, and payment method. Also allows storage of your insurance information and emergency phone numbers for police and fire. |

**TABLE A.1:** Business' Best *(continued)*

| Application | On CD? | Description |
| --- | --- | --- |
| **HelpDesk**<br>www.thinkingbytes.com<br>custsvc@thinkingbytes.com | | An easy way to record customer-service response times or order-fulfillment time. |
| **Human Resources**<br>www.thinkingbytes.com<br>custsvc@thinkingbytes.com | | Manage all aspects of Human Resources. |
| **Info Select**<br>www.miclog.com/ispdesc.htm<br>twolf@cpinews.com | X | Powerful outliner that offers organization of assorted information, fast searches, and intelligent synchronization capabilities. |
| **Job Listings**<br>www.thinkingbytes.com<br>custsvc@thinkingbytes.com | | Whether you're looking to hire somebody, you are a recruiter, or you are looking for a job yourself, this tool allows you to keep all your job listings on your Palm and exchange them on the fly. |
| **Lease-It**<br>www.pe.net/firm/dpw-designs<br>dpw-designs@pe.net | X | Fast, flexible, and easy-to-use lease calculator. Use it to help you negotiate the best possible deal on a lease, analyze where your money is going, and take the mystery out of leasing. |
| **MAM Easy**<br>www.mamsuite.com<br>info@mamsuite.com | | State-of-the-art financial management application. Allows tracking transactions in both domestic and foreign currencies. |
| **Meeting Chaser**<br>www.thinkingbytes.com<br>custsvc@thinkingbytes.com | | Relational database designed to plan and track meeting activity. |
| **My Housekeeper**<br>www.palmsoftnet.com<br>sales@palmsoftnet.com | | Tracks everything in your household. All records sorted and filtered by the categories that you define, even your rental movies. |

**TABLE A.1:** Business' Best *(continued)*

| Application | On CD? | Description |
| --- | --- | --- |
| **Pocket Pareto**<br>amsoftw.tripod.com<br>skooner@aol.com | | Allows you to analyze how much time you spend on several daily tasks and decide which need more time, which are taking too much, and which are just right! |
| **Porta Sales**<br>www.monkey-ware.com/products.html<br>sales@monkey-ware.com | | Database to store sales and commission info with detailed customer, purchasing agent, and order (product, services, other) capability. |
| **Project Punch**<br>www.geocities.com/projpunch<br>oguri_joe@bigfoot.com | | Project management program; a personal project manager with an integrated task punch clock. |
| **SalaryMate**<br>www.thinkingbytes.com<br>custsvc@thinkingbytes.com | | Tells you what the average salary of a position should be. |
| **Sales Call**<br>www.thinkingbytes.com<br>custsvc@thinkingbytes.com | | Sales Call Companies stores the company name and address of the phone sales caller. Sales Call Tracker stores the time, date, and company and keeps track if you asked them to put you on their Do Not Call list. |
| **Titrax**<br>jack.testnetz.detecon.net/software<br>Bernd.Esser@testnetz.detecon.net | | Time-management tool that helps you to keep track of time spent on various projects. |
| **TL Palm**<br>www.timeledger.com<br>xdao@attilaweb.com | | (TimeLedger Palm) Freeware; you can synchronize your Palm into www.timeledger.com, and can record time, expense, and mileage entries into your Palm. |
| **Tracer**<br>www.ptshome.com/tracer.htm<br>bhorn@ptshome.com | X | Customizable inventory program. |

**TABLE A.2:** 1,234,576$^{10}$: Calculate Anything and Everything

| Application | On CD? | Description |
| --- | --- | --- |
| **Abacus?**<br>questions.hyperlink.cz<br>antonin.holik@seznam.cz | | Simulation of an abacus; can be used to keep score in games like pool or darts. |
| **Add Util**<br>edwitkowski@hotmail.com | X | Paperless adding machine: add, subtract, or whatever just as you would on paper! |
| **Auto Lease Calculator**<br>josh@wainer.org | | Calculates monthly lease payments; provides the ability to select a negotiated price or base the lease payment on the dealer invoice price + profit amount you set − dealer hold-back %. |
| **BabyCalc**<br>dzimmer@his.com | | Helps determine the important dates during a pregnancy. |
| **Converter**<br>www.matt.oaktree.co.uk/computing/palmpilot.shtml<br>matt.marsh@bigfoot.com | | Converts miles/kilometers, Celsius/Fahrenheit, clothing and shoe sizes, radioactivity types, and more. |
| **Drunk!**<br>www.palm.freeurl.com<br>k3@iobox.fi | | Calculates the amount of alcohol in your blood. |
| **EasyCalc**<br>easycalc.sourceforge.net<br>ondrap@penguin.cz | | Scientific calculator with trigonometric functions, complex numbers, graphs, unlimited number of variables, degree/radian mode, hex/oct/bin/dec conversions, and more. |
| **Fraction Calculator**<br>mew3.com/mew3/palm/FraCalc/index.html<br>wilborne@gamewood.net | X | Four-function calculator for use with fractions. |
| **Geo Magnetic Info**<br>home.twcny.rr.com/dwbray/palm<br>dbray@twcny.rr.com | | Computes the magnetic declination, inclination, and magnitude for any location on Earth. |

**TABLE A.2:** 1,234,576[10]: Calculate Anything and Everything *(continued)*

| Application | On CD? | Description |
|---|---|---|
| **Internet Download Time Calc**<br>www.geocities.com/CapeCanaveral/Lab/9176/<br>  sumbang.html<br>arto88@dnet.net.id | | Calculates the download time for every connection speed. Also has a timer function to show remaining time for download. |
| **Lightning**<br>home.att.net/~foursquaredev/Lightning<br>foursquaredev@worldnet.att.net | | Many people know how to estimate the distance to lightning by counting the time between the flash and the thunder, and dividing by 5 to get the number of miles. Lightning is a simple app that does just that. |
| **LoanWizard Pro**<br>www.mindweave.com/loanwizpro<br>info@mindweave.com | | Versatile mortgage and loan manager; tracks multiple loans for all your customers or properties. Solve for loan amounts, monthly payments, interest rates, and duration. |
| **MedCalc**<br>medcalc.med-ia.net<br>medcalc@hotmail.com | | Medical calculator. |
| **MedMath**<br>mail.med.upenn.edu/~pcheng/medmath<br>pcheng@mail.med.upenn.edu | | Medical calculator, written by a physician for rapid calculation of common formulas in adult internal medicine. |
| **MoneyBox**<br>website.lineone.net/~caitcif<br>caitcif@lineone.net | | Sharing a house or holiday and finding it hard to split the bills? This program does all the calculations for you and reduces the number of payments to the minimum possible. It gives you a balance for each person and tells you who owes money to whom to solve all the balances. |

**TABLE A.2:** 1,234,576[10]: Calculate Anything and Everything *(continued)*

| Application | On CD? | Description |
|---|---|---|
| **Planetarium**<br>www.aho.ch/pilotplanets<br>aho@aho.ch | X | Calculates the position of the sun, the moon, and all the planets for any time and geographical position. Can also be used as a compass when the sun or moon is visible. |
| **Roman**<br>www.collectorbob.com<br>collectorbob@hotmail.com | X | Convert numbers up to 4,999 between Roman and Arabic numbers. |
| **SalaryUtil**<br>www.witkowski-design.com<br>ed@witkowski-design.com | | Calculates your *true* hourly rate (whether salaried or not) and compares it to your new job offer! |
| **Sol! II**<br>mew3.com/mew3/palm/sol/index.html<br>wilborne@gamewood.net | | Computes sunrise, sunset, day length, start and end of civil, nautical, and astronomical twilight, and length of day with twilight times added for any location on the planet. |
| **StockCalc**<br>people.ne.mediaone.net/aubin/ddt.html<br>aubin@mediaone.net | X | Calculates the number of shares, both high- and low-water stock sell price, and after-trade cash balance, given the stock purchase price and pre-trade cash balance. Even takes into account SEC and trade fees. |
| **Tax Calc**<br>www.macbride.com/pilot/index.html<br>macbride@macbride.com | | Calculates the amount of city and county transfer tax in a real estate transaction. |
| **The Athlete's Calculator**<br>www.stevenscreek.com/pilot/tac.shtml<br>sales@stevenscreek.com | X | Specialized calculator for runners, cyclists, swimmers, triathletes, and other fitness enthusiasts. |
| **Your Age In...**<br>integra_se@hotmail.com | | Your age in dog, cat, cockatiel, and turtle years. |

**TABLE A.3:** Does Anyone Really Know What Time It Is?: Clocks and Calendars

| Application | On CD? | Description |
| --- | --- | --- |
| **anaClock**<br>members.nbci.com/palmadd/index.htm<br>support@palmpadd.com | | Fills the Palm screen with a large analog clock, complete with a moving second hand. |
| **Annual Batteries**<br>members.tripod.com/yhdoo/PocketBowling.html<br>yhdoo@hotmail.com | | Battery indicators to keep annual events. Displays your important annual events, sorted so you know which is next, and counts down the days to each event. |
| **DiddleBug**<br>blevins.simplenet.com/palm<br>mblevin@debian.org | X | Electronic sticky note that you can set with an alarm to remind you of appointments or other things. |
| **Foto Timer**<br>jerusalem.usc.uni-karlsruhe.de/~exner/astro/<br>  software.html<br>Jan.Exner@gmx.net | X | Beeps every x seconds. Use it to make long-time photographic exposures. |
| **Get Ready**<br>www.palmsoftnet.com/getready/index.htm<br>sales@palmsoftnet.com | | Helps you organize your Christmas shopping and track all Christmas card send/receive status. |
| **HandBBall**<br>hotfiles.zdnet.com/cgi-bin/texis/swlib/hotfiles/<br>  info.html?fcode=001CK5&b=zdpalm | | Allows you to set up and keep score for different basketball teams. |
| **HappyDays**<br>www.jmjeong.com/palm/happydays/<br>jmjeong@oopsla.snu.ac.kr | X | Helps you remember birthdays and anniversaries of your friends and family members. |
| **HowLongToGo**<br>www.rubens.org.uk/howlong<br>paul.rubens@lineone.net | X | If you've got kids, you'll be familiar with incessant "How Long To Go till my birthday?" "Till school's out?" "Till Grandma comes to visit?" questions. HowLongToGo is powerful but simple: enter and save up to five events and see at a glance how many days to go. |

**TABLE A.3:** Does Anyone Really Know What Time It Is?: Clocks and Calendars *(continued)*

| Application | On CD? | Description |
| --- | --- | --- |
| **Less Than Zero**<br>www.palmosoft.com/palmous/index-us.htm<br>palmosoft@edisons.it | | Good for cooking pasta, for use as a timer, or for scheduling HotSync to run at night. |
| **MayaDate**<br>www.waxwolf.com/palm<br>twickel@waxwolf.com | | Ever wanted to see what day it would be on the ancient Mayan calendars? |
| **Moon Phase**<br>home.att.net/~sckienle/palm/home<br>  .html#Software#Software<br>sckienle@worldnet.att.net | | Graphically displays the phase of the moon for any day. |
| **Pocket Watch+**<br>www.focus-sw.com<br>Palmsoft@focus-sw.com | X | Turns your handheld into a pocket watch. When you turn on your handheld with the power-on button, Pocket Watch+ shows a dialog box with the current time and date for up to three seconds. |
| **Reminder**<br>home.att.net/~sckienle<br>sckienle@worldnet.att.net | | Helps you remember important dates in a manner more straightforward than trying to use your Date Book; lets you enter the date of the event, how many days' notice you want, and any other notes. |
| **SwatchHack**<br>www.quartus.net<br>info@quartus.net | X | Swatch has created a new way of measuring time, called Internet time. A day in Internet time is divided into 1,000 Swatch beats, each 1 minute 26.4 seconds long, counting from @000, which marks midnight in Switzerland. |
| **SwimTimer LT**<br>www.sundeo.com<br>paul@sundeo.com | | Times can be associated with members of the team, lane number, heat number, and event. |

**TABLE A.3:** Does Anyone Really Know What Time It Is?: Clocks and Calendars *(continued)*

| Application | On CD? | Description |
| --- | --- | --- |
| **TimeShare**<br>blevins.simplenet.com/palm<br>mblevin@debian.org | | Lets you beam the current time on your Palm to another Palm unit to set it. This way, you can push your version of the "correct time" on your friends. Also useful for international spies and bank robbers who need synchronized time schedules. |
| **Watchix**<br>www.newdatamasters.com/WatchixFree/Watchix.htm<br>info@newdatamasters.com | | Unique analog clock. It differs from other clocks in that it lets you customize its face. Select from 16 different displays (included with this package), or create your own look using the NDM Pilot Image Tool. |
| **wclockDA**<br>www04.u-page.so-net.ne.jp/zd5/kterada/pilot/<br>   index.html#wclockDA<br>kterada@iname.com | | Simple world clock; displays two clocks, which can be set to different time zones. |
| **Workout Metronome**<br>members.nbci.com/pixil/Software<br>pixel.il@usa.net | | Let Workout Metronome do the counting for you when doing repetitive exercises, such as sit-ups. |
| **Ycal**<br>www05.u-page.so-net.ne.jp/df6/kazu3/Palm/<br>   index.html<br>kazu3@df6.so-net.ne.jp | | You can see a whole year calendar in 160 x 160 screen. |
| **YearView**<br>www.eclipse.net/~reesley<br>reesley@eclipse.net | X | Displays a half year at a time. |

**TABLE A.4:** Connect from Anywhere at Any Time

| Application | On CD? | Description |
|---|---|---|
| **AccessThem**<br>www.reachthem.com<br>support@reachthem.com | X | Send a short message to anyone who has a cell phone or pager with just a click. |
| **Aileron**<br>www.corsoft.net/home.asp<br>vcare@corsoft.net | | Complete messaging support to help manage your e-mail communication with a secure, intuitive client. |
| **AreaCodes**<br>www.intrepidsoft.com/page3.html<br>cscullion@intrepidsoft.com | X | Look up area codes, geographic descriptions, and time zones by code or by state/province throughout the U.S., Canada, the Caribbean, and the Pacific. |
| **BeamBooks**<br>www.appliedthought.com/beambooks<br>support@appliedthought.com | | You can HotSync your Palm organizer with your desktop computer, but how come you can't sync your organizer with someone else's? Now you can with BeamBooks. |
| **ChaCha**<br>www.jps.net/seko/main/indexe.html<br>seko@jps.net | | Chat between two Palm via IR. |
| **Coola One-Click Doc**<br>www.coola.com<br>info@coola.com | | Helps Web sites quickly transfer documents to mobile space and wireless devices. |
| **Eudora Internet Suite**<br>www.eudora.com/internetsuite<br>eis-suggest@qualcomm.com | X | Send and receive e-mail from your Palm and Web browser. |
| **Evoke Mobile Webconferencing**<br>www.evoke.com<br>jreal@evoke.com | | Gives users the ease, convenience, and go-anywhere accessibility of the wireless world with the instant access and visual collaboration of Evoke Webconferencing. |

**TABLE A.4:** Connect from Anywhere at Any Time *(continued)*

| Application | On CD? | Description |
| --- | --- | --- |
| **Evoke Talking Email**<br>www.evoke.com<br>jreal@evoke.com | | Lets you send up to a 30-second voice message via e-mail using only a wireless device and a phone—all for free. |
| **Fax**<br>www.markspace.com/fax.html<br>brian_hall@markspace.com | X | Send and receive faxes with your Palm OS handheld. |
| **GroupPort Wireless Groupware**<br>www.groupport.com<br>support@groupserve.com | | Web-based group collaboration tool built from the ground up to support wireless technologies. Simplifies communications between project teams and mobile users, as critical business information can be accessed via any browser-based device, on any platform, from any location. |
| **IR Mail**<br>cs.wheatonma.edu/nbuggia/IrMail<br>nbuggia@wheatonma.edu | X | Allows users to beam e-mails between Palms. |
| **IrKey**<br>www.tapspring.com<br>HarryChou@TapSpring.com | X | Have you ever seen the 007 movie *Tomorrow Never Dies*? In the movie, James Bond unlocks the door of his sleek BMW with a mobile phone given to him by Mr. Q. It's cool! Now we can use our Palm III/V computer to access *any* electric door lock. |
| **IrLink**<br>www.iscomplete.com<br>Support@iscomplete.com | | Communication interface that makes infrared wireless communication possible for most programs designed to communicate with other devices via cradle. |

**TABLE A.4:** Connect from Anywhere at Any Time *(continued)*

| Application | On CD? | Description |
|---|---|---|
| **JOTbase**<br>www.chipp.com/jotbase/jotbase.htm<br>chipp@chipp.com | | JOTbase is not just another sketch-pad. In fact, it's not really a sketchpad at all. Think of it as a small notebook that you use every day to capture thoughts, phone numbers, important ideas. Later you can organize them into categories and use the filtering power of the JOTbase index to retrieve them. |
| **MonkeyTone Desktop Tool**<br>www.primatesys.com<br>support@monkeymail.com | X | Compose, edit, and install new ring-tones for your Nokia or Siemens phone from your Palm; use your own tones or select from a library of ringtones. |
| **QuickPhone**<br>www.palmpage.com/quickphone<br>quickphone@palmpage.com | | Allows you to quickly enter a phone number to your Address Book using a numeric keypad. |
| **SerialPP**<br>www.vista-software.com<br>steve@vista-software.com | | Serial port communication and file transfer program; can transfer any file through a serial connection with-out using the Palm Desktop. |
| **URL Saver**<br>hotfiles.zdnet.com/cgi-bin/texis/swlib/hotfiles/<br>   info.html?fcode=001FM6&b=zdpalm<br>shearer@popmail.com | | Keep track of those important URLs. You can also categorize URLs and rate URLs. |
| **WedgeTV**<br>home.att.net/~ah-man<br>ahmanj@worldnet.att.net | X | Palm as a remote control? Yes, it's possible today! |

**TABLE A.5:** A Place for Everything: Using Databases

| Application | On CD? | Description |
| --- | --- | --- |
| **411**<br>www.thinkingbytes.com<br>custsvc@thinkingbytes.com | | 411 keeps all your crucial telephone numbers in the palm of your hand! |
| **Airport Abbreviations DB**<br>www.pocketexpress.com<br>customerservice@pocketexpress.com | | Reference database of FAA abbreviations for U.S. airports. |
| **Barmate**<br>www.thinkingbytes.com<br>custsvc@thinkingbytes.com | | Recipes for more than 150 drinks. |
| **Bibliography**<br>take_a_break@hotmail.com | | Simple database to capture your sources when working on a research paper, book, or school assignment. |
| **eBay**<br>hotfiles.zdnet.com/cgi-bin/texis/swlib/hotfiles/<br>   info.html?fcode=00139J&b=zdpalm<br>  bluedogg19@yahoo.com | | Track bids and sales on eBay. |
| **EDrugs Database**<br>hotfiles.zdnet.com/cgi-bin/texis/swlib/hotfiles/<br>   info.html?fcode=001CZV&b=zdpalm<br>fhirning@usa.net | | Contains more than 9,000 different drug names and dosage forms, including generic name, trade names, use or class, dosage forms available, pregnancy risk category, and more. |
| **First Aid**<br>www.thinkingbytes.com<br>custsvc@thinkingbytes.com | | What to do when your baby is choking, how to treat a first-degree burn, the Heimlich maneuver, etc. |
| **Gift Shopping**<br>www.pocketexpress.com<br>customerservice@pocketexpress.com | | Keep track of gifts to buy for your friends, family, and yourself. Store names, ideas for what to get, how much to spend, where to go, what you bought last year, etc. |
| **GigTracker**<br>www.thinkingbytes.com<br>custsvc@thinkingbytes.com | | Gives the musician user the easiest way to track gigs. |

**TABLE A.5:** **A Place for Everything: Using Databases** *(continued)*

| Application | On CD? | Description |
| --- | --- | --- |
| **GolfStats**<br>hotfiles.zdnet.com/cgi-bin/texis/<br>    swlib/hotfiles/search.html<br>kellyg@trywell.freeserve.co.uk | | Helps evaluate your round of golf. Inputs the shots you played on each hole and the results rather than the score. |
| **GrowingUp**<br>www.geocities.com/webstooge<br>webstooge@yahoo.com | X | Enter the growth progress of your children. |
| **HighRoller**<br>www.thinkingbytes.com<br>custsvc@thinkingbytes.com | | Don't be fooled by people who tell you that poker depends on experience—it does not! What counts is the knowing the rules and the odds of your hand. |
| **Housesearch**<br>www.thinkingbytes.com<br>custsvc@thinkingbytes.com | | Imagine looking for a house and having to record all the details on a piece of paper... you will get tired of it after the fourth place you see. Housesearch keeps all the records and allows you to make a more intelligent decision. |
| **LiftLog**<br>www.craigcecil.com<br>Craig@craigcecil.com | X | Weightlifter's log book. |
| **Major League Baseball 2001 Schedule**<br>hotfiles.zdnet.com/cgi-bin/texis/swlib/hotfiles/<br>    info.html?fcode=001GTO&b=zdpalm<br>lani@lava.net | | MobileDB schedule for all 30 major league teams. |
| **My Quarters**<br>www.sandsusa.com/default.htm<br>Rick@SandsUSA.com | | Track your U.S. State Quarters collection. |
| **Phone List**<br>www.planet-wireless.co.uk/wio<br>info@planet-wireless.co.uk | | Freeware app to track telephone calls you have to make, that you wouldn't want to store in To Do or Address Book. |

**TABLE A.5:** A Place for Everything: Using Databases *(continued)*

| Application | On CD? | Description |
| --- | --- | --- |
| **Psycho!**<br>LoserNet@yahoo.com | | Are you a psycho? Type-A personality? Losin' it? If so, then it would be wise to log your daily transgressions. |
| **TealInfo Anniversary Gifts**<br>www.tealpoint.com<br>contact@tealpoint.com | X | Returns both modern and traditional anniversary gift themes given the correct number of years. |
| **TealInfo U.S. Postage Calculator**<br>www.tealpoint.com<br>contact@tealpoint.com | X | Calculates First Class, Priority Mail, Express Mail, and international letter postage. |
| **TealMeal Database**<br>www.tealpoint.com/software.htm<br>contact@tealpoint.com | X | Restaurant database and selection utility. Need help with the toughest decision of the day? It's where to go for lunch, of course. To the rescue comes the TealMeal, a simple and fun program that stores and manages multiple editable lists of restaurants, presents them by topic and category, and even helps choose one with the all-knowing Wheel of Food. |
| **Top Ten**<br>www.forallsystems.com<br>kjeffrey@forallsystems.com | | Makes it easy to keep track of all your top 10 lists, such as, What were the 10 best movies this year? Who are the 10 worst people to invite to dinner? |
| **WeddingDB**<br>www.thinkingbytes.com<br>custsvc@thinkingbytes.com | | So he finally proposed; now comes the hard part: caterers, florists, bakers, bands... and on and on. You can organize all your contact information, prices, and notes in one place. |
| **World Swimming Record**<br>popov.tw.to<br>ultra_sparc20@hotmail.com | X | A complete list of world swimming records. |

**TABLE A.6:** Good Words to You

| Application | On CD? | Description |
| --- | --- | --- |
| *1927*<br>www.thefittonchronicles.com/<br>  SCIENCE_FICTION_PAGE.htm<br>bfitton1@cs.com | | In this e-book, Charlie Russo is a part of the remarkable events of 1927, including Babe Ruth's quest for 60 home runs and Lindbergh's flight across the Atlantic. Jamal, from the distant future, befriends and falls in love with Charlie. |
| **Awe-Struck E-Books**<br>www.awe-struck.net<br>kdstruck1@home.com | | This commercial Web site sells almost a hundred Palm-readable e-books in categories like sf, romance, nonfiction, and paranormal. Includes *The Last Intergalactic Sighting of Melgor Lich* ("In a galaxy of law-abiding aliens, why is one little human criminal causing so much trouble?") and *Wilderness and the City* ("A thought-provoking contrast between the healing power of nature and the city."). |
| *Before the Rains Came*<br>www.alphapenguin.com<br>howard_schellenberg@yahoo.com | | In this latest serialized novel from author Howard J. Schellenberg, 1990s Seoul, Korea, provides the backdrop for murder. |
| **Curtis Weyant's e-book link archive**<br>www.angelfire.com/ny3/curtisweyant/ebook/<br>  index.html<br>dylan38@angelfire.com | | This Web site has links to text, HTML, PDF, and Palm-compatible formats of dozens of classic works, including many by Hans Christian Andersen, Jane Austen, Henry David Thoreau, and Edith Wharton. |
| *Exchange House* and *Fool's Gold*<br>www.thefittonchronicles.com<br>bfitton1@cs.com | | Two novels by Bob Fitton. In the first, there's always a danger alone in a house far away from home. In the second, a detective and the drug-dealing killer he's chasing are whisked back to frontier days. |

**TABLE A.6:**  Good Words to You *(continued)*

| Application | On CD? | Description |
| --- | --- | --- |
| ***Frankenstein***<br>level9climb@hotmail.com | | Mary Shelley's classic novel of horror, organized into chapters. |
| **Jack & Jill**<br>www.utilware.com/jackjill.html<br>BillWesterman@hotmail.com | | Ever find yourself on the road when your kids ask you to read them a nursery rhyme? Use these applications to read popular nursery rhymes to your kids, complete with text and illustrations! |
| **Jokes about Economists**<br>palm.age.com.hk<br>angusho@geocities.com | | Jokes and fun stories originally collected by Pasi Kuoppamaski. |
| **Qvadis E-Book Sampler**<br>www.qvadis.com<br>info@qvadis.com | X | The free Qvadis E-Book Sampler spotlights award-winning high-quality fiction and nonfiction books and stories. |
| **Sherlock Holmes Etext**<br>level9climb@hotmail.com | | The classic adventures of Sherlock Holmes. |
| ***Stalin's Organ***<br>www.rationalskies.com<br>admin@rationalskies.com | X | Twelve speculative short stories by David L. Major; freeware. (Site includes other fiction and nonfiction titles for sale.) |
| ***The Little Prince***<br>www.birdmen.com<br>palm@birdmen.com | | English translation, bookmarked by chapter. |
| ***The Wizard of Oz***<br>level9climb@hotmail.com | | For the first time ever, you can read the classic *The Wizard of Oz* on your Palm. Divided into chapters for easy reading, this will entertain you whenever you want, wherever you want. |

**TABLE A.7:** Having Fun

| Application | On CD? | Description |
| --- | --- | --- |
| **Conqueror**<br>hotfiles.zdnet.com/cgi-bin/texis/swlib/<br>  hotfiles/search.html<br>palm@mulliner.org | X | Turn-based strategy game. The goal is to conquer all fields (all continents) and to destroy all your opponents. |
| **Cookiz**<br>www.marilis.com<br>contact@marilis.com | | Clear the matrix with your mind! Merging objects will make identical parts disappear and clear the way to the next level. |
| **Cubik**<br>www.chipera.1stpart.com<br>ChipEra@mail.com | X | Just a small version of Rubik's Cube, 2x2x2, black and white symbols. |
| **Domino!**<br>hotfiles.zdnet.com/cgi-bin/texis/swlib/hotfiles/<br>  info.html?fcode=0015TG&b=zdpalm<br>jb.godillon@wanadoo.fr | X | A very simple dominos game. |
| **Donkey Kung Jr.**<br>www.ardiri.com<br>aaron@ardiri.com | | Donkey Kung Jr. is an implementation of the classic Nintendo game "Donkey Kong Jr." (Site includes more than a dozen other games.) |
| **Flipper**<br>www.sinz.org/Palm<br>Palm@sinz.org | | A small Othello program. |
| **FourKnights**<br>www.winisp.net/wayward.one/fourknights.htm<br>wayward.one@winisp.net | X | Object is to exchange the black knights with the white knights. |
| **Galactic Empire Builder**<br>hotfiles.zdnet.com/cgi-bin/texis/swlib/hotfiles/<br>  info.html?fcode=001AOV&b=zdpalm<br>snowzone5@hotmail.com | X | Strategy game with one simple goal: take over all the planets! But the aliens are trying to do the same thing. |
| **Hearts**<br>davemayes.hypermart.net<br>mayes@san.rr.com | | The classic card game; you compete against three Palm players. |

**TABLE A.7:** Having Fun *(continued)*

| Application | On CD? | Description |
| --- | --- | --- |
| **Hungman**<br>ki7q@arrl.net | X | Play Hangman with your Palm. |
| **Jacks Or Better**<br>hotfiles.zdnet.com/cgi-bin/texis/swlib/hotfiles/<br>   info.html?fcode=001C2J&b=zdpalm<br>kris_johnson@users.sourceforge.net | X | Video poker simulator. |
| **KQ-Pirate**<br>www.kpoole.com<br>kyle@kpoole.com | | Ever wanted to be a bloodthirsty, treasure-hungry pirate? Ever wanted to sail the high seas in your own pirate ship? Well, now you can. |
| **Lines**<br>texas.cbtdigital.com/lines<br>maiden@aha.ru | X | A classic strategy/logic game, played on a 9x9 board with tiles of different patterns. |
| **Petra-Luna**<br>www.gdprom.com<br>gdprom@gdprom.com | | Tetris-like game in which you attempt to stack bricks to make rows in order to rescue Petra-Luna. |
| **Pilot Mines**<br>www.pundt.de/pilot/index.html<br>thomas@pundt.de | | Minesweeper clone. |
| **Pocket Sotong**<br>www.geocities.com/changkin<br>changkin@geocities.com | X | Emulation of the classic Nintendo game Octopus. |
| **Robot Attack!**<br>hotfiles.zdnet.com/cgi-bin/texis/swlib/hotfiles/<br>   info.html?fcode=001CCF&b=zdpalm<br>uegarbac@mcs.drexel.edu | | You attempt to destroy all the robots on a level by forcing them to either crash into each other or walk into the fire created by two robots colliding. |

**TABLE A.7:** Having Fun *(continued)*

| Application | On CD? | Description |
| --- | --- | --- |
| **Sea War**<br>www.palm-games.com<br>william@tblabs.com | | Remake of a popular game played on paper. Your goal is to sink all of the Palm's ships by shooting to its game field. |
| **smallWare Solitaire Free**<br>www.smallware.com<br>tcain@smallware.com | | Three solitaire card games from the smallWare Solitaire collection, played with a single deck of 52 cards: Klondike Deal 3, Demon, and Baker's Game. |
| **Solskia**<br>www.kpoole.com<br>kyle@kpoole.com | | A true isometric role-playing game like those found on the PC. |
| **Sting**<br>members.nbci.com/skm1503/palm.html<br>pigmhall@hotmail.com | | Poke people. Don't poke dogs. |
| **Tatum**<br>www.palm-tatum.com<br>wniemann@t-online.de | X | Enter Castle Tatum and rescue Princess Laila Wanda from the bad magician Akran. |
| **Tetris Classic**<br>hotfiles.zdnet.com/cgi-bin/texis/swlib/hotfiles/<br>  info.html?fcode=001BYK&b=zdpalm | X | A Tetris clone that's addictive and lots of fun. |
| **Whack**<br>www.stone-age-software.com<br>frompalmgear@stone-age-software.com | X | Damsels in distress, hideous evildoers, and you in your shining armor. |
| **Yahdice**<br>www.palmspot.com/software/detail/ps7037a_9818.html<br>mirwoj@homemail.com | X | Clone of the world's most popular family dice game, Yahtzee. |

**TABLE A.8:** Seeing It All

| Application | On CD? | Description |
|---|---|---|
| **Backdrop**<br>www.twilightedge.com<br>twilight_edge@hotmail.com | | Places a customizable image in the background of your Palm OS device's screen; image will stay in place even when other apps are running, though you can set Backdrop to remove it for certain programs. |
| **Blobs**<br>www.lfw.org/pilot<br>ping@lfw.org | | This could be a screen saver for the Palm. |
| **DotEditor**<br>hotfiles.zdnet.com/cgi-bin/texis/swlib/hotfiles/<br>   info.html?fcode=000ZH3&b=zdpalm<br>unlimited@ma7.seikyou.ne.jp | | Graphic editor for Palm III. Edit PPaint image, Home's background, and Home's icon. You can also import an image of ImageView. |
| **EPaint**<br>www.pointinception.com<br>ctsiokos@cfl.rr.com | | Paint program for sketches, maps, floor plans, and other diagrams, with slide show–animation capability. |
| **Eyebeam**<br>palm.dahm.com<br>palm@dahm.com | | Can beam or convert eyemodule images to Image Viewer (now called FireViewer). |
| **Graph**<br>hotfiles.zdnet.com/cgi-bin/texis/swlib/hotfiles/<br>   info.html?fcode=000X01&b=zdpalm<br>msmith50@usa.net | | Draw $x$-$y$ plots of up to six functions simultaneously, over user-defined $x$ and $y$ ranges. |
| **My PhotoGear**<br>www.palmsoftnet.com<br>sales@palmsoftnet.com | | Tracks all your photographic equipment info: where and when you bought it, warranty expiration date, and serial number, all filtered by categories. |
| **PalmPickle**<br>homepage1.nifty.com/okuji/pickle.html<br>koji.okuji@nifty.com | | A desktop of Pickle operated by Palm. Then, what's "Pickle"? It's a naughty little fellow created by a digital illustrator. PalmPickle can "transform" into a calculator and a clock. |

**TABLE A.8:** Seeing It All *(continued)*

| Application | On CD? | Description |
|---|---|---|
| **PalmRule**<br>www.csraonline.com/pilot<br>barryc@csraonline.com | X | Displays a centimeter ruler and an inch ruler—place something on the screen and tap the screen to get the digital measurement. |
| **pbm2pfnt**<br>www.insync.net/~henke/pbm2pfnt<br>henke@insync.net | X | Set of programs that allows developers to build fonts using MetaFont and convert them to resources, which can be used in Palm applications. |
| **PilchART**<br>hotfiles.zdnet.com/cgi-bin/texis/swlib/hotfiles/<br>   info.html?fcode=000RY8&b=zdpalm<br>arto88@dnet.net.id | | PocketC applet to do bar or line charts, with an automatic function to find the best fit for the chart on screen. Up to 10 file database. Can export and import to MemoPad. |
| **Pilot Eyes**<br>www.rgps.com/PilotEyes.html<br>ron@rgps.com | X | A fun little app that will make you think your Palm is watching you. |
| **Schmear**<br>www.palmsense.com/handwatch/index.php3<br>markyang@palmsense.com | | A real-time morphing program right on your Palm! |
| **Snapshot**<br>www.strout.net/pilotsoft/snapshot/intro.shtml<br>joe@strout.net | X | Can capture any screen (grayscale or black and white) to a file in Image Viewer format. This can then be viewed on the Palm, or transferred to a desktop computer for conversion to other formats, posting on the Web, etc. Only 3K. |
| **Spirals**<br>www.enteract.com/~mwilber/palmpilot/spirals.htm<br>mwilber@enteract.com | | Generates spiral graphs. |
| **Sweetheart**<br>linkesoft.com/english/sweetheart/index.html<br>info@linkesoft.com | X | Have a picture of your beloved in your Palm! |

**TABLE A.8:** Seeing It All *(continued)*

| Application | On CD? | Description |
| --- | --- | --- |
| **Syodo**<br>www.geocities.co.jp/SiliconValley/5696/<br>  index_en.html<br>jun1@mailhost.net | | The traditional Asian character art (also Shodo). |
| **TinyLogo**<br>hotfiles.zdnet.com/cgi-bin/texis/swlib/hotfiles/<br>  info.html?fcode=0015OC&b=zdpalm<br>lipetz@netset.com | X | Programming language and program execution environment, especially friendly to beginning programmers. It is based on the Logo programming language and comes complete with Turtle Graphics. |
| **Xfont**<br>www.geocities.com/montesoft<br>montesoft@cg.yu | | Windows 9*x*/NT program that allows you to design custom fonts for Palm. |

**TABLE A.9:** Get in Shape

| Application | On CD? | Description |
| --- | --- | --- |
| **AllergyDays**<br>linkesoft.com/english/allergydays<br>info@linkesoft.com | X | Stores your daily allergy symptom observations and thus helps you to keep track of your allergies. |
| **Biorhythms**<br>www.jeffjetton.com<br>jetton@mindspring.com | | Supposedly, we all have physical, mental, and emotional cycles that start at birth and continue regularly through life. This small application will chart these cycles for any given day, using any birthday. |
| **Blood Press Mgr**<br>www.dialectica.com/bloodpressmgr<br>r.marin@dialectica.com | X | Tracks blood pressure measures, highlighted with different colors based on the pressure values. Also shows overall average statistics and weekly distribution. |

**TABLE A.9:** Get in Shape *(continued)*

| Application | On CD? | Description |
| --- | --- | --- |
| **Calorie Watch**<br>www.palmix.itil.com/newpalmix/products/<br>  calorie_home.html<br>palmix@123india.com | | Helps you to determine your ideal weight, ideal caloric intake, and body mass index depending on your age, weight, height, and lifestyle. |
| **Cyclist's Log**<br>www.fitnesslogs.com/cyclistslog/index.html<br>martyrice@pobox.com | | Complete training log designed for the casual or serious athlete. |
| **Exercise**<br>www.smasher.com/palm<br>sean@smasher.com | | Displays a rep counter, with audible indicators, for your favorite exercise routine. Enter the details of up to nine exercises and Exercise will count out your routine for you. |
| **Friend Indeed**<br>www.palmix.itil.com/newpalmix/products/<br>  friend_home.htm<br>palmix@123india.com | | Personal information system to store and monitor information like blood pressure, blood sugar, and pulse rate and to analyze them over a period of time. |
| **Herbal Zone**<br>mlongo@geotec.net | X | 100 entries of some of the most widely used herbs today, providing the ability to make an informed choice on herbal medicine. |
| **MedRules**<br>pbrain.hypermart.net<br>kwillyard@mindspring.com | | Useful clinical prediction rules taken from medical literature. |
| **PillPal**<br>www.ufp.com/pillpal/pillpal.html<br>richardl@ufp.com | | Reminds you to take your medication or vitamins. |
| **Shots**<br>pbrain.hypermart.net<br>kwillyard@mindspring.com | X | Quick-reference guide to the 2001 Childhood Immunization Schedule. |

**TABLE A.9:** Get in Shape *(continued)*

| Application | On CD? | Description |
|---|---|---|
| **Smoke History**<br>geocities.com/impauljs<br>impauljs@yahoo.com | | A tool to help you quit smoking. Whenever you have a cigarette, just tap on the button. Smoke History will keep a daily log of your cigarette counts. The point is to decrease the number of cigarettes until you quit. |
| **STAT Cardiac Risk and STAT Growth Charts**<br>www.statcoder.com<br>achen@austin.rr.com | X | Site includes several medical apps. STAT Cardiac Risk estimates coronary heart disease risk, using the Framingham Heart Study Prediction Scores, from age, sex, total cholesterol, HDL, blood pressure, smoking, and diabetes status. STAT Growth Charts calculates growth percentiles by age based on the June 2000 revision of the CDC Growth Charts for the United States. |
| **Step Counter**<br>bodotill.suburbia.com.au<br>t.harbaum@tu-bs.de | X | Enables Palms with the adxl202 acceleration sensor to count walking/jogging distances. |
| **The Baby Organizer**<br>www.geocities.com/comp2consultants/products.html<br>comp2consultants@yahoo.com | X | Tracks doctor visits, immunizations, weight, and height. Registered version can track your child's milestones, school grades, and baby feedings. |
| **Work-it-out**<br>www.planet-wireless.co.uk/wio/index.html<br>wio@planet-wireless.co.uk | | Log and track your gym workouts. |

**TABLE A.10:** Just Cool

| Application | On CD? | Description |
|---|---|---|
| **Ask President Bush**<br>www.sassypalm.com<br>support@sassypalm.com | X | Throw away your Magic 8-Ball. Put away those tarot cards. Need to find the answers to life's problems, questions, and dreams? Just ask President Bush! |
| **Cartoons Alarm Collection**<br>cnr-oxy.cnr.pmf.hr/~kdekanic<br>kdekanic@knjiga.pedos.hr | | Collection of Palm device alarms; features various tunes from popular cartoons. |
| **Delphi**<br>jove.prohosting.com/~delphi29<br>delphi29@excite.com | X | Astrology program that lets you create, view, organize, and beam birth charts. |
| **Dr. Insano's Eyes**<br>www.burmeisterconsulting.com/palmgames.html<br>richard@burmeisterconsulting.com | | Entertaining "self-hypnotism" application. |
| **freefor**<br>www.freefor.com/avatar/main/body_download.jsp<br>shahed@freefor.com | | A unique service that connects you with like-minded people in your area for your favorite activities! Creates groups of people to participate in the activities you love the most. |
| **Mr. Push Me!**<br>www.geocities.com/flaresoftware/palmsoftware.htm<br>MrGrue@hotmail.com | | Mr. Push Me! is the button with an attitude! He'll start off happy and begin to get a bit miffed. |
| **Mirror+**<br>hotfiles.zdnet.com/cgi-bin/texis/swlib/hotfiles/<br>  info.html?fcode=001C9B&b=zdpalm | | Turns your Palm into a mirror. |
| **Mystic**<br>www.rufan-redi.com/palm.phtml<br>palm@rufan-redi.com | X | Numerology calculator; give it a name, a birth date, and an event date and it gives you a reading. |
| **P-Guide**<br>www.neurontech.fr/upsilon<br>upsilon@neurontech.fr | | Retrieves movie and theater information from the Internet. |

**TABLE A.10:** Just Cool *(continued)*

| Application | On CD? | Description |
|---|:---:|---|
| **PocketRocket**<br>www.digitalfireworks.com<br>skyrocketmm@earthlink.net | X | Miniature aerial fireworks display. |
| **PortaMonkey**<br>www.eruptor.com/portapets<br>portapet@eruptor.com | X | Your very own screeching pet primate. |
| **Smiley**<br>hop.to/palm<br>Martin.viste@agderweb.no | X | A huge collection of smileys to put in your e-mail or text. |
| **Static Chicken**<br>www.sunsetandlabrea.co.uk<br>richard_chamberlain@ntlworld.com | X | Artificial life application, where you can be the keeper of your own Static Chicken! |
| **The Oracle**<br>www.quartus.net<br>info@quartus.net | | Every day, a hundred decisions. Here's something that might help. Speak your question, tap the surface of the ball, and the Oracle will give you an answer. |
| **The Simpsons**<br>www.palm3c.org<br>kingbob127@yahoo.com | | A must-have for the Simpsons fan on the go. |
| **Think!**<br>www.geocities.com/WallStreet/1028<br>pld@pld4u.com | | Do you feel that your life is wasted with important stuff filling up your time? Improve your vision of life with Think!, the fun but useless thinking tool. |
| **ThumbScan**<br>Headrush.net/palm<br>bsk@headrush.net | X | Fun application that "scans" your thumbprint on the Palm's screen. Will always fail until you hold down the special key. |

**TABLE A.10:** Just Cool *(continued)*

| Application | On CD? | Description |
| --- | --- | --- |
| **Tie**<br>hq@ccard.com.br | | If you are like me and never remember how to tie a tie, or know only one kind of knot, now you have the solution. |
| **Torch**<br>www.stone-age-software.com/product.shtml<br>frompalmgear@stone-age-software.com | X | It's dark. You are fumbling around using your Palm backlight as a flashlight, but it's just not bright enough. Torch, the world's smallest useful Palm app at 524 bytes! It makes your screen as bright as possible through judicious choice of screen coloring. |
| **WhatsOn**<br>www.palmspot.com/whatsnew<br>zucker@umunhum.stanford.edu | | Download and display TV listing data. |

**TABLE A.11:** Get Smarter

| Application | On CD? | Description |
| --- | --- | --- |
| **American Abbreviations Dictionary**<br>www.beiks.com<br>support@beiks.com | X | Simple reference program with more than 1,500 abbreviations in modern American language and their meanings. |
| **BioTables**<br>www.techfak.uni-bielefeld.de/~icschlei/pilot/<br>  biotables.html<br>chris@genetik.uni-bielefeld.de | | Lookup program for various tables from the field of biology, such as nucleotides, amino acids, or standard genetic code. |
| **DotDash**<br>break.org/gisle/PalmOS<br>sting@mix.hive.no | X | Morse code trainer with features such as Train Random Words, Learn Alphabet, Recognize Random Abbreviations, different speed settings, Morse text as you write, etc. |

**TABLE A.11:** Get Smarter *(continued)*

| Application | On CD? | Description |
| --- | --- | --- |
| **Due Yesterday**<br>www.due-yesterday.com<br>tomb@nosleep.net | X | Student organizer application; allows students to easily manage their assignments and classes. |
| **Element**<br>www.mindgear.com/element/index.html<br>sales@mindgear.com | X | Periodic table just as you would like to see it. Elements can be selected via tapping directly in the table, or by selecting via name, symbol, weight, or atomic number. Data for 25 element properties. |
| **Handheld Leadership**<br>www.empoweringtechnologies.com<br>solutions@empoweringtechnologies.com | X | How would you like to be a better leader? Here's an interactive tutorial that will help you learn the basic leadership skills you need. |
| **Internet Acronyms**<br>hotfiles.zdnet.com/cgi-bin/texis/swlib/hotfiles/<br>   info.html?fcode=001C3A&b=zdpalm<br>fhobiz@yahoo.com | | What is AWHFY? When someones tell you a joke, should you ROTFLOL? Get more Internet acronyms here. |
| **Jtutor**<br>www.land-j.com/jtutor.html<br>support@land-j.com | | Quiz application. Features multiple choice, true/false, and flashcard modes. Also retains the date and scores of the last five attempts at each quiz. |
| **Kanji Hanabi**<br>www.neth.com/hanabi.html<br>sam@neth.com | | Powerful learning tool for students of the Japanese language. |
| **Mahatma Gandhi's Quotes**<br>www.memoware.com<br>PalmaServ@topmich.com | | "Man becomes great exactly in the degree in which he works for the welfare of his fellow-men."<br>—Mahatma Gandhi. More than 250 quotes. |
| **Memorizer**<br>www.geocities.com/ResearchTriangle/Node/9238/<br>   index.html<br>shiyan@worldonline.nl | | Notepad with fast lookup and flashcard-like support for memorizing words, expressions, etc. |

**TABLE A.11:** Get Smarter *(continued)*

| Application | On CD? | Description |
| --- | --- | --- |
| **Mental Maths**<br>members.aol.com/TJLivett<br>TJLivett@aol.com | X | Designed to test your mental arithmetic through a series of skill levels from simple addition to very challenging. |
| **Name Meanings Dictionary**<br>www.beiks.com<br>support@beiks.com | | List of over 1,700 names and their meanings. |
| **Noah Lite English Dictionary**<br>www.arslexis.com<br>arslexis@pobox.com | X | The biggest English dictionary for Palm. |
| **PalmASL**<br>www.zoosware.com/palmasl.html<br>info@zoosware.com | | Learn American Sign Language (ASL). Gradually progress from basic alphabets and numbers to the sign spell feature: You type in the words, and PalmASL will show you the words using ASL. |
| **PalmAtlas**<br>astro.isi.edu/palmatlas<br>brian@isi.edu | | Interactive star atlas. |
| **PALMSensei**<br>my.bawue.de/~jtesch/sensei/palm<br>joachim@tesch.com | | Helps you learn the Japanese hiragana and katakana alphabets. |
| **PocketGreek**<br>www.cadvision.com/southpaw<br>southpaw@cadvision.com | X | Flashcard program that will help you to learn Greek vocabulary. |
| **Spell It**<br>soark.net/~slg/index.html<br>palm@mycroft.cmhnet.org | X | Check word spelling; easy to use and comes with an 850-word database of commonly misspelled words. |
| **Thesaurus**<br>www.beiks.com<br>support@beiks.com | | Based on latest edition of WordNet's lexical database and contains 55,000 words. |

**TABLE A.11:** Get Smarter *(continued)*

| Application | On CD? | Description |
|---|---|---|
| **Trivopaedia**<br>3lib.ukonline.co.uk/pocketinfo/index.html<br>slitchfield@ukonline.co.uk | X | The ultimate encyclopedia of useful trivia, this freeware features a mountain of information. |
| **VISitOR**<br>www.sildelta.com/products/VISitOR%20Compass%20&%<br>   20Locater.html<br>david@sildelta.com | | Complete scientific compass and geographic locator; allows you to easily get the location you are currently in and, by orienting your Palm or Visor based on the position of the sun, moon, or stars, to quickly determine North. |
| **Wine Terms Dictionary**<br>www.beiks.com<br>bgk@altavista.net | | Free dictionary that contains most frequently used wine terms and their explanations. |
| **World Geography**<br>www.thomasgredig.com<br>tiger7g@yahoo.com | X | Learn the capitals, areas, and populations of the countries of the world with multiple-choice questions. |

**TABLE A.12:** Getting the Most from Your Palm: Tools and Utilities

| Application | On CD? | Description |
|---|---|---|
| **4T Personal**<br>www.fortsoft.com<br>support@fortsoft.com | | Full-featured personal information storage application; stores the information needed when purchasing an automobile or house, filling out a credit application, etc. |
| **Accu4Pilot**<br>www.luebeck.com/~kolz/proge.htm<br>Uwe.Kolz@luebeck.com | | With this program, you can use rechargeable batteries with your Palm, without the risk of losing data or damaging the rechargeables. |
| **AlwaysOn**<br>www.persicke.de/pilotfre.htm<br>rps@persicke.de | X | Simple little program that lets you change the auto-off time of your Palm to values other than those possible with the built-in preferences. |

**TABLE A.12:** Getting the Most from Your Palm: Tools and Utilities *(continued)*

| Application | On CD? | Description |
| --- | --- | --- |
| **Application Usage Hack**<br>www.benc.hr/appusage.htm<br>bozidar.benc@sb.tel.hr | | Runs in the background and keeps a tally on the number of times different applications are used, the total time those applications have been used, and a grand total time. |
| **Backup Bitster**<br>www.geocities.com/katz_karsai<br>katz_karsai@yahoo.com | | Protect all your Palm's data and applications! Provides full control over which data and applications are backed up during a HotSync. |
| **CD List**<br>piprograms.com<br>oomen@piprograms.com | | Browse through your compact disc inventory. |
| **Cruise Control**<br>www.bluenomad.com<br>sales@BackupBuddy.com | X | Using Cruise Control may allow you to speed up your Palm Organizer by as much as 50%. |
| **CryptInfo**<br>www.normsoft.com/cryptinfo/index.shtml<br>tim@normsoft.com | | Remembers all of your passwords, account numbers, and more! |
| **DVD Trak-R**<br>www.jet-ware.com/dvdtrakr.html<br>jetware@jet-ware.com | | Helps you keep track of your DVDs (and video games, VHS titles, home movies, CDs...). |
| **GadgetHack**<br>ourworld.compuserve.com/homepages/mcdan/<br>  gadgethack.html<br>mcdan@csi.com | | Control your Palm handheld within the current application, make the backlight "sticky," invert the screen for easy reading, jump back and forth between utility apps, and keep instant track of the time, date, and voltage! Turns the current application's title into an information bar where you can see the time, date, and weekday. |

**TABLE A.12:** Getting the Most from Your Palm: Tools and Utilities *(continued)*

| Application | On CD? | Description |
|---|---|---|
| **Graspeedy**<br>ourworld.compuserve.com/homepages/mcdan/<br>  graspeedy.html<br>mcdan@csi.com | | Write Graffiti. Faster! Define a custom area to write capital letters. Graspeedy can also perform "Graffiti monitoring," and automatically substitute incorrect letters with the correct replacements. |
| **Hi-Note**<br>www.cyclos.com/hi-note.htm<br>palmspot@cyclos.com | | Combines the capabilities of an outliner program, a notepad program, and a drawing program to let you store text and pictures in a hierarchical format. |
| **International KeybHack**<br>www.palmgear.com/software/<br>  showsoftware.cfm?&prodID=9239<br>jonatanf@home.se | | Turns your keyboard into an International keyboard in respect to how you type accented characters like ë, á, õ, û, and ì. |
| **Linkdragon**<br>hotfiles.zdnet.com/cgi-bin/texis/swlib/hotfiles/<br>  info.html?fcode=0011NC&b=zdpalm<br>sergio.carvalho@mail.pt | | Fills a major gap in Palm apps: allows associations to be made between pairs of records. With only two programmable strokes, you can easily establish hyperlinks and navigate between apps. |
| **Palm-Job**<br>www.monkey-ware.com/products.html<br>sales@monkey-ware.com | | Applying for a job or jobs? Palm-Job tracks resumes, interviews, salary info, Web sites, headhunters, company info, and more. |
| **PrintMemo**<br>www.homestead.com/rayrodrick/PalmPilot.html<br>rayrodrick@iform.com.au | | Print a memo to the serial port, or save it in a file on a PC using a Terminal program such as HyperTerminal on a Windows 95 computer. |

**TABLE A.12:** Getting the Most from Your PalmPilot: Tools and Utilities *(continued)*

| Application | On CD? | Description |
| --- | --- | --- |
| **ReDo**<br>www.probe.net/~rhuebner/redo.html<br>rhuebner@probe.net | | Cures a serious lack in the built-in To Do List: the inability to schedule recurring reminders. It adds a powerful and flexible repeat capability to the To Do List program, so that you can set up reminders that automatically insert themselves into your To Do List on any required repeating basis. |
| **SilverScreen**<br>www.pocketsensei.com<br>mpeters@pocketsensei.com | | The first and only application launcher that's every bit as distinctive as your Palm device. Meticulously designed themes transform the graphical interface into a feast for the eyes. |
| **Survey/Quiz Mate**<br>www.thinkingbytes.com/products/surveymate.asp<br>armando@thinkingbytes.com | | Electronic questionnaire/quiz system; gathers information, counts it, charts it, and compiles the results in three different formats. |
| **TakeHome**<br>soft.syclonix.net/TakeHome<br>webmaster@syclonix.net | X | Lets you quickly jot down what you need to take home (or anywhere else) from school, from books and binders to documents. |
| **vBattery**<br>hotfiles.zdnet.com/cgi-bin/texis/swlib/hotfiles/<br>   info.html?fcode=001424&b=zdpalm<br>ramel@PalmMate.com | | Displays your Palm battery status in voltage or percentage (switch modes by clicking the battery). |
| **Volume**<br>home1.pacific.net.sg/~kokmun/pilotpgm.htm<br>kokmun@pacific.net.sg | | Utility to control the sound volume of the Palm. |

**TABLE A.12:** Getting the Most from Your Palm: Tools and Utilities *(continued)*

| Application | On CD? | Description |
|---|---|---|
| **Word Doc Converter**<br>hotfiles.zdnet.com/cgi-bin/texis/swlib/hotfiles/<br>   info.html?fcode=001424&b=zdpalm<br>pontius@free.net.nz | | This Word add-in will display a new toolbar to convert Word documents to Palm Doc, iSilo, or RichReader format, or from Palm Doc format to Word. |
| **WordSmith**<br>http://www.bluenomad.com/ws<br>sales@bluenomad.com | X | A fully featured word processor for your Palm. |

**TABLE A.13:** Tour the World

| Application | On CD? | Description |
|---|---|---|
| **Abroad!**<br>www.geocities.com/SiliconValley/Peaks/9768/<br>   Pilot.html#anchor95817<br>ykanai@kagi.com | X | Abroad! is a suite of three applications: Currency Exchange, Unit Conversion and World Clock, and a powerful Country Information Database, designed to help you when you go abroad. |
| **AirInfo Wireless**<br>www.rovenet.com<br>maureen@rovenet.com | | Heading to the airport? Getting ready to leave for a trip? Want to know what to really expect? Now you can know what the airlines know. Access real-time airport status info for all major cities. |
| **Airlines Performance**<br>www.thinkingbytes.com<br>custsvc@thinkingbytes.com | X | Want to know which airline is on time? How about the statistics on luggage loss? |
| **City Guide**<br>www.palmgear.com/software/showsoftware<br>   .cfm?sid=44358820010131114716&prodID=12172<br>software@anima3d.com | X | City Guide will help you decide on many activities around town. This program works for everyone around the world. It is not built for a specific city; it is global. |

**TABLE A.13:** Tour the World *(continued)*

| Application | On CD? | Description |
| --- | --- | --- |
| **CityZen**<br>www.cs.man.ac.uk/~hancockd/CityZen<br>hancock@cs.man.ac.uk | | Interactive world map. Scroll and zoom with the buttons or stylus. Find cities or countries by name from the thousands in the database, or use the quiz mode to improve your world geography knowledge. |
| **Commute**<br>www.liii.com/~koehler/pilot.htm<br>koehler@liii.com | | Manage your bus, train, and ferry schedules. |
| **Highway Manager Pro**<br>tinystocks.com/highway.html<br>cvandend@zorglub.com | X | Gas mileage application (metric and imperial measurements); amount of gas per distance (MPG) or distance per amount. |
| **JunglePort**<br>www.junglesoft.com<br>bkahn@JungleSoft.com | | Personalizable mobile portal, including personalized dining guides, yellow pages, and maps for 39 cities. |
| **Limo Wireless**<br>165.254.148.22/limo.htm<br>maureen@rovenet.com | | Book dependable car service trips, airport pickup, and limos. Service by 1-800-Book-A-Limo worldwide. |
| **MapBook**<br>www2.wbs.ne.jp/~pilotdev/down.htm<br>uruki@mail.wbs.ne.jp | | Map display and GPS navigation program. |
| **Mobile Motion**<br>www.mobilemotion.com/index.html<br>techsupport@mobilemotion.com | X | Business and entertainment directory. Taxi, limo, horseback riding, bicycle/skate rental, go-cart, helicopter, hot air balloon, skydiving, glider, pleasure boat, canoe, ice skating, and many more! |
| **Palm Globe**<br>www2.hursley.ibm.com/pglobe/pglobe.html<br>support@pc.ibm.com | | Displays the Earth as a globe. |

**TABLE A.13:** Tour the World *(continued)*

| Application | On CD? | Description |
| --- | --- | --- |
| **PalmWorld**<br>www.users.globalnet.co.uk/~ewenjc/palmworld.html<br>ewenjc@globalnet.co.uk | | Use your pen to explore the world; PalmWorld will show you the nearest city, the time, the phone code, its longitude and latitude, and how far away it is. |
| **Parking Buddy**<br>www.geocities.com/CapeCanaveral/Lab/9176/<br>  sumbang.html<br>arto88@dnet.net.id | | PocketC applet to calculate your parking bill. |
| **Roadfood.com Memorable Eateries**<br>www.handmark.com<br>sales@handmark.com | | Use this MobileDB database to find the most memorable local eateries along the highways and back roads of America. |
| **TourMate (English to French)**<br>www.palmix.itil.com/newpalmix/products/<br>  tmfrench_home.htm<br>palmix@123india.com | | Companion for anyone who seeks to converse with people in French. |
| **TourMate (English to Italian)**<br>www.palmix.itil.com/newpalmix/products/<br>  tmitalian_home.htm<br>palmix@123india.com | | Companion for anyone who seeks to converse with people in Italian. |
| **TourMate (English to Spanish)**<br>www.palmix.itil.com/newpalmix/products/<br>tmspanish_home.htm<br>palmix@123india.com | | Companion for anyone who seeks to converse with people in Spanish. |
| **Travel Data**<br>www.geocities.com/travel_data<br>eugene86@magix.com.sg | X | Too many trips to keep track of? With Travel Data, you will never forget them again! Contains just about anything you need to manage your travels. |

# INDEX

**Note to the Reader:** Page numbers in **bold** indicate the principle discussion of a topic or the definition of a term. Page numbers in *italic* indicate illustrations.